www.wadsworth.com

wadsworth.com is the World Wide Web site for
Wadsworth and is your direct source to dozens of
online resources.

At *wadsworth.com* you can find out about supplements,
demonstration software, and student resources. You can
also send email to many of our authors and preview
new publications and exciting new technologies.

wadsworth.com
Changing the way the world learns®

THEORY ESSENTIALS
VOLUME I WITH CD

An Integrated Approach to
Harmony, Ear Training,
and Keyboard Skills

Connie E. Mayfield
Kansas City Kansas Community College

THOMSON

SCHIRMER

Australia • Canada • Mexico • Singapore • Spain
United Kingdom • United States

Publisher: *Clark G. Baxter*
Assistant Editor: *Julie Iannacchino*
Editorial Assistant: *Jonathan Katz*
Technology Project Manager: *Jennifer Ellis*
Marketing Manager: *Mark Orr*
Marketing Assistant: *Justine Ferguson*
Advertising Project Manager: *Brian Chaffee*
Project Manager, Editorial Production: *Dianne Toop*
Print/Media Buyer: *Robert King*

Permissions Editor: *Roberta Broyer*
Production Service: *A-R Editions, Inc.*
Text Designer: *Patrick Devine Design*
Copy Editor: *Barbara Norton*
Cover Designer: *Patrick Devine Design*
Cover Image: *©I Burgum/P Boorman/Stone/Getty Images*
Cover Printer: *Malloy Lithographing, Inc.*
Compositor: *A-R Editions, Inc.*
Printer: *Malloy Lithographing, Inc.*

For more information about our products, contact us at:
Thomson Learning Academic Resource Center
1-800-423-0563
For permission to use material from this text, contact us by:
Phone: 1-800-730-2214   **Fax:** 1-800-730-2215
Web: http://www.thomsonrights.com

ISBN 0-534-57231-6

Wadsworth/Thomson Learning
10 Davis Drive
Belmont, CA 94002-3098
USA

Asia
Thomson Learning
5 Shenton Way #01-01
UIC Building
Singapore 068808

Australia
Nelson Thomson Learning
102 Dodds Street
South Melbourne, Victoria 3205
Australia

Canada
Nelson Thomson Learning
1120 Birchmount Road
Toronto, Ontario M1K 5G4
Canada

Europe/Middle East/Africa
Thomson Learning
High Holborn House
50/51 Bedford Row
London WC1R 4LR
United Kingdom

Latin America
Thomson Learning
Seneca, 53
Colonia Polanco
11560 Mexico D.F.
Mexico

Spain
Paraninfo Thomson Learning
Calle/Magallanes, 25
28015 Madrid, Spain

TABLE OF CONTENTS

Preface

The study of music theory is a rite of passage for all college-level music students. The subject matter is often difficult and is usually undertaken at the very beginning of your college career. Each topic must be mastered and retained, because it will be needed if you are to understand the next idea. This cumulative process can be extremely daunting for a first-year music student, especially if you do not enter college with a thorough mastery of the fundamentals of reading music and understanding musical patterns such as scales, intervals, and chords.

Music theory is a study of the nuts and bolts of music—an in-depth look at the components that make up the language of music. It is also a study of the manner in which those components interact in musical compositions. The study of theory includes many aspects of reading and performing music. These include harmony, rhythm, and listening skills (often called "aural" skills). It is also possible to apply theoretical concepts to the keyboard, a subject that is sometimes included in the music theory curriculum as keyboard harmony. All of these elements of musical training work together to teach you the mechanics of music, combining abstract and intellectual thought processes with the practical realities of musical performance.

If this sounds like an intimidating course of study, it is! But all serious musicians should embrace the study of this subject, because it will increase your understanding of and appreciation for the art that you love.

Theory Essentials is intended to be your partner in this process. Unlike many college textbooks that you encounter during your years as a student, this book is intended to be user friendly and easy to read. If you start college without an extensive background reading and performing music, this book will help you gain a firm foundation of music fundamentals. Even if you already read music and understand patterns such as scales, you will probably discover new ideas and concepts as you read.

This book includes the content usually covered during the first year of college-level music theory studies. It encompasses the subject matter for both notation studies (usually called theory or harmony classes) and the material for your aural skills classes (usually called sight-singing, ear training, or musicianship classes). Each chapter contains two major sections: Theoretical Skills and Aural Skills. The final page of each chapter gives you an opportunity to apply what you have learned to the keyboard.

The book provides regular evaluations of your progress called Practice Boxes. These are included after each major concept is presented. They will give you an opportunity to assess your understanding of each concept. Your instructor may ask you to do these exercises as nongraded assignments or ask you to complete them during class. Practice Box answer keys are included in the back of the book. You should use these exercises to judge your own progress. If everything in the Practice Box makes sense, then you should be confident of your mastery of that topic. If not, read the text again and ask questions. Almost always, if you do not attain mastery of each topic, the next one will be harder or even impossible to understand.

This book is different from other music theory textbooks because of the inclusion of theoretical and aural skills under the same cover. Although you may be enrolled in separate courses for these two subjects, they are essentially varied applications of the same topics. In this book, the theoretical topics that you study will be emphasized in sight-singing and dictation exercises within the same chapter.

Another feature of this textbook is the inclusion of a large number of musical figures and examples throughout the text. Those designated "figures" are written by the author to demonstrate and illustrate concepts presented in the text. Those designated "examples" are excerpts from music by composers spanning many centuries and representing a variety of styles from classical to jazz to popular music. All of the music labeled "example" is included on the audio compact disc that accompanies this book, giving you an opportunity to hear a performance of everything you are studying. This wide variety will give you a chance to see and hear all concepts presented in the text in actual musical form—exactly the kind of music that you will be studying and performing as a musician for the rest of your life.

I have been a theory teacher for many years, and this book is the result of years of experimentation with my own students. You might be interested in knowing that my own students have actually contributed many of the thoughts and ideas in this book. One of the highlights of my career as a theory teacher is the knowledge that my students usually develop a love of the study of music theory. I hope that this book will help you become a successful theory student and help you to appreciate the importance of this subject in the grand scheme of your musical training.

Before writing this preface, I asked my own students what words of advice they could give to other music students using this book. Here are a few of the things they had to say:

> *"Theory is the most important aspect of music. Using this book has furthered my understanding of music greatly. The way Dr. Mayfield organizes the book is very simple and step-by-step to make the learning of theory easy. The language she uses is very easy to understand, as if she is there speaking the words to you one on one. The most important first thing to understand, as we all have to know, are the key signatures. After that, it gets easier!"*

> *"This book is very detailed, easy to read and to understand. Consider it as a complete guide to music. It can be challenging, but it is worth the time."*

> *"Work through all of the Practice Boxes. Pay close attention to every detail. Repetition is the key to get the hang of things."*

> *"These first chapters are the fundamentals, elements in the process of creating music. Drill these lessons into your mind. These basics will not change. They are the beginning and the end."*

You are embarking on a long journey when you begin the study of music theory. It is a journey that will last through your entire career as a musician. Take your study of theory seriously, because it will enable you to speak the language of music and it will make you a better musician for having endured the challenge of mastering this material.

Acknowledgments

So many people have contributed support and encouragement for me and for this book that I may never be able to thank them enough. I would like to begin by thanking Clark and Abigail Baxter of Wadsworth Publishing, who have worked with me throughout the development process. They have given me many sage words of advice that have helped make the book what it is today.

I have also received an amazing amount of support from the college where I teach, Kansas City Kansas Community College. Many thanks are due the administration of the college, including the Board of Trustees; Dr. Thomas Burke, president; and Dr. Kaye Walter, vice president of academic services, who granted me a sabbatical in the early stages of writing this book. My current dean, Dr. Amy Fugate, gives me constant moral support, and my former dean, Dr. James Brown (now dean at Lakeland Community College, Kirtland, Ohio), encouraged me to believe in myself and follow my dreams.

My colleagues in the music department have supported me with advice, encouragement, and patience during the years that I have been writing the book. I want to thank all of my colleagues who have read, critiqued, and contributed ideas that have made their way into this edition. In particular, I would like to mention Ian Corbett, Jim Mair, Dale Shelter, Ronda Ford, and Dr. Paul Hidgon, who have all shared their thoughts and ideas throughout this process. I would like to particularly thank two of these colleagues for special contributions to the book: Jim Mair, who contributed the voice-overs heard on the audio CD, and Ian Corbett, who composed *Check-In To Go* as an excellent illustration of the twelve-bar blues.

I also must acknowledge the professors who have influenced me in my theoretical studies through the many years that I was a student. In particular these include Professors Arnold Whittall and Kofi Agawu, with whom I studied at King's College, University of London, and my theory professors at the University of Kansas. In particular at KU, Dr. Stanley Shumway, Dr. Mark Holmberg, Dr. Charles Hoag, and Dr. John Pozdro played an enormous part in shaping my philosophy of music theory pedagogy. I am extremely grateful to them for their interest and involvement in my doctoral studies and the guidance they gave me that has helped me become a successful teacher of music theory.

Perhaps the biggest group of contributors, and those to whom this book is truly dedicated, are my students. My life has been inspired, enriched, and enlivened by the students who have come through my music theory classrooms over the years. It was their combined voices that originally motivated me to write a theory textbook, when I discovered that they had special needs that were not being met. My students have struggled and endured right alongside me as this book grew from an inspiration into a reality. They have brought me their ideas and their innovations and I have incorporated so many of their wonderful ideas into this text. I have truly learned as much from them as they have from me. As we worked with many preliminary versions of the text, they have done the bulk of the proofreading for me.

Four particular students need to be singled out for the intense technical work and research that has helped me write the book. These four young men are all graduates of the Music Technology program at Kansas City Kansas Community College and have worked as lab assistants in our technology studios. Their technical expertise in a variety of areas, including notation software, Internet research, and recording technology, have made this book a physical reality. Aaron Crawford, Chip Knighton, Luiz Moreira, and Phil Park have contributed so many hours of work to the book that I can never repay them. They are four of my finest students. My pride in their accomplishments and gratitude for their help is endless. I particularly want to recognize the work that Luiz Moreira contributed in recording and engineering the audio CD that accompanies the book.

Finally, it is not possible to write these acknowledgments without mentioning my parents, Ben and Fern Mayfield, who taught me the importance of education and self-discipline, and who supported me financially and emotionally throughout my own college career. They have continued to be the best parents in the world, helping me with everyday things in my life that would have slipped by because of the hours I have spent at the computer writing and finishing *Theory Essentials*. Everything that I have accomplished in life is really due to them.

MUSICAL EXAMPLES

TABLES

chapter 1

The Basics of Reading Music

THEORETICAL SKILLS

Definition of Theory

Music theory is the study of patterns and formulas that make up musical languages. It is also a study of the way in which those patterns and formulas are put together to create real music. It is called "theory" because although the patterns and formulas are predetermined, the manner in which they can be used together is as varied as any composer cares to make it.

In the study of music theory, as indicated by the definition above, the starting place is to understand the facts. One must be able to read music, know how to write it on paper, and know most of the basic formulas such as scales, intervals, and chords. Then the student of theory is ready to look at real music and study how all the various elements can be combined, or as stated in the definition above, related to one another.

Historical Overview

Western music has been recorded on paper since about the ninth century. Almost as soon as human beings figured out a way to notate musical sounds, they also began to write about music. They speculated about the way in which the elements were put together to create certain effects, they wondered why it worked the way it did, and they pondered what formulas made the music good (or bad). People who write about music in this manner are called **theorists.** Theorists have been trying to explain music from the ninth century right up to the present day. The styles of music have changed, but the desire to explain music has always been present among curious musicians.

This volume is primarily concerned with the study of tonal music, which is often called music of the Common Practice Period. This span of music history includes three major style periods, roughly covering the years 1600–1900. Table 1 shows a time line that will help you understand where this time fits into the larger picture of music history. Can you name any of the composers who lived during these time periods?

Table 1.   *Dates and names of major style periods of music history. Although these dates are approximate, they are useful when discussing musical style.*

450–1450	1450–1600	1600–1750*	1750–1820*	1820–1900*	1900–present
Middle Ages	Renaissance	Baroque	Classical	Romantic	Contemporary

* Common Practice Period 1600–1900

Music Notation

The most basic symbol of musical sound is called a **note.** Its shape is simply that of an oval. This symbol tells a performer to make one musical sound, such as striking any key on the piano one time. Several notes written one after the other tell the performer to make successive sounds.

Notes have not always been shaped as ovals. The earliest types of music notation date from the medieval period, when the notes where shaped as squares, diamonds, and rectangles. See Figure 1.1.

1

Figure 1.1. Note shapes used in early music

Notes can also have lines attached to them, called stems, and flags may be attached to the stems. Notes can also be shaded black. These alterations in the appearance of notes are shown in Figure 1.2. Changes in appearance of the note affect the duration of the sounds.

Figure 1.2. Notes with stems, flags, and shaded note heads

The note alone gives us very little information about the musical sound that is to be created. The note must also indicate two other aspects of musical sound: pitch and rhythm.

Pitch is the aspect of sound that distinguishes high sounds from low sounds. If you play piano keys at the far right side of the keyboard, you will hear high sounds. Keys played at the extreme left side will result in low sounds. Even when two white keys side by side on the piano keyboard are played, it is possible to distinguish which one is higher.

A **staff** (Figure 1.3) is a graphic symbol used to distinguish high notes from low ones. It is a series of five horizontal parallel lines and can be thought of as a musical ladder. This ladder can very clearly distinguish high from low, just as each rung of a ladder takes the climber one step higher. (Note: the plural of staff is **staves.**)

Figure 1.3. Staff

Notes can be placed on a staff in only two ways, on a line and between two lines. These are called, respectively, line notes and space notes. As you can see in Figure 1.4, the direction of notes is easy to discern; notes that climb toward the top of the staff are getting higher in pitch and those that move toward the bottom get lower in pitch.

Figure 1.4. Line and space notes on a staff

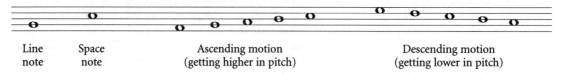

| Line
note | Space
note | Ascending motion
(getting higher in pitch) | Descending motion
(getting lower in pitch) |

Musical sounds are named with letters A through G of the alphabet. These seven letters are called the **musical alphabet.** On a full-size piano keyboard, the key that is farthest to the left is the letter A. The key to its right is B, the next is C, and so on. After using each letter of the musical alphabet, the names start over with A again. Therefore there are many As on the piano, many Bs, and so on. See Figure 1.5.

Figure 1.5. The musical alphabet on the piano keyboard

Left edge of
an acoustic
piano keyboard

When thinking of the musical alphabet and the manner in which the seven letters repeat, it is helpful to think in terms of a clock. When you think of a clock's face, it seems normal that the numbers "12" and "1" are side by side. Similarly, on the "musical clock" (see Figure 1.6), the letters G and A are next to each other. Going up in pitch signifies that you are going clockwise around the musical clock. Going down in pitch signifies counter-clockwise motion.

Figure 1.6.   A regular clock compared to a "musical" clock

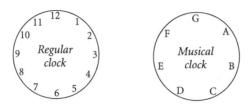

It is important that you be able to say the musical alphabet backward as easily as you can say it forward. One way to practice this is to build it up a letter at a time. Repeat C–B–A several times. Then repeat D–C–B–A several times, then E–D–C–B–A, and so on until it becomes easy.

Naming Notes

When you refer to a specific sound such as the lowest A on the piano keyboard, you are referring to a single pitch. When you discuss all of the As on the keyboard, you are referring to a **pitch class**. Pitch class is a collective term that associates all the musical sounds that bear a single name. The pitch C that is closest to the center of the piano keyboard is known as **middle C**.

In order to give letter names to the notes placed on a staff, another type of symbol is used. It is called a **clef** sign. There are several different types of clef signs. Each type is named with a letter of the musical alphabet. They are C clef, F clef, and G clef. In addition, all of the clef signs have nicknames, which are commonly used in place of their proper names. These clefs are pictured in Figure 1.7.

Figure 1.7.   Clefs

All clefs are movable (up or down) on the staff, although the only clef that is typically moved is the C clef (Figure 1.8). When a clef is moved, it is given a different nickname.

Figure 1.8.   C clefs

The clef sign is used to place one specific letter name on the staff. On the staves above, the line that is touched by the center of the clef is given the name C. In fact, it is not just any C, but specifically middle C. Therefore, depending on whether an alto, tenor, or mezzo-soprano clef is used, the middle C could be placed on any of the middle three lines of the staff.

The most common clefs are the **treble** and the **bass,** so we will begin with those. (C clefs will be covered in depth later.) All clefs give their real names to one line of the staff (see Figure 1.9). So the treble clef gives its name, G, to a specific line, the second line from the bottom. Likewise, the bass clef gives its name, F, to the second line from the top.

Figure 1.9.   *Clefs impart their names to a staff line*

This note is   This note is
named G.   named F.

It is important to notice which G and which F these notes represent. They do not stand for just any G or F, but specifically the G that is five notes up from middle C and the F that is five notes down from middle C.

If we know the name of one note on a staff, it is very easy to name all the others. A line note and a space note that touch the same line of the staff always represent two adjacent letters of the musical alphabet. These notes will also always represent white keys of the piano that are side by side. Therefore, the space on the staff directly below the given note is the preceding letter of the alphabet, and the space above it is the next letter of the alphabet. See Figure 1.10.

Figure 1.10.   *Naming adjacent notes on the staff*

F   **G**   A   E   **F**   G

One line and one space note always represent adjacent letters of the alphabet. In other words, if F is a space note, the G next to it on the piano keyboard must be a line note. If F is a line note, G must be a space. Figure 1.11 shows how it is possible to use this principle to name all notes on the treble and bass clef staves.

Figure 1.11.   *Naming treble and bass clef notes*

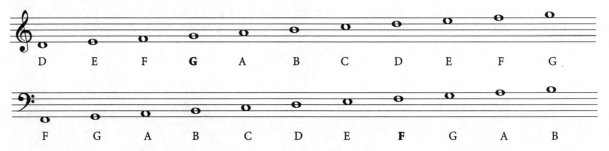

D   E   F   **G**   A   B   C   D   E   F   G

F   G   A   B   C   D   E   **F**   G   A   B

If you know one letter name, it is possible to figure out any other name by working forward or backward in the musical alphabet (clockwise or counterclockwise on the musical clock). With practice, you should soon be able to easily name any note on the staff just by glancing at it. Alternatively, you may choose to use the following mnemonic devices. (These are just a few of the many word phrases that can be used.)

The names of the four space notes on the treble staff spell a word:

    F   A   C   E.

The names of the five line notes on the treble staff can be identified this way:

    E-very   G-ood   B-oy   D-oes   F-ine.

The names of the four space notes on the bass staff can be identified this way:

    A-ll   C-ows   E-at   G-rass.

The names of the five line notes on the bass staff can be identified this way:

    G-ood   B-urritos   D-on't   F-all   A-part.

Practice Box 1.1

Name the following notes.

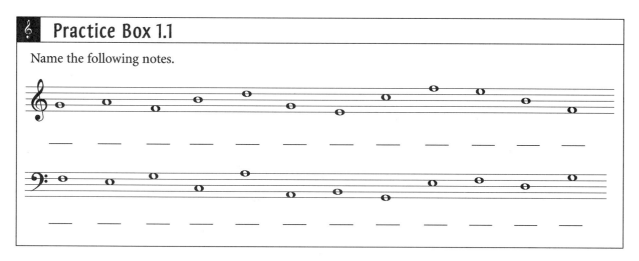

The alto clef is the most commonly used of the C clefs. It uses middle C as its reference point on the middle line of the staff. Figure 1.12 shows how the other lines and spaces are named from middle C.

Figure 1.12.   Naming alto clef notes

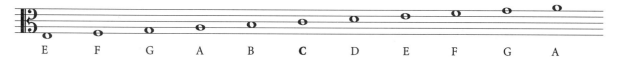

E   F   G   A   B   **C**   D   E   F   G   A

Try creating some mnemonic devices of your own to name the lines and spaces of the alto clef.

Ledger Lines and the Grand Staff

The staff contains only five lines and four spaces, so only nine different pitches can be written on a staff (or eleven, if you count the space notes above and below the staff). Obviously there are many more than nine possible pitches (take a look at a piano keyboard). Music for instruments or ensembles using a large range of pitches (such as a piano or a choir) is typically written on something called a **grand staff.** See Figure 1.13.

A grand staff is constructed with two staves, two clef signs, an initial bar line (a vertical line that connects the two staves together), and a bracket. Since the piano encompasses both high and low sounds, both a treble clef and a bass clef are typically used. Generally, the piano player uses the right hand to play notes on the treble staff and the left hand for the bass staff. The grand staff can also be used to represent choral music, with the parts for the high voices written on the upper treble staff and the parts for low voices written on the lower bass staff.

Figure 1.13.   The grand staff, with middle C written as a treble-clef note and as a bass-clef note

However, there is still only enough space on a grand staff for twice as many notes as on a single staff, so **ledger lines** are used. These are short extensions of the staff and are used to represent notes that are above, below, or in between the notes of the treble and bass clefs. Middle C (shown in Figure 1.13) is an example of a ledger-line note.

Middle C is written on the first ledger line below the treble staff and the first ledger line above the bass staff. Both of the notes in Figure 1.13 represent middle C. Figure 1.14 demonstrates some more ledger-line notes.

Figure 1.14.   Ledger lines on the grand staff

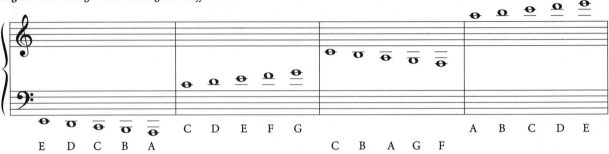

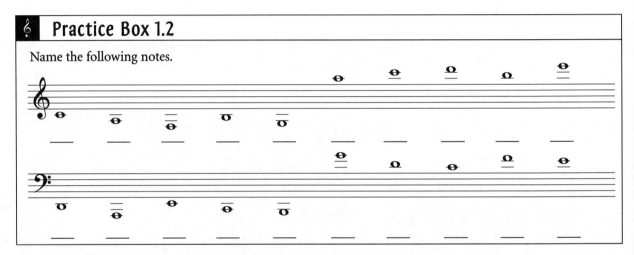

♭ Practice Box 1.2

Name the following notes.

Ledger-line notes that appear above the bass staff can also be written as treble-clef notes. Likewise, ledger lines below the treble staff can be rewritten as bass-clef notes, as shown in Figure 1.15. Each pair of notes represents exactly the same pitch, or exactly the same key on the piano.

Figure 1.15.   Rewriting ledger-line notes on the staff

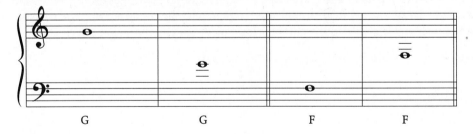

♭ Practice Box 1.3

In the measure following each given note, draw a ledger-line equivalent on the opposite staff.

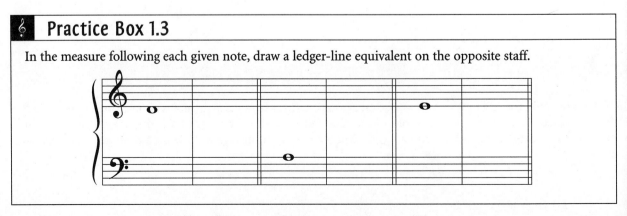

The symbol *8va* may be used to avoid writing ledger-line notes. The symbol stands for the Italian term *ottava* (in English, octave) and refers to the distance between two pitches that have the same letter name, for example, A to A. When the symbol is placed *above* a single note or group of notes, it changes those pitches by the distance of one octave. That means the written note is to be played or sung on the next higher pitch of the same letter name. This symbol is demonstrated in Figure 1.16.

Figure 1.16.   *The 8va sign*

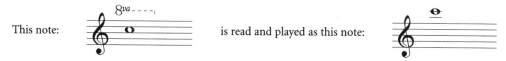

When written *below* a single pitch or group of pitches, the *8va* symbol signifies that the indicated pitches are to be played an octave lower than written.

Sometimes the symbol is written *8ve* or *8*. All versions of this symbol are interpreted the same way. When written underneath a staff you may also occasionally see *8va bassa* (or rarely, *8vb*), which means an octave lower.

Occasionally the symbol *15ma* is used. This refers to the Italian term *quindicesima*, meaning "at the fifteenth." This symbol is used when the note is to be played two octaves higher than notated, as seen in Figure 1.17.

Figure 1.17.   *The 15ma sign*

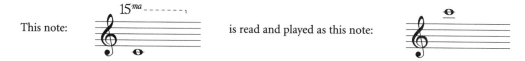

Octave Identification

Each of the octaves on the piano has a particular designation so that each can be uniquely identified. Because there are so many keys on the piano, this allows specific reference to a single key within an octave. There are several systems of octave identification, but the one that will be introduced here designates the lowest C on the piano as C^1. Designations for each higher octave raise the superscript number. For the notes below C^1, the superscript 0 is used. Middle C is designated C^4. Designations and names for all octaves are shown in Figure 1.18.

Figure 1.18.   *Octave identification*

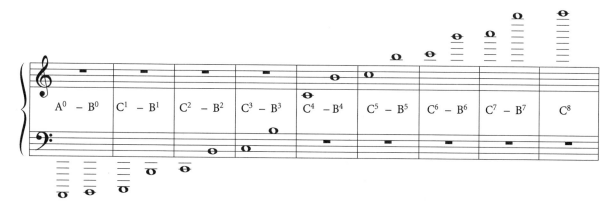

Half and Whole Steps

The pitches represented by the musical alphabet are not evenly spaced in their distances from one another. When you look at the piano keyboard, you will see that E and F sit beside each other with no black key in between them. But there is a black key in between C and D. The sound represented by this black key makes C and D more distant in pitch than E and F.

The distance between E and F is called a **half step.** Two half steps occur naturally in the musical alphabet, between B and C and between E and F. The other distances, A–B, C–D, D–E, F–G, and G–A, are called **whole steps.** The whole steps occur where there are black keys in between the white keys. This information is also demonstrated in Figure 1.19.

Figure 1.19.   Half steps on the piano keyboard. The other distances between white keys are whole steps.

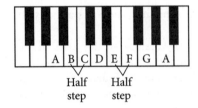

The half steps are represented with an arrow symbol above. Notice the absence of a black key where the half steps are marked. All of the other distances between the white keys are considered to be whole steps, because there is an intervening black key between the white keys.

Half steps can also occur between a white key and the closest black key. In other words, a half step is the closest that any two pitches can be placed. A whole step occurs when two pitches are separated by one other pitch; therefore, the adjacent black keys between F and G are a whole step apart, as are B and the black key to the right side of C. See Figure 1.20.

Figure 1.20.   Half and whole steps using black keys

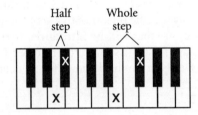

Accidentals

The black keys of the piano can take the name of either of the white keys that surround them. In order to name the pitches that are represented by the black keys, we use one of two new terms in addition to a letter of the musical alphabet: **flat** or **sharp.** The word "sharp" is used to represent a pitch that is one half step higher than the chosen letter name (or the key to the right on the keyboard). The word "flat" is used to represent a pitch that is one half step lower than the chosen letter name (or the key to the left on the keyboard).

The symbol used for a sharp is ♯. This symbol is used to raise a pitch by one half step. The symbol used for a flat is ♭. This symbol is used to lower a pitch by one half step.

One additional word is used when you wish to refer to a regular member of the musical alphabet after having discussed the same letter name as a sharp or flat. That word is **natural.** A natural sign cancels a sharp or a flat. The symbol used for the word natural is ♮.

For example, using the word natural is a way of ensuring that you distinguish between C-sharp and plain C (or C-natural). These three symbols are referred to as **accidentals.**

When writing or talking about music, the words and written symbols are always placed after the letter names, such as C-sharp, C♯; D-natural, D♮; and B-flat, B♭. However, when a sharp or flat is placed on a staff next to a note, it must come first, on the left side of the note. Since the sharp or flat symbol affects the note it sits beside, by either raising or lowering it in pitch, it must be written first. See Figure 1.21.

When writing notes on the staff, you must also be careful to place your sharps and flats precisely on a line or space in front of the notes to which they belong. Name these six notes.

Figure 1.21.   Placing accidentals on a staff

♭ Practice Box 1.4

1. The closest key to the right side of F is _____.

2. The closest key to the left side of A is _____.

3. The closest key to the right side of C is _____.

4. The closest key to the left side of G is _____.

5. The closest key to the right side of A is _____.

6. The closest key to the left side of B is _____.

Write the following pitches on the staff, with the correct accidental beside them.

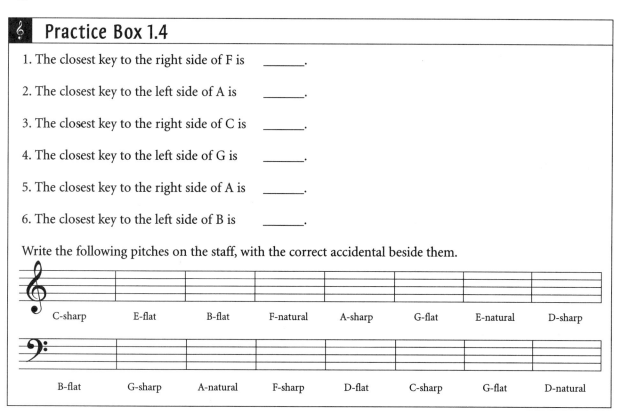

When any accidental (sharp, flat, or natural) is placed into a measure of music, it stays in effect on that particular line or space until the end of the measure, a segment of music delineated by a vertical line crossing all lines of the staff. It does not affect any other line or space on the staff, including other lines or spaces that have the same letter name. It is canceled by the next bar line. This is an important rule to remember when naming notes, because a single accidental can affect several other notes within a measure. See Figure 1.22.

Figure 1.22.   The accidental affects more than one note in the first measure

The first measure of this example contains two F♯s. Because the bar line cancels each accidental, it is necessary to repeat it in each subsequent measure to create another F♯.

If any line or space has recently had an accidental, then a reminder is often placed next to that note in the new measure to help you remember that it has reverted to its original status. That reminder is called a **courtesy accidental**. Its use is demonstrated in Figure 1.23.

Figure 1.23.   *Courtesy accidental in second measure*

Enharmonic Names

All black keys on the piano can be referred to by more than one name. The black key between C and D can be called either C♯ or D♭. *It is important to remember that nothing in the definition of the words sharp or flat says that these pitches have to be black keys.* The definition simply says that these symbols change a musical pitch by raising or lowering it one half step. Therefore, B♯ is the same pitch as C. And F♭ is the same pitch as E.

When the same pitch can be given two different names, these names are said to be **enharmonic.** Enharmonic names are just two ways of spelling the same sound. Therefore, F♯ is an enharmonic name for G♭. In addition, all of the F♯s and G♭s are considered to be the same pitch class. A pitch is a specific letter of the musical alphabet occurring in a specific octave, such as C^3. However, a pitch class refers to any C occurring in any octave and includes all the enharmonic respellings of that note, such as B♯.

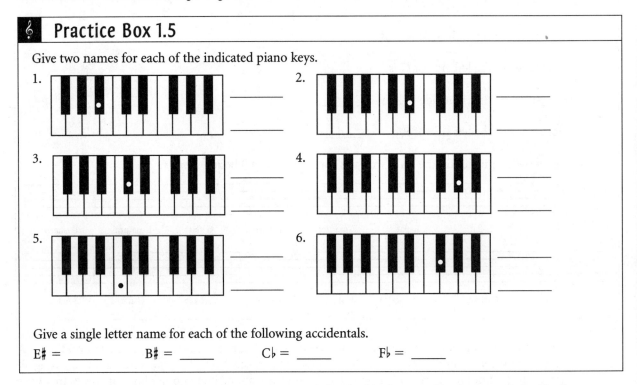

Give two names for each of the indicated piano keys.

Give a single letter name for each of the following accidentals.

E♯ = _____   B♯ = _____   C♭ = _____   F♭ = _____

Additional accidentals include the **double sharp** and the **double flat.** Double sharps and double flats are not as commonly used as regular sharps and flats. All of these symbols can be canceled by a natural sign.

The symbol used for a double sharp is ✕. This symbol is used to raise a pitch by one whole step. The symbol used for a double flat is ♭♭. This symbol is used to lower a pitch by one whole step.

Any octave can be divided into twelve equal half steps. The representation of this division on a staff is known as the **chromatic scale.** A *scale* is a stepwise series of notes that form a distinctive pattern. The chromatic scale provides an excellent opportunity to make use of the enharmonic names that you have learned. Traditionally, the chromatic scale is spelled with sharps representing the black keys when the scale ascends, and with flats representing the black keys when the scale descends.

Music Manuscript

As a theory student, you will be writing a great deal of music by hand. It is important to know how to draw all musical symbols correctly and to be able to do it quickly and legibly. The following rules will be helpful.

1. When you draw notes, it is important to make your notes very easily distinguishable as line notes or space notes. Make sure that your line notes are centered around a line and that your space notes only touch the surrounding lines, not cross them.

2. When you place stems on notes, the notes that are high on a staff generally have stems that go down. The notes that are low on a staff generally have stems that go up. The idea is to draw the stem in the direction of the maximum number of staff lines. Notes on the middle line of the staff usually have stems that go down. See Figure 1.24. These rules may be overridden if there is a specific reason, such as demonstrating which hand should be used to play a particular note in a composition for piano. For a demonstration of this, see Example 1.1.

Figure 1.24.   Normal stemming of notes on a staff

3. The length of the stem is usually three lines or three spaces. As you look at the examples above, you will see that on line notes, the stem crosses three lines of the staff in addition to the line on which the note is written. For space notes, the stem crosses three spaces of the staff.

4. Clef signs should be practiced until you can make them easily, especially the treble clef, which is somewhat complicated. The treble clef can be drawn in a single motion, starting at the bottom of the symbol, or in two motions, starting with a straight line and then going back to the top and drawing the curved portion of the symbol. The bass clef is not hard to draw, but you should make certain that you do not draw it backward like the letter C. (When studying manuscripts of certain composers, it should be noted that some of them consistently wrote their bass clef symbols "backward.")

🎼 Practice Box 1.6

Draw several of each of the following clef signs.

    treble clef   bass clef   alto clef

Draw several notes of each of the types specified below the staff.

| low line notes | high line notes | low space notes | high space notes |
| (stems up) | (stems down) | (stems up) | (stems down) |

Music for Analysis

In each chapter, you will have one or more compositions to analyze for particular features. Name each pitch in the following piece. If the pitch includes an accidental, your answer should include that symbol.

Example 1.1.   *Johann Sebastian Bach*, Little Prelude

Track 1, 0:00

AURAL SKILLS

Melody

Exercise 1. You will hear single pitches, which you will be asked to sing.

Exercise 2. You will hear a series of short melodies, four or five notes in length. After you have heard the melody once, you will be asked to sing it back as accurately as possible. Use the syllable "la" as you sing each pitch.

Exercise 3. You will hear two notes played at the same time. Sing each of those two individual pitches, one after the other. It does not matter which pitch you sing first. Sing the pitches in the register (area) of your voice that is most comfortable for you.

Rhythm

The word "rhythm" can mean any aspect of music that deals with time. Because of that broad definition, rhythm might refer to the duration of individual pitches or the manner in which those durations are organized.

You were introduced to the concept of notes, which are oval shapes that represent single musical sounds. You saw that notes could be drawn in several semblances: as a plain oval, with a stem, blackened in the middle, or with a flag on the stem. These different ways of drawing the oval shape represent different durational values. In other words, when the oval is manipulated by attaching a line or flag to it, or by filling it in, the sound will be heard for a different amount of time. The names given to different ways of drawing the original oval shape are shown in Figure 1.25.

Figure 1.25. Note names

Double whole note   Whole note   Half notes   Quarter notes   Eighth notes

All of these shapes have the oval as part of the symbol, but the half notes, quarter notes, and eighth notes have been manipulated in various ways. The half note is drawn as a whole note with a stem. The direction of the stem can go up or down. When flags are attached to notes, they always are drawn on the right side, no matter the direction of the stem.

Each note drawn above has an exact mathematical relationship to the following note. It sounds for exactly twice as long as the next note to the right. Another way to say this is that each note sounds for half as long as the previous one in the list. Various ways to illustrate the mathematical proportions of pairs of notes are given in Figure 1.26.

Figure 1.26. Proportional relationships between notes

o = ♩ + ♩   ♩ = ♩ + ♩   ♩ = ♪ + ♪

𝄞 Practice Box 1.7

Do the following musical math by drawing a single whole, half, or quarter note in each blank space.

1. _____ = ♩ + ♩ + ♩ + ♩

2. _____ = ♩ + ♩

3. _____ = ♪ + ♪ + ♪ + ♪

4. _____ + _____ + _____ + _____ = ♩

5. _____ + _____ = ♩

6. _____ + _____ + _____ + _____ = o

Pulse and Meter

Virtually all music has a background beat, sometimes called a pulse. This is similar to the pulse in your own body. A heartbeat is regular and steady, or at least it ought to be if the heart is working correctly. The same characteristics apply to a musical pulse. It should be regular, with the same length of time between each beat or pulse, and it should be steady, meaning that it should not speed up or slow down. It is very easy to achieve this effect by tapping your foot. Your leg muscles pull your foot up and down in a very steady manner, raising it the exact same distance each time and moving at the same speed. This creates a steady beat and that is an important skill for all musicians to develop.

In order to keep track of the beats or pulses in music, every so often one beat is **accented.** That means it is made louder or more important than the beats surrounding it. This accent usually happens in a regular pattern, such as every three beats or every four beats. This is called the **meter** of the music. These regular accents are demonstrated in Figure 1.27 with a series of notes and musical symbols called *accents*.

Figure 1.27.   Demonstration of recurring accents

The arrowhead symbols above the quarter notes are the accent marks. Let us suppose that each of these quarter notes represents one beat of the music. Then this line represents a quadruple meter, which means that there is an accent on every fourth beat. A triple meter would have an accent on every third beat, and a duple meter would have an accent on every second beat.

When music is notated on a staff, these regularly recurring groups are shown through the use of vertical **bar lines.** The bar lines divide music up into segments of equal duration. These segments are called **measures,** and are labeled in Figure 1.28.

Figure 1.28.   Measures

Each measure of music has the same number of pulses and therefore occupies the same amount of time. The number of pulses contained in each measure is indicated at the beginning of the music by a symbol called a **time signature.** The time signature is a pair of numbers written like a fraction. It is written directly after the clef sign (see Figure 1.29). Each of these two numbers gives a different type of information about the rhythm of the piece.

Figure 1.29.   Time signature

In this time signature, both of the numbers are four. This time signature is read as "four-four" time.

The top number of the time signature determines how many beats or pulses there will be in every measure. Provided that it is *not* a multiple of three greater than three itself, the top number will always represent the number of beats per measure. Numbers that are commonly used as the top number of a time signature are 2, 3, and 4. In Figure 1.30, the number is 4, so there will be four beats or counts in every measure.

Figure 1.30.   Counting beats in ⁴⁄₄ time

The bottom number is more difficult to understand, because although it is written as a numeric figure, it does not represent a quantity. It is actually a code for one of the types of notes that we have previously discussed, such as eighth, quarter, or half. It is responsible for determining which type of note gets a single beat. For the time signatures described in the preceding paragraph, where the top number is *not* a multiple of 3 greater than 3 itself, Table 2 shows the meaning of the bottom number of the time signature.

Table 2. *Explanation of bottom number of various time signatures*

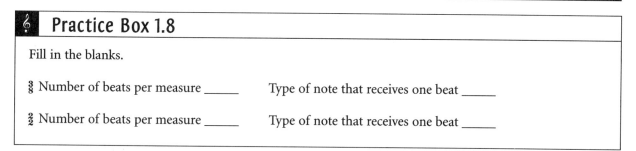

Bottom number of the time signature	What it means
The number 2 stands for a half note.	♩ = 1 count
The number 4 stands for a quarter note.	♩ = 1 count
The number 8 stands for an eighth note.	♪ = 1 count

Practice Box 1.8

Fill in the blanks.

³⁄₈ Number of beats per measure _____   Type of note that receives one beat _____

²⁄₂ Number of beats per measure _____   Type of note that receives one beat _____

Figure 1.31 has a time signature that is read as ⁴⁄₄. The top number is 4, and that tells you that there will be four beats or pulses in every measure. The bottom number is also 4, and that tells you that every quarter note will receive one count.

Figure 1.31. *Counting beats in ⁴⁄₄ time*

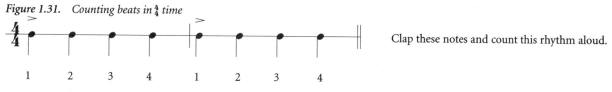

Clap these notes and count this rhythm aloud.

1   2   3   4   1   2   3   4

When you clap and count the subsequent exercise (and all others from now on) your hands and mouth will be doing different things. The words you speak will represent every possible beat within the measure and will be responsible for keeping track of a steady flow of pulses. The hands will clap the notes that actually appear on the staff. It is important to understand the distinction between the two actions.

Figure 1.32 shows how other combinations of whole, half, and quarter notes can be combined in a single measure.

Figure 1.32. *Counting other rhythms in ⁴⁄₄ time*

Clap and count this rhythm.

1 2 3 4   1 2 3 4   1 2 3 4   1 2 3 4

The time signature that we have been using thus far, ⁴⁄₄ time, is also sometimes known as **common time**. This is frequently abbreviated as the letter C when it is written on a staff. See Figure 1.33.

Figure 1.33. *Symbol for common time*

The **C** stands for common time or ⁴⁄₄.

Practice Box 1.9

Rhythmic exercises are often written on a single line staff without a clef sign. Write the counts under these lines of music, and then clap and count each line aloud.

Additional Rhythms

For extra practice, clap and count these longer exercises in common time.

Dictation

You will hear pairs of notes. Circle the note that is higher.

1.	1st	2nd
2.	1st	2nd
3.	1st	2nd
4.	1st	2nd
5.	1st	2nd
6.	1st	2nd
7.	1st	2nd
8.	1st	2nd
9.	1st	2nd
10.	1st	2nd

You will hear groups of three notes. Circle the note that is highest.

1.	1st	2nd	3rd
2.	1st	2nd	3rd
3.	1st	2nd	3rd
4.	1st	2nd	3rd
5.	1st	2nd	3rd
6.	1st	2nd	3rd
7.	1st	2nd	3rd
8.	1st	2nd	3rd
9.	1st	2nd	3rd
10.	1st	2nd	3rd

You will hear groups of four notes. Circle the note that is highest.

1.	1st	2nd	3rd	4th
2.	1st	2nd	3rd	4th
3.	1st	2nd	3rd	4th
4.	1st	2nd	3rd	4th
5.	1st	2nd	3rd	4th
6.	1st	2nd	3rd	4th
7.	1st	2nd	3rd	4th
8.	1st	2nd	3rd	4th
9.	1st	2nd	3rd	4th
10.	1st	2nd	3rd	4th

Conducting Patterns

The terms "downbeat" and "upbeat" are used to refer to various components of a measure, but they come from terminology associated with conducting. When a conductor moves his or her hands and arms to guide an ensemble, the patterns of movement are associated with specific meters, but they all share certain elements in common. The first beat of the measure is always represented with a downward movement, hence the term "downbeat." The final beat of the measure, regardless of the meter, is always represented with an upward movement, hence the term "upbeat."

Figure 1.34 diagrams duple, triple, and quadruple conducting patterns. Conducting these patterns is an activity that can be added to many of the aural exercises in all subsequent chapters of this book.

Figure 1.34.   *Conducting patterns*

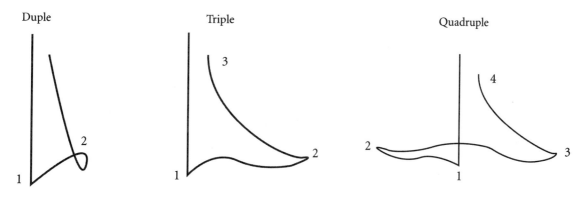

KEYBOARD APPLICATIONS

In order to learn your way around the piano keyboard, you must notice how the black keys are arranged in groups of twos and threes. These groups alternate over the whole length of the keyboard, no matter whether you are playing a small electronic keyboard or a full-size acoustic piano.

Play each of the letters of the musical alphabet on the piano keyboard. The picture will help you locate the correct key. For each letter, play all the keys you can find on your keyboard that look like the picture. In addition, answer the questions beside each keyboard picture, basing your answers on a full-size acoustic piano.

1.

How many Cs are on the keyboard? _____

The letter C sits beside a group of two black keys and is on the left side of the entire group.

2.

How many Fs are on the keyboard? _____

The letter F sits beside a group of three black keys and is on the left side of the entire group.

3.

How many Bs are on the keyboard? _____

The letter B sits beside a group of three black keys and is on the right side of the entire group.

4.

How many Ds are on the keyboard? _____

The letter D sits within a group of two black keys and is the key between the two black keys.

5.

How many As are on the keyboard? _____

The letter A sits within a group of three black keys and is between the two black keys on the right.

6.

How many Es are on the keyboard? _____

The letter E sits beside a group of two black keys and is on the right side of the entire group.

7.

How many Gs are on the keyboard? _____

The letter G sits within a group of three black keys and is between the two black keys on the left.

2 Major Scales and Key Signatures

THEORETICAL SKILLS

Tonality

Frequently, music is said to be in a **key**. You may have heard people refer to a piece being in the key of D major, or in the key of E minor. That is a musical expression referring to the scale on which the composition is based. So if a piece is said to be in D major or in the key of D major, that simply means that most of its pitch content comes from a scale called D major. It also means that the piece will end on the pitch class D or on a combination of pitches that includes D. The last pitch that is heard in any composition is an important one, since it is the thing that leaves the final impression on the listener. Most pieces of music end on the name of the scale from which the piece is derived. This pitch, which forms the first note of the scale and the last note of the composition, is known as the **tonic**. Music that is written in a major or minor key is called **tonal music**. In this chapter, you will study major scales.

The origins of tonality, or the practice of writing tonal music, are in the baroque period. The practice of writing music in major and minor keys evolved over a period of many years and gained widespread acceptance during the latter half of this period. Jean-Philippe Rameau was the first theorist to write about tonal music, and Johann Sebastian Bach played an important role in the widespread adoption of the tonal system. Bach wrote two collections of keyboard music, known as *The Well-Tempered Clavier*, Books I and II. Each of these collections contains twenty-four preludes and fugues, one in each major and minor key. Bach wrote these collections to demonstrate the possibilities inherent in the tonal system, as well as the new tuning system known as "equal temperament," which divides the octave into twelve equal half steps and is still in use to this day. The books of *The Well-Tempered Clavier* are considered masterpieces of keyboard literature.

Major Scales

The study of music theory involves learning many patterns that make up music. You have learned the building blocks that make up patterns that are called scales. You should recall that a **scale** is a series of pitches, usually presented in a stepwise arrangement, that together form a recognizable pattern. One characteristic of a scale is that it begins and ends on the same letter of the musical alphabet.

The word **major** actually refers to a particular eight-note pattern of whole and half steps. The most basic major scale is found on the piano keyboard from C to C, using only white keys. It is known as the C major scale. Figure 2.1 shows this pattern on a keyboard diagram.

Figure 2.1.   C major scale on keyboard

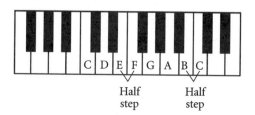

pattern of whole and half steps:
WWHWWWH

The pattern, known as major, can be abbreviated as shown in Figure 2.1. Notice the placement of the half steps from the third to the fourth notes of the scale and from the seventh to the eighth notes of the scale. All other distances between notes of the scale are whole steps. This eight-note pattern is actually made up of seven *different* pitches, the eighth letter name of the pattern being a repeat of the first.

It is possible to move, or **transpose**, the pattern to other starting pitches. All transposed major scales will need one or more accidentals in order to create this same pattern of whole and half steps. For example, if we start on F, a whole step up will take us to G, another whole step up will take us to A, and a half step will take us to a pitch that has two possible names, A♯ or B♭. The choice between the two enharmonic names is determined by this principle: when writing scales, the letter names of the musical alphabet must be written in sequence, with no letter name being duplicated.

Another way to state this same idea is to say that all of the distances between notes of the scale must be diatonic steps, as opposed to chromatic steps. The word **diatonic** means "in a scale" and refers specifically to major scales (and minor scales, which will be studied later). A diatonic half step would be the distance from A to B♭. The same distance spelled as A to A♯ would be considered a chromatic half step (the type of half step that would appear in a chromatic scale). Although these two pairs of notes sound the same, their meaning is different in the context of a scale. Because all of the distances from note to note in the F major scale must be diatonic, its fourth note must be called B♭. After this note, the rest of the pattern is C, D, E, and F. In Figure 2.2, the half steps are marked with arrows above the keyboard.

Figure 2.2. *F major scale on keyboard*

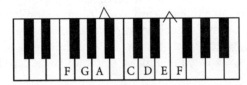

On a staff, the F major scale will look like the pattern in Figure 2.3.

Figure 2.3. *F major scale on staff*

When writing any major scale, there are several rules to remember. First, every major scale is based on the same pattern of whole and half steps: W–W–H–W–W–W–H. Second, always alternate line notes and space notes when you write the scale on the staff. This means you must use all seven letters of the musical alphabet when writing the scale. It also means that no letter will be omitted or duplicated. Finally, you must be certain that you *do not mix sharps and flats in the same scale.* This is true of all major scales.

🎼 Practice Box 2.1

Write the following major scales, placing accidentals beside the required notes. Be careful with F♯ major, since it uses an enharmonic name for one of the white keys of the piano.

G major scale

1.

F♯ major scale

2.

E♭ major scale

3.

Introduction to Intervals

Distances between pitches can be represented numerically; these distances are called **intervals.** They are always represented as ordinal numbers. The ordinal number (for example, second or 2nd) refers to the distance between the letter names of the two notes. F and G are next to each other in the musical alphabet, so there is no letter name in between them. The pair of letter names, with no letter in between them, is called the distance of a second (2nd).

If we describe the distance between two other pitches, like F and A, the distance would be different. F and A are not next to each other in the alphabet, and they are also farther apart on the piano keyboard. By counting both of the letters given to us, plus all the letters in between, we come up with three. Therefore, as shown in Figure 2.4, the distance between F and A is a third (3rd).

Figure 2.4. *Calculating intervals*

F	(G)	A		C	(D	E	F)	G
1	2	3		1	2	3	4	5

This distance is called a third.   This distance is called a fifth.

Modifying words can be used to represent different distances that use the same letters of the alphabet. For example, E to F is a second; so is E to F♯. We have referred to the first interval as a half step and the latter as a whole step. They are both seconds, although they are different types of seconds. A more sophisticated way of referring to a whole step is to call it a "major" second. A half step is commonly known as a "minor" second.

When these names are written, it is common to abbreviate the words major and minor. A capital letter "M" is generally used for the word major. When abbreviating the word minor, you should write the abbreviation as a lowercase letter "m." Some people prefer to abbreviate minor as "mi," since it is sometimes difficult to distinguish between an uppercase and a lowercase "m." You should always write your abbreviations for major and minor legibly, so that those who read your writing are sure to understand what you mean.

Key Signatures with Sharps

The term "key signature" may look somewhat familiar to you, since we have already discussed something with a similar name. Like the time signature, the key signature is written near the beginning of a piece of music and gives vital information about the organization of that piece.

A **key signature** is a type of shorthand that tells you the name of the scale on which the composition is based. Each major scale uses a unique combination of sharps or flats in order to put the whole and half steps in the proper position in the pattern. By writing this combination at the beginning of the piece, the person reading the music can quickly identify the name of the major scale being used. The key signature is written between the clef sign and the time signature on any staff.

Since sharps and flats are never combined in any major scale, they are also not combined in any key signature. Sharps or flats are written in the key signature in a particular order. That order is determined by the name of the scale and its distance from the C major scale, which has no key signature because the scale has no sharps or flats. Every time a scale is started five notes higher (from the starting pitch of C), a sharp is added to the key signature.

First we will determine the order in which we should consider the scales, and then we will use that order to figure out key signatures. The fifth note of the C major scale is G. The pitch G can also be said to be a fifth up from C. The scale that begins on G requires one sharp, an F♯, to create the correct pattern of half and whole steps. Therefore, its key signature is one sharp.

The fifth note of the G major scale is D. You can also say that D is up a fifth from G. Proceeding in this manner, we organize the names of the scales by ascending intervals of a fifth. The pattern of scale names for key signatures containing sharps is C, G, D, A, E, B, F♯, and C♯. The last two keys have the word "sharp" in their names because those sharps have already been added to the key signature. In addition, there are different types of fifths, just as there are major and minor seconds. The type we need is called a perfect fifth and must be the fifth note of the preceding scale. F♯ is the fifth note of the B major scale, and C♯ is the fifth note of the F♯ major scale. The perfect fifth contains seven half steps. (Note: when counting half steps in an interval, do not count the first note.)

Now we will consider the accidentals used for each of these scales in our order based on fifths. Table 3 shows the manner in which sharps are added to each successive major scale. As you progress upward by the distance of a fifth, another sharp is added to the key signature, keeping all the sharps that were used in the previous scales.

Table 3.   *Sharps used in major key signatures*

Name of major scale	C	G	D	A	E	B	F♯	C♯
Number of sharps in scale	0	1	2	3	4	5	6	7
Names of the sharps used in scale		F♯	F♯	F♯	F♯	F♯	F♯	F♯
			C♯	C♯	C♯	C♯	C♯	C♯
				G♯	G♯	G♯	G♯	G♯
					D♯	D♯	D♯	D♯
						A♯	A♯	A♯
							E♯	E♯
								B♯

From this chart you can see that the A major scale has three sharps, the F♯ major scale has six sharps, and so on. Notice that in each scale, the new sharp added is the letter in the musical alphabet just before the name of the scale. The sharps are placed in a key signature in the order in which they appear as you read down this chart. In other words, a piece of music based on a C♯ major scale would have seven sharps, and they would be written in the order F–C–G–D–A–E–B. You might want to use a saying such as *F*-red *C*-an *G*-o *D*-own *A*-nd *E*-at *B*-reakfast to help you learn the **order of the sharps.** The lines drawn through the sharps in Figure 2.5 should help you remember their placement on the staff.

Figure 2.5.   *Writing sharps on the treble and bass staves*

It is important to realize that sharps are not written in a key signature according to the order in which they occur when performing a scale. Both the chart and the examples above show you the order of the sharps, and you must memorize it. Then when you are asked to write a key signature that needs only one sharp, you will know that it must be F♯.

The sharps must be written into the key signature exactly as they appear above. F♯ must be written on the top line of the treble staff, not on the bottom space, and so on.

Practice Box 2.2

Copy the sharp key signature shown in Figure 2.5 on each of these grand staffs. Repetition will improve your accuracy and your ability to do this fluently.

For extra practice, use your own staff paper to copy the sharp key signature several more times.

If you know the order of the sharps and can name the scales up in intervals of a fifth, then you can easily learn to match all the major scales with their corresponding key signatures.

Key Signatures with Flats

Key signatures can contain flats as well as sharps. Most of the preceding discussion on sharp key signatures can also be applied to flat key signatures. The only difference is the way in which the circle of fifths is formed for flats. Instead of starting with C major and going up by the interval of a fifth, for flat keys we start with C major and go *down* a fifth. The note a fifth down from C is F, as shown in Figure 2.6. (Remember that notes that go down in pitch go backward in the musical alphabet.)

Figure 2.6.   *Interval of a 5th down from C*

$$F \quad (G \quad A \quad B) \quad C$$
$$5 \quad 4 \quad 3 \quad 2 \quad 1$$

backward in the musical alphabet

Proceeding in this manner, the pattern of scale names goes as follows: C, F, Bb, Eb, Ab, Db, Gb, and Cb. Remember that the type of fifth we need is called a perfect fifth and has to have seven half steps in it. That is the reason most of these scale names use the word "flat" in their names.

Based on the order for the flat scales, Table 4 shows the accidentals used in each flat key signature.

Table 4.   *Flats used in major key signatures*

Name of major scale	C	F	Bb	Eb	Ab	Db	Gb	Cb
Number of flats in scale	0	1	2	3	4	5	6	7
Names of the flats used in scale		Bb	Bb	Bb	Bb	Bb	Bb	Bb
			Eb	Eb	Eb	Eb	Eb	Eb
				Ab	Ab	Ab	Ab	Ab
					Db	Db	Db	Db
						Gb	Gb	Gb
							Cb	Cb
								Fb

From this chart you can see that the F major scale has one flat, the G♭ major scale has six flats, and so on. The order of flats in a key signature is B–E–A–D–G–C–F. You might use a saying such as *B*-efore *E*-ating *A D*-onut *G*-et *C*-offee *F*-irst. You might also notice that the first four flats spell a word, "bead." This should help you memorize the **order of the flats.**

Do you notice any relationship between the order of the sharps and the order of the flats? If you do, this relationship should help you to memorize the two lists. (They are opposites of one another.)

When written on a staff, the flats look like Figure 2.7. The lines should help you remember the placement.

Figure 2.7.   Writing flats on the treble and bass staves

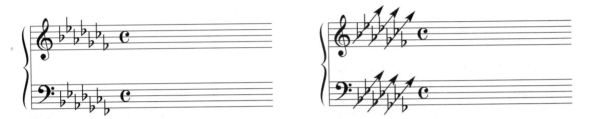

Like sharps, flats are not written in a key signature according to the order in which they occur when performing a scale. They must be written into the key signature exactly as they appear above.

♪ Practice Box 2.3

Copy the flat key signature shown in Figure 2.7 on each of these grand staffs. Repetition will improve your accuracy and your ability to do this fluently.

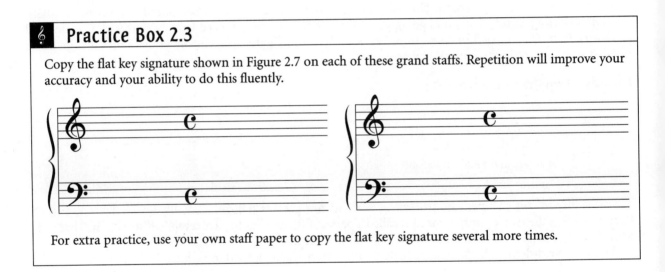

For extra practice, use your own staff paper to copy the flat key signature several more times.

The information presented in Tables 3 and 4 demonstrate an idea in music that is often called the **circle of fifths.** As the names of the scales go up by fifths, the number of sharps in the key signature increases. As the names of the scales go down by fifths, the number of flats in the key signature increases.

The circle of fifths represents both sharp keys and flat keys on the same diagram. Figure 2.8 shows the fifteen possible major keys and demonstrates those that are enharmonic. You should notice that there are twelve major keys and fifteen different ways to notate them. Three of the major keys have enharmonic spellings. The enharmonic pairs are found near the bottom of the circle of fifths.

Figure 2.8.   The circle of fifths

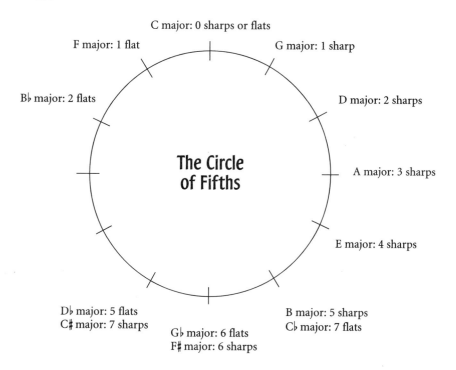

Identifying Keys and Key Signatures

There are some tricks that might help you learn the association between keys and key signatures. For sharp key signatures, the name of the key (scale) is always up one half step from the last sharp. If there are two sharps in the key signature, they will be F♯ and C♯. The last one in this group is C♯. Now think of the piano keyboard. If you play a C♯ anywhere on the piano and slide up (to the right) to the very closest key, you will land on D. So a key signature with two sharps means the key of D major.

If you are asked to name the key when there are flats in the key signature, a different trick applies. As long as there are two or more flats in the key signature, the name of the next to last flat is the name of the key. If there are three flats in the key signature, they will be B♭, E♭, and A♭. The next to last flat in this order is E♭. Therefore, the name of the key is E♭ major. When you use this trick, the name of the key (or scale) will always contain the word "flat." This is very important to remember, because E♭ major has a very different key signature from E major.

Practice Box 2.4

Name the following keys by looking at the key signature.

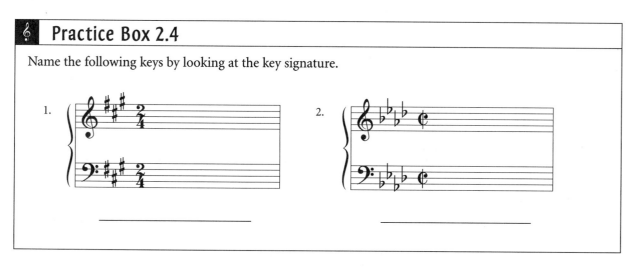

Practice Box 2.4 (continued)

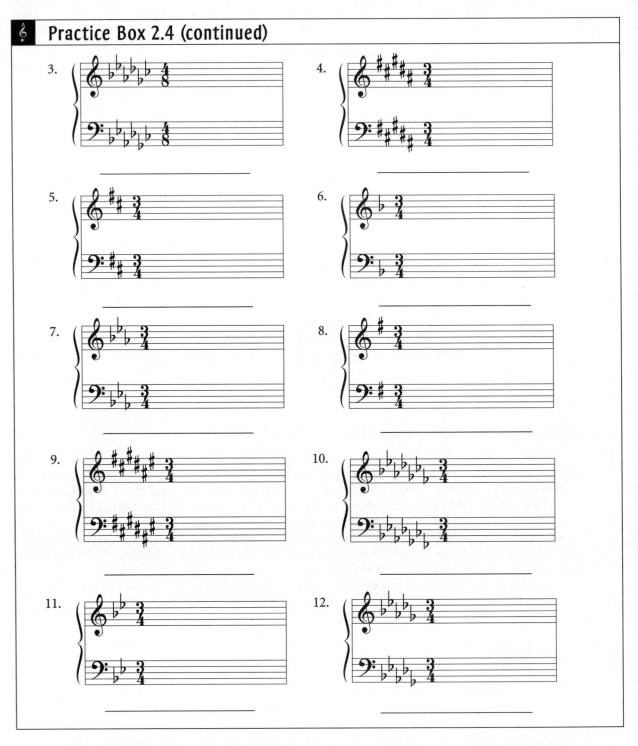

You should memorize the tricks described on the previous page and use them to easily name most key signatures. There is no easy trick for two of the key signatures. These two keys are C major, which has no key signature, and F major, which has only one flat (and therefore has no next to last flat). These two key signatures should be memorized.

Sometimes you will be asked to create the key signature for a given key or scale. Before you can do this, you must have memorized the order of the sharps and flats. Next, you must remember one common-sense rule. If you are asked to create a key signature for a key whose name contains the word "flat," the key signature must contain flats, not sharps. Most of the keys that have sharps in the key signature are named with single letters (that is, there are no accidentals in the name). Of course, F♯ major and C♯ major will have sharps in the key signature. F major is the only key with flats that does not contain the word "flat" in its name.

When you are asked to create a key signature that you know must contain sharps, add sharps in the correct order until you have written the letter of the musical alphabet that comes just *before* the name of the key. For example, if you are asked to write the key signature for E major, you will add sharps until you get to D♯. That means that you will write four sharps in the key signature.

When you are asked to create a key signature with flats, you will add flats until you have written a flat with the same name as the scale, and then you must add one more flat. The only exception to this rule is the key of F major, which contains only one flat.

Practice Box 2.5

Create a key signature for each of the following keys. Write the accidentals in both the bass and treble clef.

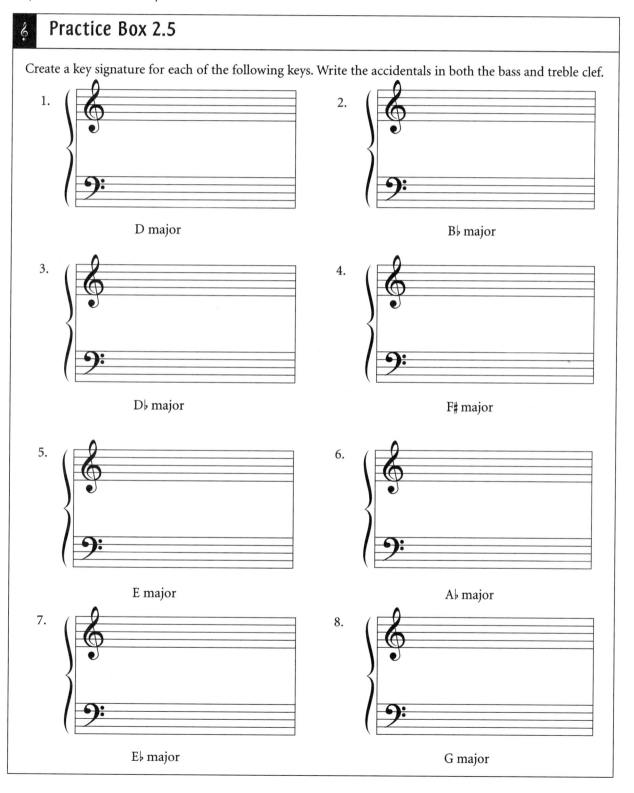

1.   D major

2.   B♭ major

3.   D♭ major

4.   F♯ major

5.   E major

6.   A♭ major

7.   E♭ major

8.   G major

Music for Analysis

Name the key for the following excerpts. After you have studied the Aural Skills section of this chapter, you should also practice naming the solfege syllables (or scale degree numbers) for both lines of the Bach example and the melody of the Chaminade example.

Example 2.1.   *Wilhelm Friedemann Bach, Minuet, mm. 13–20*

Key _____   Track 2, 0:00

Example 2.2.   *Cécile Chaminade,* The Silver Ring, *mm. 63–73*

Key _____   Track 2, 0:26

AURAL SKILLS

Melody

When we sing notes that are associated with a pattern such as a scale, it is typical to assign them syllables that reflect their position in the pattern. The syllables shown in Figure 2.9 may already be familiar to you.

Figure 2.9. Solfege for the major scale

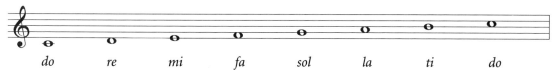

These words come from a system of singing known as **solfege** or **solmization**. This system comes to us from the Middle Ages. A monk named Guido of Arezzo used the first syllable and the first pitch from each sentence of a chant melody that was widely known and sung in his time. By learning this series of pitches, he was able to teach his students how to sing patterns. (His patterns actually consisted of six notes, so they were known as **hexachords.**) These syllables, which are written under the scale in Figure 2.9, were the first words of each of the sentences of the chant melody.

Guido's original system of solmization used the syllable *ut* for the first note of the pattern. Today, the lowest note of the pattern is always given the name *do*. It is the lowest pitch of the scale. The other names follow in order up the steps of the scale. Therefore, in this C major scale, for example, C is always *do*, D is always *re*, E is always *mi*, and so on. This is true no matter what order the actual pitches appear.

We will begin by singing patterns that use only the lowest five notes of the scale. This pattern is called a **pentachord.** The word itself refers to a five-note (penta-) group of pitches (-chord). In Figure 2.10, sing them as they appear, in order from *do* to *sol*. Then sing the same pattern starting on other pitches.

Note: It is also possible to assign numbers to the notes of the scale, singing 1–2–3–4–5–6–7–8 (or 1) in place of the solfege syllables.

Figure 2.10. Solfege for the lowest 5 notes of the major scale

Figure 2.11 shows another pattern, this time using skips instead of steps. Sing the pattern as written and then starting on other pitches.

Figure 2.11. Solfege pattern using skips

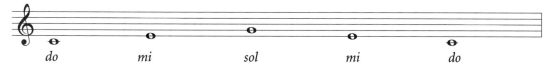

Here are some more patterns using the C major pentachord. Sing each of these patterns using solfege syllables, but try not to have to write the syllables under the notes.

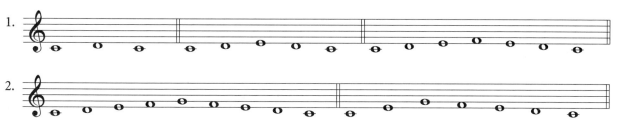

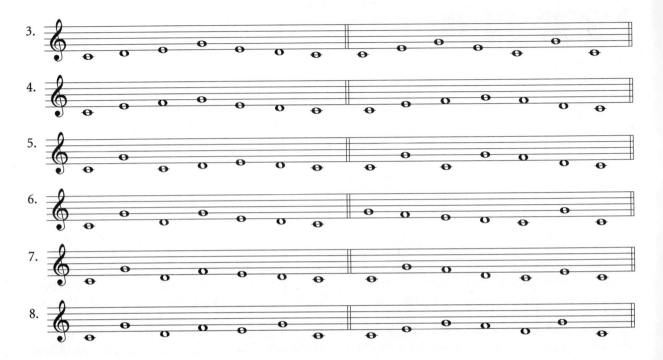

The following patterns involve steps and skips using the major scale. Sing them in various keys. Two of these exercises go below middle C to B. What is the proper solfege syllable to sing on that note?

1. Major scale

2. Skips

3. Leaps

4. Corkscrew

Practice Box 2.6

Use these staves to create your own melodies. Use a different pentachord for each staff and make your melody five or six notes in length. Use any clef and label each pentachord that you use.

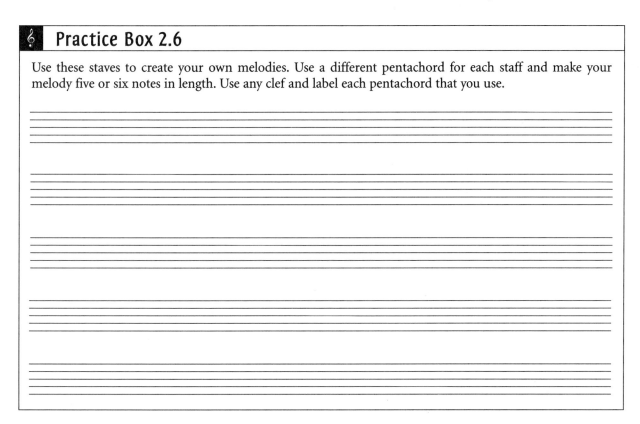

Rhythm

There are many possible time signatures other than ⁴⁄₄. The top number of the time signature tells you how many beats there are in each measure. If the top number changes, the way you count each measure will also change. Two other frequently used time signatures are ²⁄₄ and ³⁄₄ time. Figure 2.12 demonstrates ²⁄₄ and ³⁄₄ time.

Figure 2.12.   Rhythms in ²⁄₄ and ³⁄₄ time

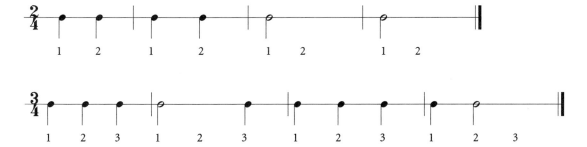

Now we will look at time signatures that have different numbers on the bottom. If there is an 8 as the bottom number, an eighth note will occupy a single beat. In this time signature, the eighth note will then behave exactly as a quarter note did when the time signature was ¼. Figure 2.13 shows an example of 4/8 time.

Figure 2.13. *Rhythm in 4/8 time*

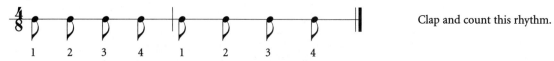

Clap and count this rhythm.

Since in any time signature a quarter note always receives twice as many counts as an eighth note, in 4/8 time a quarter note will receive two counts. A half note will receive four counts. Clap and count the rhythm in Figure 2.14. Is it possible to use a whole note in 4/8 time? (The answer is no, because it would receive twice the number of beats possible in each measure of this time signature.)

Figure 2.14. *Another rhythm in 4/8 time*

Finally, if there is a 2 on the bottom of the time signature, every half note receives a single beat. (See Figure 2.15.) If the time signature is 4/2, there can be four half notes in every measure. Each whole note would receive two counts.

Figure 2.15. *Rhythm in 4/2 time*

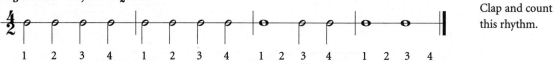

Clap and count this rhythm.

The time signature 2/2 is also known as **cut time**, or ***alla breve.*** Like common time, it has a special symbol that is sometimes used in place of the regular time signature, as shown in Figure 2.16.

Figure 2.16. *Cut time*

The ¢ stands for cut time or 2/2

Practice Box 2.7

Write the counts under these lines of music, and then clap and count aloud each line.

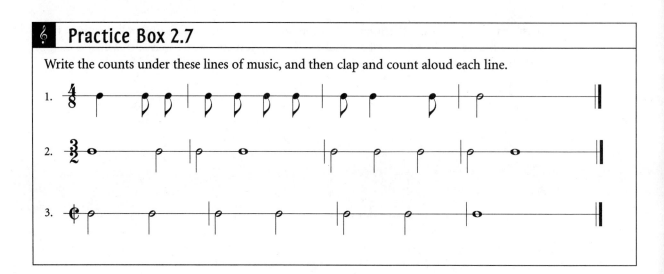

Rests

A note is a symbol of sound, but sometimes it is necessary to have silence in music. The symbol used to represent silence is called a **rest**. Figure 2.17 demonstrates the rests that correspond to the notes you have learned. Just like notes, there are whole, half, quarter, and eighth rests.

Figure 2.17. Rests

| Whole rest | Half rest | Quarter rest | Eighth rest |

Pay particular attention to the whole and half rests, since they are so similar in appearance. The whole rest sits under a line (in a hole) and the half rest sits above a line (like a hat). The similar-sounding words in parentheses may help you remember the names of these rests.

Each rest receives the same number of beats as its corresponding note in any time signature. Even though a rest is a symbol of silence, that silence must be measured as carefully as a note. Write the counts under Figure 2.18 and then clap and count it aloud.

Figure 2.18. Rests in ⁴⁄₄ rhythm

Frequently a whole rest is used in time signatures other than ⁴⁄₄ to represent a complete measure of silence. Clap and count Figure 2.19.

Figure 2.19. Whole rest used to represent complete measure in ³⁄₄ time

Practice Box 2.8

Write the counts under these lines of music, and then clap and count.

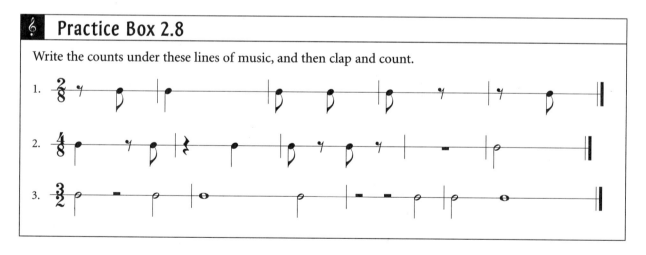

Dots and Ties

Any note can have a **dot** placed beside it. The dot lengthens the note in a specific manner. The dot adds half of the original number of beats to any note it is placed beside. Study Figure 2.20. (These examples assume that the bottom number of the time signature is four.)

Figure 2.20. Counts received by dotted notes

$$\mathbf{o} = 4 \qquad\qquad \textstyle\d = 2$$

$$\mathbf{o.} = 4 + 2 = 6 \qquad \d. = 2 + 1 = 3$$

𝄞 Practice Box 2.9

In the given time signatures, figure the value of the dotted notes. Write your answer as a number.

1. $\frac{8}{4}$ 𝅝. = _____

2. $\frac{4}{2}$ 𝅝. = _____

3. $\frac{3}{4}$ 𝅗𝅥. = _____

4. $\frac{4}{8}$ 𝅗𝅥. = _____

Do you notice anything about the number of counts received by the dotted notes?
Do the following musical math. Fill in each blank space with a single note.

5. _____ = ♩ + ♩ + ♩

6. ____ + ____ + ____ = 𝅗𝅥.

7. _____ = 𝅗𝅥 + 𝅗𝅥 + 𝅗𝅥

8. ____ + ____ + ____ = 𝅝.

A symbol called a **tie** is used to connect the values of two notes into a single musical sound. The tie symbol is a curved line that connects two note heads. It can be drawn as an upward curve or a downward curve, depending on where the notes are placed on the staff. (The tie usually goes in the direction opposite the stem.)

The tie is often used to make a note continue sounding past the end of one measure. It must connect two notes that are on the same line or the same space. (See Figure 2.21.) *If a curved line connects notes of different pitch, it is not a tie.*

Figure 2.21.   Ties

When you clap and count the $\frac{3}{4}$ example above, you will speak all six of the beats, but you will only clap four times, because the tie joins together the third and fourth notes to make a single note that takes up two counts. In the $\frac{4}{8}$ example above, you will clap only three times, because the second and third notes are tied.

If a tie connects a note with an accidental to the next measure, the second note does not need to have another accidental placed beside it. Figure 2.22 demonstrates the fact that it automatically retains the altered pitch from the previous measure.

Figure 2.22.   Notes tied across a bar line

There are two final things to understand about writing rhythmic notation. The first is that the time signature is only written on the first line of the piece. On any subsequent line or **system** of music (the two staves of a grand staff make up one system) the time signature is not repeated. That means you must make a mental note of the time signature when you look at the beginning of a piece of music and remember it throughout the remainder of the music. The only exception to this rule is when the time signature changes within the piece. (Note: unlike the time signature, the key signature is repeated at the beginning of every staff system.)

The final thing to mention about rhythmic notation concerns the bar lines. The bar lines divide the music into segments of equal length, but the final bar line of a piece of music is written in a special manner. This symbol is called a double bar line, and in printed music, it consists of a thin line followed by a thick line. You have already seen several double bar lines, such as the examples on the preceding page. When you write a double bar line in your own manuscripts, you typically will write two thin lines, because it is easier and faster.

Additional Rhythms

For extra practice, clap and count these exercises.

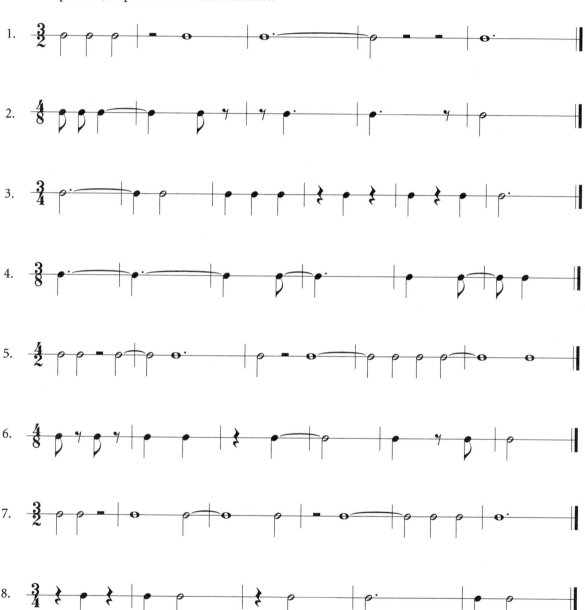

Dictation

Melodies are often described according to their **contour**, or shape. Contour is a way of describing the shape of a melody. The motion within a melody can be described as either conjunct, also known as stepwise movement, or disjunct, which is movement that involves leaps. When asked to draw the contour of a melody, you will draw a line that shows the direction of the movement and represent whether the movement is conjunct or disjunct. Here are some examples. In Figure 2.23, the straight line represents the placement of the starting pitch.

Figure 2.23.   *Two melodies with contour lines*

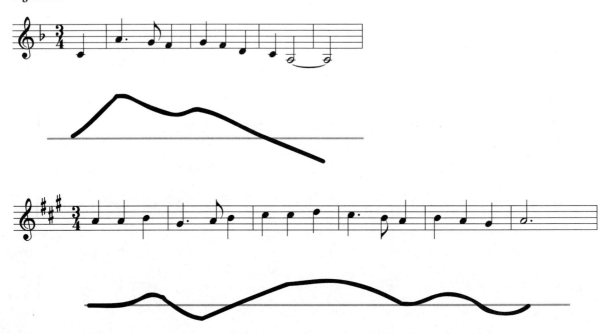

Now you will hear several melodies. Describe their contour with a line as shown above. Each melody will be four measures in length. Listen to the melody once before you begin to draw your contour.

1. _____

2. _____

3. _____

4. _____

Error Detection

The following rhythms contain one or more errors. There may be dots or ties missing, or the actual note values may be incorrect. Listen and correct the errors that you see. Write the corrected version under each staff.

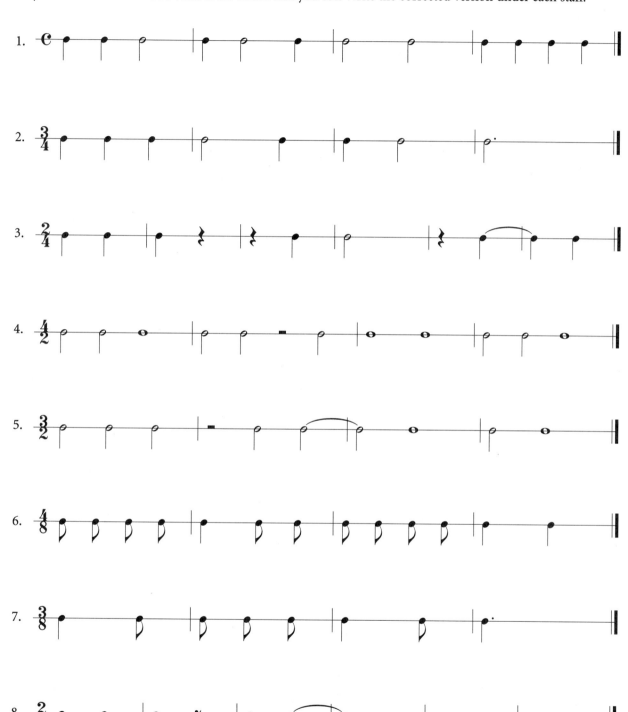

KEYBOARD APPLICATIONS

Pentachords form an excellent introduction to playing musical patterns on the keyboard. (See definition on page 29.) A pentachord is a very convenient shape to play on the piano, because we have five fingers on each hand. A major pentachord is the first five notes of a major scale. Play each of the following pentachords on the piano, one hand at a time. Start the left hand groups with the fifth finger (pinky) and the right hand groups with the first finger (thumb). You may play these patterns hands together or separately.

There are eight more major pentachord hand positions on the piano. Use blank staff paper if you need to write them out for both hands before playing them.

Looking Ahead

There are patterns other than scales that are built on stepwise motion. Patterns known as *modes* were used during the Middle Ages and Renaissance, before the major and minor scales were developed. Modes can be thought of as white-key patterns other than C major and A minor. Modes can be built on D, E, F, G, and B. The names of these modes are as follows:

Dorian   D to D
Phrygian   E to E
Lydian   F to F
Mixolydian   G to G
Locrian   B to B

All of these modes except Locrian were in constant use from the earliest Gregorian chants through the end of the Renaissance. During the Baroque era, the major-minor system of tonality began to replace the use of modes. The Locrian mode is a twentieth-century invention that was never used during the medieval and Renaissance periods.

Modes will be studied in depth in volume 2 of *Theory Essentials*.

chapter 3 Intervals

THEORETICAL SKILLS

Intervals

The term "interval," introduced in the previous chapter, refers to a measure of distance between two pitches. Intervals are always named with ordinal numbers, using words such as third, fifth, or ninth. The only exception is the distance of the eighth, which is usually referred to as an **octave**, and the unison, which is usually called a **prime**.

The process of determining the size of an interval is very easy and was briefly described in chapter 2. To identify the ordinal number that represents the size of the interval, you must count each of the given letters plus any letters that occur between these two pitches in the musical alphabet. You should count forward in the alphabet from the lowest note to the highest. Figure 3.1 shows the manner of determining the interval between F and C. Notice that the size of the interval changes depending upon whether F or C is the lowest note of the pair.

Figure 3.1. Calculating intervals on a staff

| 5th | 5th | 4th | 4th |

Eighths, or octaves, are special intervals. When you start with any letter of the musical alphabet as the first note of an interval and count up to eight, you will discover that you always finish with the same letter of the alphabet. Octaves have a special musical sound, caused by the two notes blending so perfectly (the two sounds differ only in their relative highness and lowness). The word octave is abbreviated *8ve* or *8va*.

There is a handy rule of thumb that can be used when naming intervals on a staff. Even-numbered intervals, such as seconds, fourths, and so on, will always consist of one line note and one space note. Odd-numbered intervals, such as thirds and fifths, will always consist of two line notes or two space notes. This information is shown in Table 5.

Table 5. Size of interval in relationship to staff lines and spaces

Line-to-space note Space-to-line note	Line-to-line note Space-to-space note
2nd	Prime (unison)
4th	3rd
6th	5th
8ve	7th

Remember, in order to name an interval, always determine the lowest note of the pair, whether it comes first or last, then count up to the higher note. In this manner, you will always correctly name the size of the interval. It is also important to note that the presence of an accidental beside any note of the interval does not affect the size of the interval.

Practice Box 3.1

Name the size of the interval (ordinal number) for the following pairs of notes.

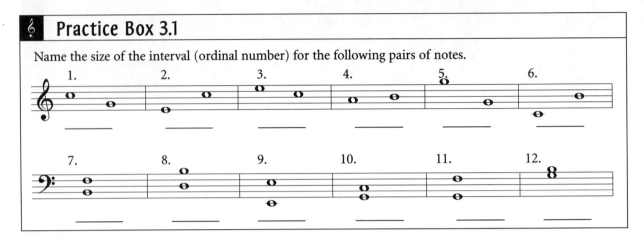

Look at Practice Box 3.1. The notes in the first staff are written side by side. Intervals constructed in this manner are known as "melodic" because their constituent pitches appear one after the other like notes in a melody. The second staff contains "harmonic" intervals, which are stacked one on top of the other like notes in a typical chord. The notes of melodic intervals are heard sequentially, and the notes of harmonic intervals are heard simultaneously. This distinction does not affect the manner in which the intervals are named.

Intervals of the Major Scale

The quantitative aspect of intervals is not the only one that we must study. The other aspect is the qualitative one, which describes the exact distance between the musical sounds, not just the distance between the letter names. Whenever the word **quality** is used, it is usually in reference to one of the following five terms: major, minor, perfect, diminished, and augmented. In chapter 2, we used the words "major" and "minor" to refer to the exact size of intervals of the second. We can use the same words to discuss other intervals that occur within the major scale. For now, we will deal only with ascending intervals.

The word "major" is used to describe the size of an interval from the first note of the major scale to certain other notes of the scale. So, for example, in a C major scale, C to D is a major second, C to E is a major third, C to A is a major sixth, and C to B is a major seventh. The intervals that can take the name "major" are seconds, thirds, sixths, and sevenths.

The word "perfect" is used to describe the size of an interval from the first note of a major scale to the fourth, fifth, or eighth note of that scale. Therefore, C to F is a perfect fourth, C to G is a perfect fifth, and C to C is a perfect octave. (Also, two Cs that have *exactly* the same pitch—for example, if you play middle C on the piano and use your own voice to sing middle C—are called a perfect unison or a perfect prime.) Figure 3.2 shows the intervals of the major scale on a staff. All of these are ascending intervals.

Figure 3.2.   *Ascending intervals of the major scale*

| Major 2nd | Major 3rd | Perfect 4th | Perfect 5th | Major 6th | Major 7th | Perfect 8ve |

If you are wondering why the intervals of a single scale are named with two different qualities, play the sounds on the piano and listen to the differences. The fourths, fifths, and octaves are neutral sounds, neither pleasant nor unpleasant. In fact, these intervals have an open or empty quality because the relationship between the frequencies (or sound-wave vibrations) that form these intervals are exact mathematical ratios. Therefore, the fourths, fifths, and octaves are given the name **perfect.**

The thirds and sixths are very pleasant-sounding intervals; they sound as if they are at rest. These are referred to as consonant sounds, or consonances. The seconds and sevenths are very harsh sounds and full of tension. They are called dissonant sounds, or dissonances. These four intervals from the major scale are always given the name "major." Perfect intervals never take the name "major," and major intervals never take the name "perfect."

Did you notice that each pair of intervals discussed above adds up to the same number? This trick might help you remember which intervals take which names. $(4 + 5 = 9 \quad 3 + 6 = 9 \quad 2 + 7 = 9)$

If you need to create a major or a perfect interval that begins on any other pitch, all that is necessary is to think of a major scale that begins on that letter name. For example, a major third that has D as its lowest note would be created with the third note of the D major scale. Therefore, the interval would be D to F♯. A perfect fifth that has B♭ as its lowest note would be created with the fifth note of the B♭ major scale, which is F. These intervals are shown with their respective scales in Figure 3.3.

Figure 3.3.   *Construction of major and perfect intervals from a scale*

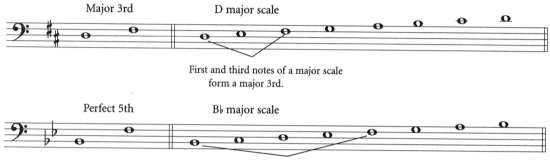

Practice Box 3.2

Write the note necessary to create the following intervals. The notes you write should all be the same as or higher than the given note. Write your notes as melodic intervals.

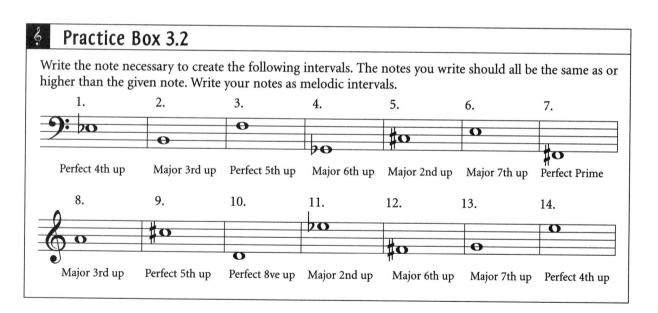

A few pitch classes do not have major scales associated with them. These include D♯, A♯, and G♯. When asked to build a major or perfect interval up from one of these pitches, it might be helpful to imagine the interval built from D, A, or G, respectively. Then, once you have created the interval that way, raise both pitches by a half step, and you will still have the quality that you are seeking. In Figure 3.4, the goal is to build a perfect fourth up from A♯.

Just as in algebra, where you can do the same thing to both sides of an equation without changing the nature of the equation, you can place the same accidental on both notes of an interval without changing its quality. Think of this procedure as "musical algebra." Since A to D occurs in an A major scale, it is a perfect fourth. Therefore, the correct answer is that to create a perfect fourth up from A♯, you need a D♯.

Figure 3.4. Create a perfect 4th up from A♯

Perfect 4th   Perfect 4th

Practice Box 3.3

Using "musical algebra," build the following intervals up from the given notes.

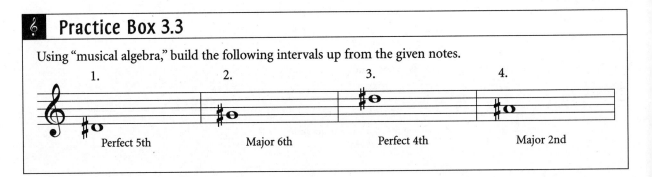

1.   2.   3.   4.

Perfect 5th   Major 6th   Perfect 4th   Major 2nd

Minor Intervals

Consider the following intervals: C up to E and C up to E♭. Both of these intervals are thirds, since both use the same two letters of the musical alphabet. However, they cannot be exactly the same interval, since the two pairs of notes are not equally far apart on the piano keyboard. A descriptive word other than major or perfect must be used to describe the distance between C and E♭.

Whenever a major interval is made smaller by a half step, the interval is called **minor**. Therefore, the distance from C to E♭ is called a minor third. When we say that an interval is made smaller, that means that the two notes move closer together, as on the piano keyboard. This can be accomplished in one of two ways: by moving the bottom note up a half step, or by moving the top note down a half step. Either process reduces the distance between the two pitches. Of course, the letter names used to name them must remain the same as the ones used in the major interval. In other words, C to D♯ is not a minor third, even though the sound of the two pairs of notes is identical. See Figure 3.5.

The numeric designation of an interval is referred to as its size. The other designation given to an interval, including the words major, minor, or perfect, is known as its quality.

Figure 3.5. Major vs. minor intervals

Major 3rd   Minor 3rd   Also 3 half steps,
4 half steps   3 half steps   but not spelled as a 3rd

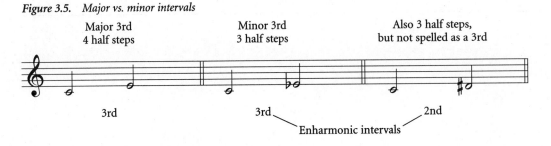

3rd   3rd_____   _____2nd
                               Enharmonic intervals

In Figure 3.6, major intervals are given as the first intervals of each pair. The top note of the interval is lowered by one half step, creating minor intervals.

Figure 3.6.   *Creating minor intervals by lowering the top note of a major interval*

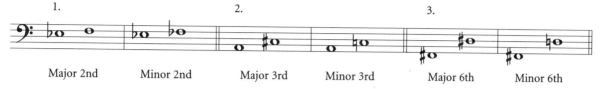

In Figure 3.7, the bottom note of each major interval is raised by one half step. In the final interval, the pitch Cx (C double-sharp) is enharmonically equivalent to D.

Figure 3.7.   *Creating minor intervals by raising the bottom note of a major interval*

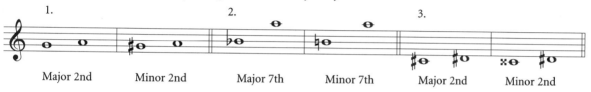

Practice Box 3.4

Identify the following intervals by size and quality. Remember that if the pair of notes does not occur in the major scale that begins on the lower of the two notes, you should not identify it as a major interval.

Example: __M2__   ____   ____   ____   ____   ____

In exercises 7–12, the pair of notes descends. Naming intervals that descend is a process that is no different from the process of naming ascending intervals. Simply calculate your answer from the lower of the pair of notes. Name these intervals by size and quality.

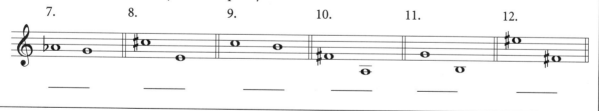

____   ____   ____   ____   ____   ____

Altering Perfect Intervals

It is also possible to change one note of a perfect interval so that the notes are closer together and the interval becomes smaller. When this procedure is done to a major interval, the resulting interval is called minor. However, a perfect interval that is made smaller *never* takes the word minor. Instead, it is called a **diminished** interval. The word "diminished" means "made smaller."

The intervals that take the name perfect are: unisons (also called primes), fourths, fifths, and octaves. Therefore, when the lower note is raised or the top note lowered, these intervals are then called diminished fourths, diminished fifths, or diminished octaves. (In fact, the diminished octave is rarely used.) The word "diminished" can be abbreviated "dim" or "d," or with a small circle drawn like a degree symbol (°). The second of each pair of intervals in Figure 3.8 is a diminished interval that has been created by raising or lowering one note of the preceding perfect interval.

The first example uses a double-flat to create the diminished interval. The pitch A♭♭ is enharmonically equivalent to G. In each of these examples, notice whether the upper or lower note of the interval is altered.

Figure 3.8.   *Creating diminished intervals from perfect intervals*

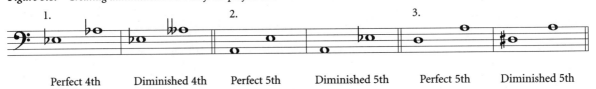

    Perfect 4th   Diminished 4th   Perfect 5th   Diminished 5th   Perfect 5th   Diminished 5th

It is also possible to make a perfect interval larger by moving the two notes farther away from each other. These intervals are called **augmented**. The word "augmented" means "made larger." When an interval is augmented, the top note of a perfect interval is raised or the bottom note of a perfect interval is lowered. (Just as with the diminished intervals, the augmented octave is rarely used.) The word "augmented" can be abbreviated "aug" or just "A" or with a small plus sign (⁺).

The second of each pair of intervals in Figure 3.9 is an augmented interval that has been created by raising or lowering one note of the preceding perfect interval. Again, you should notice which note is altered to make the augmented interval.

Figure 3.9.   *Creating augmented intervals from perfect intervals*

    Perfect 4th   Augmented 4th   Perfect 5th   Augmented 5th   Perfect 4th   Augmented 4th

Practice Box 3.5

Name the following intervals. There will be perfect, diminished, and augmented intervals. There is a mixture of ascending and descending melodic intervals.

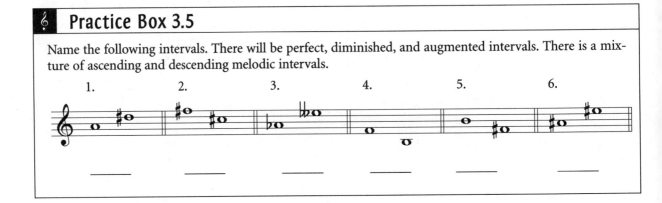

Practice Box 3.5 (continued)

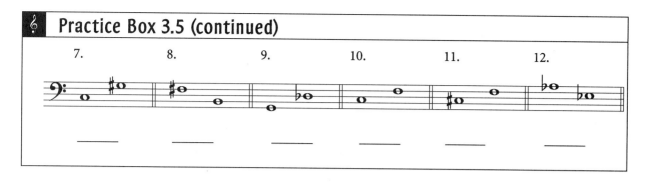

Altering Major and Minor Intervals

Consider the intervals in Figure 3.10. All of them are thirds, but they are all different qualities because they contain differing numbers of half steps.

Figure 3.10.   Various qualities of 3rds

The first pair forms a major third, because it represents the distance between the first and third notes of an A major scale. The second interval is a minor third since the distance has been made smaller by one half step. The third interval is yet smaller. Since it is spelled with the letters A and C, it is still a third even though it sounds like a major second when played on the keyboard. This interval is called a diminished third.

When minor intervals are made smaller by a half step, they are given the name diminished. The names of all these intervals are shown in Figure 3.10.

Figure 3.11 shows two more intervals. The first is a familiar major third. The second interval is also a third, but the notes are farther apart than those of the major third. It sounds like a perfect fourth when played on the keyboard, because enharmonically it could be respelled A–D.

Figure 3.11.   Various qualities of 3rds

Here the major third is made bigger by one-half step in the second interval. The resulting interval is called an augmented third. When major intervals are made larger by a half step, they are given the name augmented. The names of these two intervals are given in Figure 3.11.

Practice Box 3.6

The first interval is given to you. Create the intervals requested in the second measure by altering only the top note of the second interval.

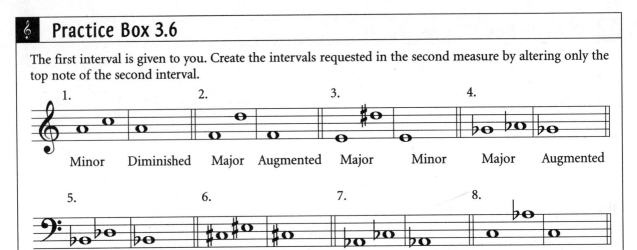

Minor	Diminished	Major	Augmented	Major	Minor	Major	Augmented

Minor	Diminished	Major	Augmented	Minor	Diminished	Minor	Diminished

Just as there are enharmonic pitches, it is possible to have enharmonic intervals. Several are described in the preceding paragraphs. A diminished third is enharmonically equivalent to a major second. An augmented third is enharmonically equivalent to a perfect fourth.

Two specific intervals, the augmented fourth and the diminished fifth, are enharmonically equivalent and are occasionally given the name **tritone**. This term refers to the fact that a tritone (whether spelled as an augmented fourth or diminished fifth) is comprised of three (*tri-*) whole steps (*-tone*). The term originated in the Middle Ages, when this sound was called "the devil in music." This supposedly evil sound was avoided by composers of that day and gave rise to a practice called *musica ficta,* where accidentals were used to alter specific notes to avoid the tritone. Today we can find tritones in major scales from *fa* up to *ti* (the fourth to the seventh notes of the scale, forming an A4) and from *ti* up to *fa* (the seventh to the fourth notes of the scale, forming a d5).

Practice Box 3.7

Name a major or minor interval that is enharmonically equivalent to the intervals listed below.

Augmented 2nd _____   Augmented 5th _____

Diminished 4th _____   Augmented 6th _____

All intervals can take the names diminished or augmented. However, not all intervals can take the names major, minor, or perfect. The names major and minor are only used with seconds, thirds, sixths, and sevenths. The name perfect is only used with unisons, fourths, fifths, and octaves. This is shown in Table 6.

Table 6. *Relationships between qualities of intervals*

	2nds, 3rds, 6ths, 7ths	**Unisons, 4ths, 5ths, 8ves**
Larger	Doubly augmented (rare)	Doubly augmented (rare)
↑	Augmented	Augmented
distance	Major	
between		Perfect
notes	Minor	
↓	Diminished	Diminished
Smaller	Doubly diminished (rare)	Doubly diminished (rare)

Remember, the words major, minor, perfect, diminished, and augmented refer to the *quality* of the interval. Whenever you are asked a question regarding the quality of an interval, one of these words will always be the appropriate response.

There is one final, although rare, possibility for interval qualities. If an augmented interval is made bigger by one half step, it is known as a doubly augmented interval. If a diminished interval is made smaller by one half step, it is known as a doubly diminished interval. You will not encounter these terms very often, but it is helpful to be acquainted with them. These rare qualities are included in Table 6.

Inversion of Intervals

Although it may seem surprising, the interval from C to F is not the same as the interval from F to C. Assuming that both intervals are ascending, the first one is a fourth and the second one is a fifth. This is due to a phenomenon in music known as **interval inversion.**

The process of inverting intervals is not used often in the study of real music, but it is a very useful trick in naming intervals, especially large ones. Switching the order of any two musical pitches always creates an interval inversion. In essence, you are turning the notes of the interval upside down, hence the term "inversion." If you know the quality of interval that you start with, by using interval inversion you will be able to predict the quality of the inverted pair.

As you saw above, fourths become fifths when inverted. Notice that the numbers 4 and 5 add up to 9. This is true of all inverted pairs. Table 7 shows the inversions for all interval sizes.

Table 7. *Inversions for all interval sizes*

Original interval	**Inverted interval**
Unison	8ve
2nd	7th
3rd	6th
4th	5th
5th	4th
6th	3rd
7th	2nd
8ve	Unison

As you can see, the size of the original interval and the size of the inverted interval always add up to nine. This can be an aid for figuring larger intervals if they are not as easy for you as smaller ones. In the example below, B down to D is an easy interval to name because the notes are close together on the staff. The second interval, D up to B, is not as easy because the notes are spread far apart on the staff. However, if you know the interval inversions shown in Table 7, it is easily identifiable as a sixth. Remember that in order for interval inversion to be effective, you must always use pairs of notes that have exactly the same two pitch classes. The only difference between the pairs should be that the pitches occur in a different order from top to bottom. Both of the intervals in Figure 3.12 use the same pitch classes; only the direction of the interval has changed.

Figure 3.12.   Interval inversion: size only

This same technique will also work on the qualities of intervals if you know the specific conversions that occur. Table 8 demonstrates the inversion of interval qualities.

Table 8.   Inversions for all interval qualities

Original interval	Inverted interval
Perfect	Perfect
Major	Minor
Minor	Major
Diminished	Augmented
Augmented	Diminished

Here are some examples. If you invert a diminished fourth, you will get an augmented fifth. (See Figure 3.13.) If you invert a minor sixth, you will get a major third. The main thing to remember is that perfect intervals can never become anything other than perfect when inverted. It means that when you invert a perfect fourth, although the size of the interval will change to a fifth, the quality will always remain perfect.

Figure 3.13.   Interval inversion: size and quality

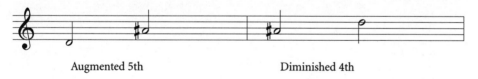

Practice Box 3.8

Name the following intervals. The second interval of each pair is an inversion of the first.

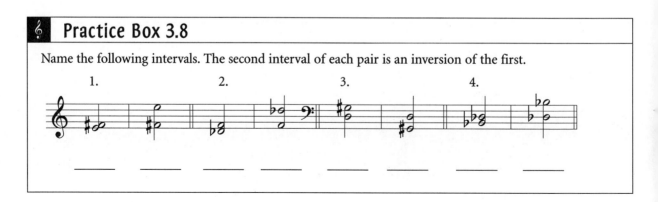

Creating Descending Intervals

To this point, you have been asked to name the size and quality of descending intervals, but not to create them. The principle of interval inversion can be used to make this an easy process. You should now be able to create any ascending interval. To create descending intervals, think of its interval inversion and then reverse the direction. For example, to create a descending minor third, think first of the note that would create an ascending major sixth. Then, instead of writing that note above the given note, write it lower than the given note. This example is demonstrated in Figure 3.14.

Figure 3.14. Ascending major 6th used to create a descending minor 3rd

Ascending
major 6th

Descending
minor 3rd

In Figure 3.14, you should write an E on the bottom line of the treble staff. The first measure of the figure shows you how to think of this answer. The major sixth up from G gives you the answer of E. To turn the interval into its inversion, simply write the answer E lower than the given note G.

An alternative way to create minor intervals also involves interval inversion. When we started our study of intervals at the beginning of this chapter, you learned the intervals of the ascending major scale. (See Figure 3.2.) When the descending intervals of the major scale are written, instead of forming major and perfect intervals, they form minor and perfect intervals. This is demonstrated in Figure 3.15. The same letter combinations that formed major intervals in the ascending version now form minor intervals. The perfect intervals remain perfect.

Figure 3.15. Descending intervals of the major scale

Minor 2nd   Minor 3rd   Perfect 4th   Perfect 5th   Minor 6th   Minor 7th   Perfect 8ve

Practice Box 3.9

Write the note necessary to create the following intervals. The notes you write should all be *lower* than the given note.

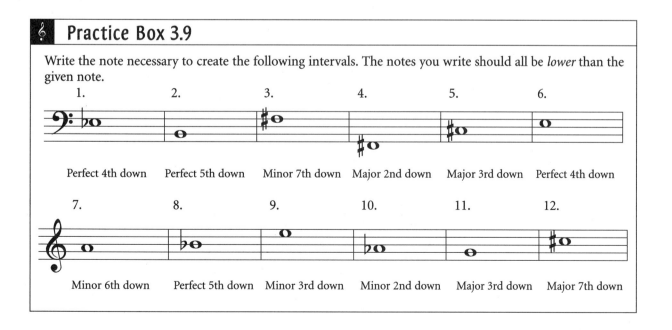

1.   2.   3.   4.   5.   6.

Perfect 4th down   Perfect 5th down   Minor 7th down   Major 2nd down   Major 3rd down   Perfect 4th down

7.   8.   9.   10.   11.   12.

Minor 6th down   Perfect 5th down   Minor 3rd down   Minor 2nd down   Major 3rd down   Major 7th down

Compound Intervals

It is also possible to have intervals that are larger than an octave. These are called **compound intervals,** as opposed to simple intervals that are equal to or smaller than an octave. The most common compound intervals are ninths and tenths, but it is possible to refer to intervals as big as elevenths, twelfths, and thirteenths. Some compound intervals are shown in Figure 3.16.

Figure 3.16.   *Simple and compound intervals compared*

| Major 2nd | Major 9th | Minor 3rd | Minor 10th |

In this case, the ninth takes the same quality as the smaller interval that uses the same pitches. This is true of all compound intervals—to determine their qualities, use the same name that you would use for a simple interval with the same pitches. In most aspects of musical study, a compound interval can be considered equivalent to its simple counterpart. Occasionally the simple interval name is used in place of the compound name. You will always add seven to the interval number of a simple interval to determine its compound equivalent.

Practice Box 3.10

Name the following compound intervals by size and quality.

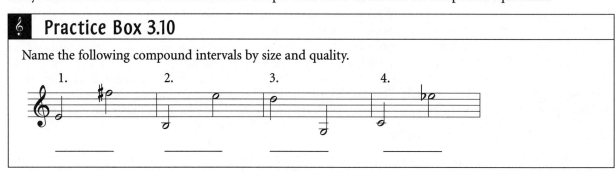

Music for Analysis

Determine the size and quality of each interval.

Example 3.1.   *Béla Bartók,* Mikrokosmos, *Book V, "Free Variations," mm. 14–24*

Track 3, 0:00

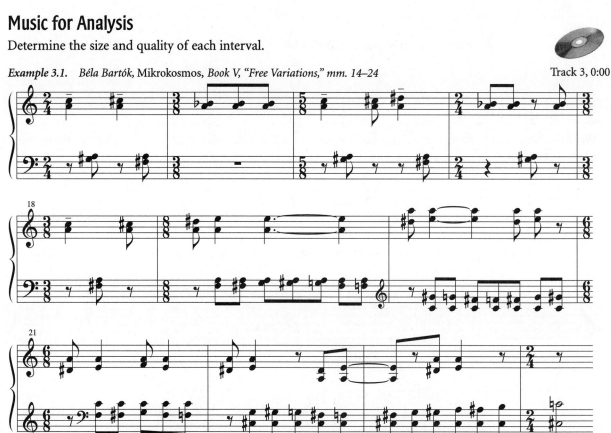

AURAL SKILLS

Melody

Solfege syllables or scale numbers can be used with patterns that begin on pitches other than C. All of the melodic lines below are based on major pentachords. The lowest note of the pattern is always *do*, and the other syllables are used as you move stepwise up in the pattern.

Each of these examples begins with *do*. For each, name the key, based on the key signature. For extra practice, speak the syllables as you read the music without singing.

1.

2.

3.

4.

5.

6.

7.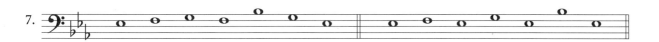

8.

Intervals

Practice singing the following intervals up from a variety of pitches. You can sing the words "la-la" or use the suggested solfege syllables to help associate each sound with the major scale. Try to think of other tunes that begin with these same intervals.

Major 2nd: *do-re.* "Frère Jacques" is a tune that begins with a major second.

Major 3rd: *do-mi.* "Michael, Row the Boat Ashore" is a tune that begins with a major third.

Perfect 4th: *do-fa.* "Here Comes the Bride" and "Amazing Grace" are tunes that begin with this interval.

Perfect 5th: *do-sol.* The theme from the movie *Star Wars* begins with this interval.

Major 6th: *do-la.* The NBC signature tune begins with this interval.

Major 7th: *do-ti.* The song "Bali Ha'i" (from the musical *South Pacific)* creates this interval with the opening three notes.

Perfect 8ve: *do-do.* "Somewhere over the Rainbow" begins with this interval.

Do the same set of exercises for the descending intervals of the major scale. They are minor second, minor third, perfect fourth, perfect fifth, minor sixth, minor seventh, and perfect octave.

Rhythm

Any musical pulse can be divided, causing each of the notes contained in that beat to receive less than a single count. When a beat of music is divided into two or three equal parts, we call those notes **divisions of the beat.** The top number of a time signature indicates whether the normal division for that meter is two or three equal parts.

When the top number of a time signature is 2, 3, or 4, the normal division of the beat is into two notes of equal length. A time signature with any of these numbers on top is called a **simple meter.** The bottom number of the time signature does not play a role in determining whether the meter is simple. Table 9 shows examples of simple meters.

Note: It is also possible to divide a beat into three equal parts. This kind of time signature will have as its top number a multiple of 3 greater than 3 itself, such as 6 or 9. A time signature with any of these numbers on top is called a **compound meter.** These will be studied later.

Table 9. Simple meters

Time Signatures			Characteristics
$\frac{2}{2}$	$\frac{2}{4}$	$\frac{2}{8}$	These meters are considered to be duple simple. Duple refers to the fact that there are two beats per measure. Simple refers to the possible division of each beat into two equal parts.
$\frac{3}{2}$	$\frac{3}{4}$	$\frac{3}{8}$	These meters are considered to be triple simple. Triple refers to the fact that there are three beats per measure. Simple refers to the possible division of each beat into two equal parts.
$\frac{4}{2}$	$\frac{4}{4}$	$\frac{4}{8}$	These meters are considered to be quadruple simple. Quadruple refers to the fact that there are four beats per measure. Simple refers to the possible division of each beat into two equal parts.

When a beat note is divided, each of the resulting notes received one half of a count. When represented on the staff in actual musical notation, divisions of beat in $\frac{2}{4}$ time look like Figure 3.17. Notice that instead of putting a flag on the stem of each individual eighth note, as we have done in the past, the eighth notes are beamed together at the ends of their stems. This is done so that the notation actually indicates the division, showing that two of them must be added together to equal an entire count.

Figure 3.17.   Divisions of the beat in $\frac{2}{4}$ time

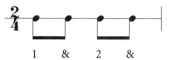

In simple meters that have 4 as the bottom number of the time signature, the division of the beat will always be an eighth note.

When counting divisions, the first of the pair of notes will *always* take a number that represents the location in the measure on which the division begins. The second of the pair will *always* take the word "and." In order to count divisions accurately, you should say the "and" after every beat of the measure. By doing this, you will be thinking and speaking a steady pulse of divisions (whereas before you were thinking and speaking a steady pulse of beats). When divisions of the beat occur in music, the hardest part of counting is not the shorter notes that form the divisions, but the longer notes in each measure. By counting each beat number plus the "and" of every beat, you will count the long notes more accurately.

When the two eighth notes are part of the same beat, they are typically written with a *beam* connecting them, instead of with individual flags. When both notes of a beamed pair are on or above the middle staff line, the stems are drawn down from the note heads. If they are below the middle line, the stem goes up. If they are on opposite sides of the middle line, the note farthest from the middle line determines the direction. See Figure 3.18.

Figure 3.18.   Beaming eighth notes

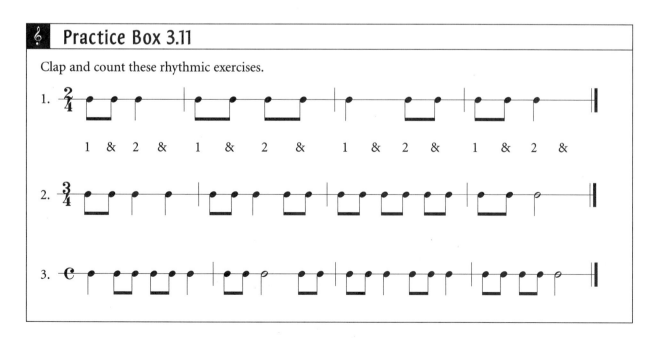

Upbeats

It is possible to begin a piece of music with an incomplete measure. The note or notes that appear before the first strong beat of a musical segment are called an **anacrusis** or, more commonly, a **pick-up** or upbeat. The first beat of the measure is the strongest pulse, and the term **downbeat** refers to the movement a conductor makes on that beat. Any other pulse in the measure can be considered an **upbeat.**

To begin a piece of music in the middle of a measure, the beats are borrowed from the final measure of the piece. For example, if a piece in $\frac{4}{4}$ time starts with a single beat before the first full measure, that beat is borrowed from the end of the last measure, meaning it is the fourth count in the measure. See Figure 3.19.

Figure 3.19.   *Upbeat*

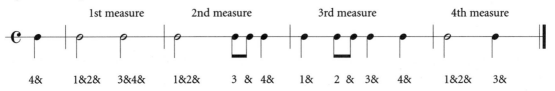

In Figure 3.19, the final beat has been borrowed from the end of the piece and placed at the beginning. There are still only four measures of music; the anacrusis at the beginning is not considered the first measure of music because it does not contain a first beat. Whenever an upbeat is used, the last measure of the piece will have fewer counts than the time signature specifies. The final measure plus the upbeat(s) must add up to a complete measure. When counting an upbeat, you will never begin with beat number 1.

Practice Box 3.12

Add any combination of notes or rests to complete the final measure of each line, then clap and count.

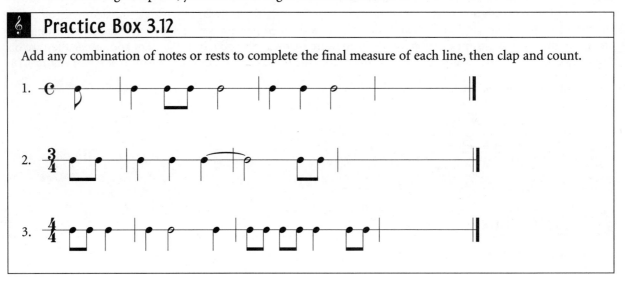

Dotted Quarter Notes in $\frac{4}{4}$ Time

In any meter, when a dot is placed beside a note, it adds half of the original value to the note. In all simple meters, when a *beat note* is tied to a note that represents a *division of the beat,* the result is always a note that equals one and a half counts. When counting such a note, it is necessary to speak three words, such as "one-and-two" or "three-and-four." Even though the words are not spaced evenly in Figure 3.20, your manner of counting them should be as steady as possible.

Figure 3.20.   *Dotted quarter rhythms*

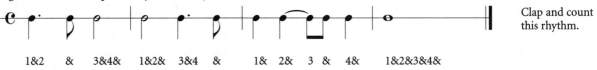

Clap and count this rhythm.

Following each of the dotted quarter notes in Figure 3.20, notice that there is a subsequent eighth note completing the second half of the beat used in the dotted note. This note that follows the dotted note will always be a division note, and it will always take the word "and."

Notice that in the third measure of Figure 3.20, a tie creates a combined note value of one and a half beats (the same as a dotted quarter note). In a quadruple meter, the third beat is considered to be a secondary accent. The strongest beat of the measure is always the first beat, but beat 3 begins the second half of the measure and therefore is considered the next strongest beat of the measure. The use of a tie rather than a dotted note allows the third beat to be shown in the measure, making it easier to read.

It is also possible to reverse the order of the pair of notes and have the division note precede the dotted note, as seen in Figure 3.21.

Figure 3.21.   More dotted quarter rhythms

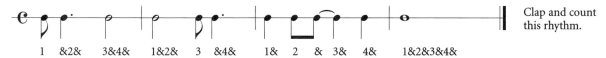

Clap and count this rhythm.

Rests and ties are treated in the same manner as that which we learned before, even when dotted notes are present. In simple meters, dotted rests can be used, but it is more typical to see two rests of unequal value represent one and a half beats, especially if it makes the rhythmic structure of the measure easier to read.

Practice Box 3.13

Clap and count these rhythms. Can you find the tied notes that are equivalent to dotted quarters?

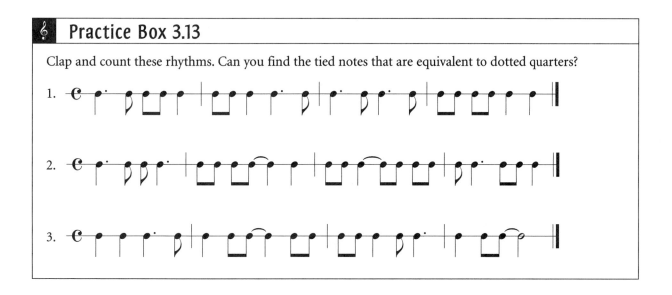

Additional Rhythms

For extra practice, clap and count these exercises.

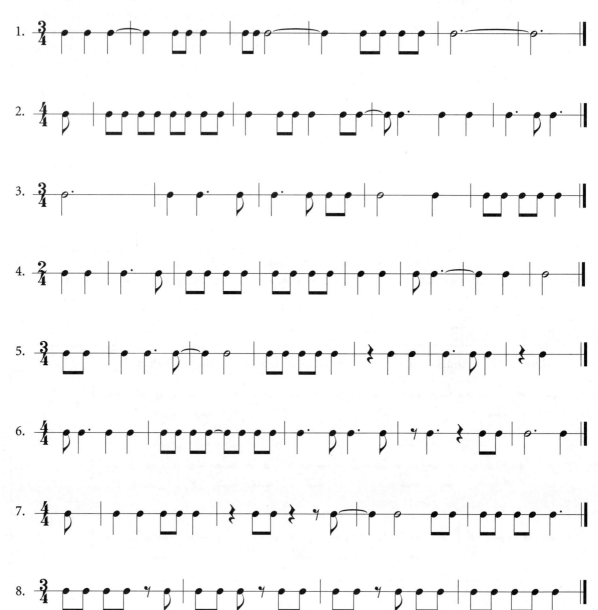

Dictation

You will hear pentachord melodies that are five pitches in length. The first note of each melody is given to you, and it is the lowest note of the pentachord. You will hear each melody three or four times. First, identify the key based on the key signature. Try to hear the melody in your head and see if you can assign syllables to what you hear. Then begin to write down the pitches that you hear. Write all of your notes as plain ovals (no stems or flags).

Combinations of sounds are referred to as consonances or dissonances, depending upon whether they are pleasant or unpleasant to our ears. A **consonance** is a combination of sounds that is pleasant, typically thirds and sixths. A consonant sound is considered to be "at rest." A **dissonance** is a combination of sounds that is unpleasant. Seconds and sevenths are typically considered to be dissonances. Within the context of tonal music, a dissonant sound requires *resolution,* or movement toward a consonant sound. Perfect intervals such as fourths and fifths are not considered to be either consonances or dissonances. They have a characteristic hollow sound that is neither pleasant nor unpleasant.

You will hear an interval that is either a consonance or a dissonance. Circle the correct choice.

1. consonance	dissonance
2. consonance	dissonance
3. consonance	dissonance
4. consonance	dissonance
5. consonance	dissonance
6. consonance	dissonance
7. consonance	dissonance
8. consonance	dissonance
9. consonance	dissonance
10. consonance	dissonance

You will hear an interval that is either a consonance, a dissonance, or a perfect interval. Circle the correct choice.

1. consonance	dissonance	perfect
2. consonance	dissonance	perfect
3. consonance	dissonance	perfect
4. consonance	dissonance	perfect
5. consonance	dissonance	perfect
6. consonance	dissonance	perfect
7. consonance	dissonance	perfect
8. consonance	dissonance	perfect
9. consonance	dissonance	perfect
10. consonance	dissonance	perfect

You will hear a variety of seconds and thirds. Circle the correct choice for the interval size and whether or not it is harmonic or melodic.

1.	2nd	3rd	harmonic	melodic
2.	2nd	3rd	harmonic	melodic
3.	2nd	3rd	harmonic	melodic
4.	2nd	3rd	harmonic	melodic
5.	2nd	3rd	harmonic	melodic
6.	2nd	3rd	harmonic	melodic
7.	2nd	3rd	harmonic	melodic
8.	2nd	3rd	harmonic	melodic
9.	2nd	3rd	harmonic	melodic
10.	2nd	3rd	harmonic	melodic

You will hear seconds, thirds, and fourths. Circle the correct choice.

1.	2nd	3rd	4th
2.	2nd	3rd	4th
3.	2nd	3rd	4th
4.	2nd	3rd	4th
5.	2nd	3rd	4th
6.	2nd	3rd	4th
7.	2nd	3rd	4th
8.	2nd	3rd	4th
9.	2nd	3rd	4th
10.	2nd	3rd	4th

You will hear fifths, sixths, and sevenths. Circle the correct choice.

1.	5th	6th	7th
2.	5th	6th	7th
3.	5th	6th	7th
4.	5th	6th	7th
5.	5th	6th	7th
6.	5th	6th	7th
7.	5th	6th	7th
8.	5th	6th	7th
9.	5th	6th	7th
10.	5th	6th	7th

Error Detection

The following rhythms contain one or more errors. There may be dots or ties missing, or the actual note values may be incorrect. Listen and correct the errors that you see. Write the corrected version under each staff.

KEYBOARD APPLICATIONS

It is possible to study groups of notes that are subsets of major scales. You have already played pentachords at the keyboard. Another subset of a major scale is a tetrachord, which is a four-note group. One interesting thing about tetrachords from major scales is the relationships that appear as you go around the circle of fifths. The upper tetrachord of any scale is the lower tetrachord of the next scale around the circle.

Play the following exercise, paying careful attention to the abbreviations LH for left hand and RH for right hand. The numbers beneath the notes refer to fingers of the hand. The thumb of each hand is finger 1, and the ring finger of each hand is finger 4. The last four notes on the first staff are the same as the first four notes on the next staff. For extra practice, play this exercise backward as well as forward.

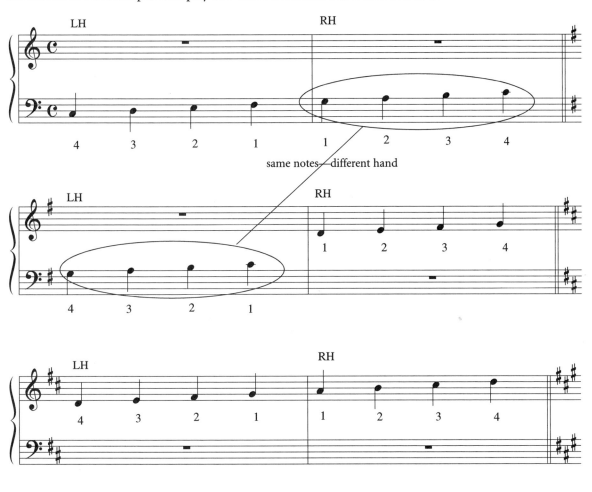

same notes—different hand

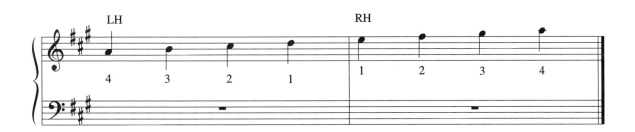

Tetrachord exercises using other major scales will appear in chapters 4 and 5.

chapter 4

Minor Scales and Key Signatures

THEORETICAL SKILLS

Relative Key Signatures

We have learned all the possible key signatures, and we have learned how to associate them with the names of the major keys. However, each key signature can also be associated with a different key. The new keys that can be associated with each key signature are *minor*. Therefore, each of the key signatures that you have learned will now represent two possibilities, major or minor.

The two keys represented by each key signature are called **relative keys,** because they share the same key signature. A specific technique is used to determine the names of relative keys. You already know how to identify the name of the major key associated with a key signature. Once you have identified the major key, count to the sixth note of the major scale, also referred to as the "sixth scale degree." This note will give you the name of the relative minor key that also uses that same key signature (see Figure 4.1).

Figure 4.1. Identifying relative minor key

The up-arrow symbols, called "carets," over the numbers above refer to scale degrees, meaning the note's position in the scale. In this C major scale, C is the first scale degree, D is the second scale degree, and so on. The sixth scale degree is A. Therefore, A is the note that gives us the name of the relative minor key. We would say it this way:

The relative minor of C major is A minor.

There are fifteen minor keys, just as there are fifteen major keys. As mentioned earlier, another way to think of this concept is that there are only twelve possible minor keys and fifteen ways to notate them, with three of the keys having enharmonic spellings. The enharmonic pairs are G♯ and A♭ minor, D♯ and E♭ minor, and A♯ and B♭ minor.

Practice Box 4.1

1. The 6th note of the F major scale is _____.   The relative minor of F major is   _____.

2. The 6th note of the A major scale is _____.   The relative minor of A major is   _____.

There is another method of naming relative minor keys that is very useful if you are sitting at a keyboard or can visualize scales on the keyboard. You can arrive at the correct answer by playing the name of the major scale on the keyboard, then moving down (left) three half steps, which is the distance of a minor third (see Figure 4.2). The note you land on will be the name of the relative minor key. This is analogous to singing the major scale downward from *do* to *la* (*do–ti–la*). There is one important thing to remember if you use this method: you must always skip a letter of the musical alphabet between the name of the major key and the name of the minor key. This method works because the major sixth up used in the previous method is the interval inversion of the minor third down used in this method.

Figure 4.2.   Identifying relative minor key

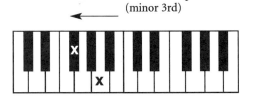

The black X is on the name of the major key, A major. The white X has been drawn three half steps lower, on the first note of the group of three black keys. This note can take either the name F♯ or G♭. Because you cannot use the letter name next to A in the alphabet, which would be G (remember, the distance must be a third), the name of the relative minor must take the letter name F; therefore, the relative minor of A major is F♯ minor.

🎼 Practice Box 4.2

Name the relative minors by counting backward on the keyboard 3 half steps or a minor 3rd.

1. G major _____   2. B major _____

The method of counting half steps is also useful if you are given the name of a minor scale and need to determine its relative major. You can arrive at the correct answer by playing (or thinking of) the name of the minor scale on the keyboard and counting up (right) three half steps, as shown in Figure 4.3.

Figure 4.3.   Identifying relative major key

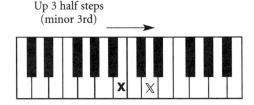

In the above example, the black X is the name of the minor scale, B minor. By counting three half steps to the right, you can determine its relative major, which is D major.

No matter whether you are starting with the name of a major or minor key, you can always use the trick of counting half steps. The name of the major scale is always to the right of the name of the minor scale on the keyboard. Count down to find the name of a relative minor key; count up to find the name of a relative major. There is one final piece of information that is helpful to remember: Unlike the numbering of intervals, when you count half steps you do not number the starting note.

🎼 Practice Box 4.3

Name the relative majors by counting up on the keyboard 3 half steps.

1. G minor _____   2. F minor _____

Determining Keys

Any key signature can represent two different keys, one major and one minor. If you are asked to name the key of a piece of music, the key signature will help you determine these two possibilities. However, the key signature cannot tell you which of these two possible keys is the correct answer for that piece.

In order to determine the key of a composition, you must look at its pitch content. In particular, the last note should tell you with certainty the name of its key. As you learned in an earlier chapter, a piece of tonal music should end on the name of its key or scale. By looking at the final note or combination of notes in a composition, you should gain a clear idea of whether it is based on the major or the minor scale that is associated with its key signature. If the composition ends with a chord (a combination of pitches often found in a vertical arrangement), the lowest note of the chord will form the name of the key.

If you are asked to name the two possible keys associated with the key signature, as in the practice box below, it is important that your answers include the words "major" and "minor." For example, if you say that a composition is in the key of D, it is an incomplete answer. Now that we have broadened our knowledge base to include relative keys, it does not give enough information about the scale or key. The correct answer would be D major or D minor.

♭ Practice Box 4.4

Name the two possible keys and then circle the correct answer based on the notes of the piece.

1. _____   2. _____

Example 4.1.   *John Henry Hopkins, Jr., "We Three Kings of Orient Are"*

Track 4, 0:00

Consider the number of simultaneous pitches on each beat. How many people would it take to sing this example? In measures 12 and 14, what is the purpose of the stems that are drawn in seemingly wrong directions?

Natural Minor Scales

Because the notes of a scale can be inferred from its key signature, we can now write a minor scale. C major and A minor are considered relatives, and since C major has no sharps or flats in its key signature, neither will A minor. An A minor scale is written on the staff in Figure 4.4.

Figure 4.4.   *The A minor scale*

As you study the pattern of whole and half steps in this scale, you will see that it is a different pattern from that of a major scale. In this minor scale, the pattern is WHWWHWW. Although it is possible to memorize this pattern and learn to create minor scales using the pattern of half and whole steps, it is easier and more efficient to learn to identify the key signature of the minor scale based on its relative major and create the scale from the key signature.

Using the example above, an F♯ minor scale will use the same key signature as A major—three sharps.

Figure 4.5.   The F♯ minor scale

The minor scale sounds different from the major scale because of the placement of half steps within the scale pattern. One of the aspects of any major scale that gives it such a satisfying sound is that it ends with a half step. Because of the half step at the end of the scale, the next to last note pulls, or leads, to the final note of the scale. This tendency of the seventh scale degree to pull upward toward the tonic is one of the most important aspects of "tonal music," or music that is written in a key. In fact, the seventh scale degree is often called the **leading tone** because of its tendency to lead upward to the tonic.

Look at the minor scales demonstrated above. The distance between the seventh and eighth notes of the scale is a whole step, not a half step. The seventh note does not lead toward the tonic because it is not a half step away. This makes the sound of the pure minor scale quite different (and, some would say, less satisfying) than the major scale.

Usually in the course of an actual piece of music, the seventh note of a minor scale is altered with an accidental that raises it a half step. This alteration creates a leading tone, causing the seventh scale degree to pull toward the tonic. This alteration is always written beside the actual notes of the piece of music, not in the key signature.

The form of the minor scale that we have looked at on preceding pages is called **natural minor** or **pure minor.** Since this scale does not contain a leading tone, it is almost never used for tonal compositions. Nevertheless, it is the form of the minor scale that agrees exactly with the key signature, and therefore, it must be learned as a necessary component of music theory.

𝄞 Practice Box 4.5

Write the following natural minor scales. Use a key signature. (First determine the relative major.)

1. G natural
   minor

2. C♯ natural
   minor

3. E natural
   minor

4. F natural
   minor

Other Forms of the Minor Scale

There are two important variations of the natural or pure minor scale. Both of these variants use an accidental within the scale to raise the seventh scale degree by a half step, thus creating a leading tone. This accidental is never a part of the key signature of the scale. All three versions of the scale use exactly the same key signature.

The **harmonic minor** form of the scale adds just this one accidental to the natural minor scale, as shown in Figure 4.6.

Figure 4.6.   A natural minor changed to A harmonic minor

A natural minor   A harmonic minor

We write the accidental in the scale to represent the way it would be used in a piece of music. It would never appear in the key signature of the piece. If a composition were in the key of A minor and based on the harmonic minor version of the scale, all of the Gs in the piece would have the sharp written beside them.

The G♯, which creates a leading tone in the A minor scale, cannot be placed in the key signature for the following reasons:

1. G can only be used in a key signature as the third sharp in the order.
2. F and C must be present in the key signature in order to have a G.
3. This scale does not use F♯ or C♯. The third scale degree is C♮ and the sixth scale degree is F♮.

For ease in learning how to raise seventh scale degrees to create leading tones in minor scales, keep the following rules in mind:

1. If the seventh scale degree is a natural in the key signature (like G in the A minor scale above), it will need a *sharp* to become a leading tone.
2. If the note is a flat in the key signature, it will need a *natural* to become a leading tone.
3. If the note is a sharp in the key signature, it will need a *double-sharp* to become a leading tone.

𝄞 Practice Box 4.6

Write the following harmonic minor scales. Use a key signature plus the appropriate accidental within the scale.

1. C harmonic
   minor

2. F♯ harmonic
   minor

3. B♭ harmonic
   minor

4. D♯ harmonic
   minor

The final form of the minor scale is called **melodic minor.** It is the most complicated form and *the most commonly used form of the scale.*

The most significant difference between melodic minor and the other two forms is that melodic minor uses different accidentals depending on whether it is ascending or descending. It also places accidentals beside more notes of the scale than just the seventh scale degree.

When the scale is ascending, both the sixth and seventh scale degrees are raised a half step higher. When the scale descends, the sixth and seventh scale degrees are lowered back to their original position. When descending, the melodic scale has the same pitches as the natural minor scale—identical to the key signature. Figure 4.7 shows the difference between the ascending and descending versions of the melodic minor scale.

Figure 4.7.   A melodic minor

It is a very good idea to write the accidentals beside the notes in the descending version of the melodic minor scale, even those notes that are within the key signature, to indicate very clearly that the accidentals used in the ascending half of the scale are being canceled. Figure 4.8 provides another example.

Figure 4.8.   G melodic minor

You will notice in the scale above, as in the harmonic minor scale, that the accidentals are placed into the music in addition to whatever sharps or flats are in the key signature. The descending half of the melodic minor scale is always identical to the pitches of the natural minor scale.

𝄞 Practice Box 4.7

Write the following melodic minor scales. Use a key signature plus the appropriate accidental within the scale.

1. B melodic
   minor

2. D melodic
   minor

3. E♭ melodic
   minor

4. G♯ melodic
   minor

There are several reasons that the melodic form of the minor scale is the one most commonly used. One reason has to do with the melodic options that are inherent in the scale. There are nine distinct pitch classes available within this form of the scale. (Remember, a pitch class is defined as a collective term that associates together all the musical sounds that bear a single name, so both of the Gs in the G minor scale on page 65 count as the same pitch class.) All other forms of the minor scale have only seven pitch classes. The melodic minor scale has more pitch resources from which to choose when constructing a minor melody. Similarly, when constructing chords from a scale, the melodic minor form provides much greater harmonic resources than any other form.

Parallel Key Relationships

When two keys share a common key signature, they are said to be relative keys. The tonic notes of relative keys are never the same letter name. It is possible, though, to describe another kind of relationship between scales and keys that share a starting note name instead of a common key signature. This kind of relationship is called a **parallel relationship,** and the keys involved are called **parallel keys.**

For example, C major and C minor are said to be parallel keys. Their key signatures are quite different—no sharps or flats for C major as opposed to three flats for C minor. The relationship is in the starting note of their scales. Parallel keys always begin their scales on the same letter name of the musical alphabet. It is important to note that some keys do not have parallel counterparts; for example, D♭ major does not have a parallel minor.

Practice Box 4.8

1. The relative minor of A major is _____.

2. The parallel minor of A major is _____.

3. The relative minor of E major is _____.

4. The parallel minor of E major is _____.

5. The relative minor of F♯ major is _____.

6. The parallel minor of F♯ major is _____.

7. The relative major of G minor is _____.

8. The parallel major of G minor is _____.

9. The relative major of B♭ minor is _____.

10. The parallel major of B♭ minor is _____.

Scale Degree Names

Each scale degree in a major or minor scale has a specific name that is often used in place of its numerical name. You have already learned two of these names. The first scale degree of any scale is always called the tonic. The seventh scale degree, provided that it sits specifically a half step away from the tonic, is called the leading tone.

Table 10 shows the complete list of **scale degree names.** These names are an important part of musical terminology and should be committed to memory. The words will be used in future discussions of chords and harmony.

Table 10. Scale degree names

Tonic	1st scale degree	Major & minor scales
Supertonic	2nd scale degree	Major & minor scales
Mediant	3rd scale degree	Major & minor scales
Subdominant	4th scale degree	Major & minor scales
Dominant	5th scale degree	Major & minor scales
Submediant	6th scale degree	Major & minor scales
Subtonic	7th scale degree	Minor scales only (must be a whole step lower than tonic)
Leading Tone	7th scale degree	All major scales and in minor scales where the note is raised

Music for Analysis

Determine the key of each of the following excerpts and the type of scale used if the key is minor.

Example 4.2. *Ludwig van Beethoven, Sonatina no. 5, 1st movement, mm. 61–71*

Key: _____

Track 4, 0:29

Example 4.3. *J. S. Bach,* Notebook for Anna Magdalena Bach, *Polonaise, mm. 10–16*

Key: _____

Track 4, 0:52

Example 4.4.   *Johannes Brahms, Hungarian Dance no. 5, mm. 95–104*

Key: _____

Track 4, 1:14

Example 4.5.   *Franz Schubert, Waltz, op. 9, no. 3, mm. 1–8*

Key: _____

Track 4, 1:36

AURAL SKILLS

Melody

Minor pentachords are sung with the same syllables as major pentachords, except for the middle note of the pentachord. Remember that the middle note of the minor pentachord is lower by a half step. Because of that change in pitch, the third note of the pattern takes a different syllable, *me* (pronounced "may"). Name the key of each exercise below, then sing the melodies.

Key: _____

1.

do   re   me   fa   sol

Key: _____

2.

Key: _____

3.

Key: _____

4.

Key: _____

5.

Key: _____

6.

Key: _____

7.

Key: _____

8.

Clap and count each example. Then identify the key of each example. There are major and minor keys. Name the keys and then sing the examples using syllables, being sure to keep the rhythm correct. You might tap your foot as you sing to help keep track of the pulses.

1. Key: _____

2. Key: _____

3. Key: _____

4. Key: _____

5. Key: _____

6. Key: _____

7. Key: _____

8. Key: _____

Rhythm

When the bottom number of the time signature changes, the type of note that becomes the division of the beat will change. Figure 4.9 demonstrates the division of the beat in time signatures with 2 as the bottom number.

Figure 4.9.   Divisions of the beat in cut time

In simple meters that have 2 as the bottom number of the time signature, the division of the beat will always be a quarter note. In all simple meters where the beat is a half note, the divisions of the beat are more difficult to read. In previous examples, where the divisions were eighth notes, the beaming showed you the pairs of notes that go together to form a single beat. In this meter, since the divisions are quarters, they cannot be beamed together. You must be well aware before you begin to count that the beat is a half note, because the notation itself will not aid you in seeing the groups of notes that make the divisions.

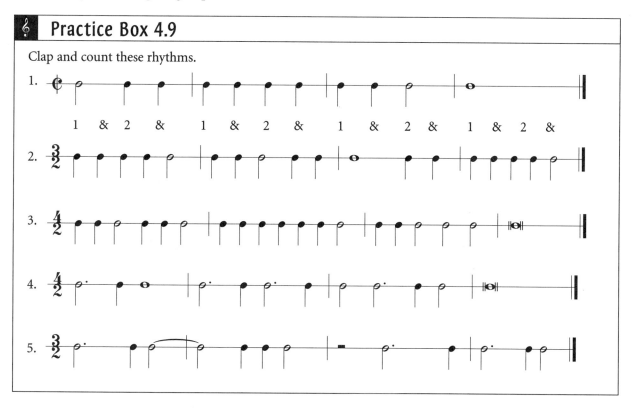

When the bottom number of the time signature is 8, the division of the beat is a note value that has not yet been introduced in this book. The note value that is equal to half the length of time occupied by an eighth note is called a sixteenth note and is shown in Figure 4.10.

Figure 4.10.   Sixteenth notes

Sixteenth notes

Notice that the sixteenth note looks a great deal like an eighth note but has two flags where the eighth note has only one. Likewise, when sixteenth notes appear in pairs, they are beamed together with two beams instead of one. Figure 4.11 shows how eighth note beats in $\frac{2}{8}$ time divide into sixteenth notes.

Figure 4.11. Divisions of the beat in $\frac{2}{8}$ time

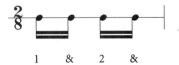

Like the meters that use 4 as the bottom number, the divisions of the beat in $\frac{2}{8}$ time are easy to read because the notes are beamed together.

The sixteenth rest, shown in Figure 4.12, looks similar to an eighth rest, except for the addition of a second flag on its stem.

Figure 4.12. Sixteenth rest

Sixteenth rest

Practice Box 4.10

Clap and count these rhythms.

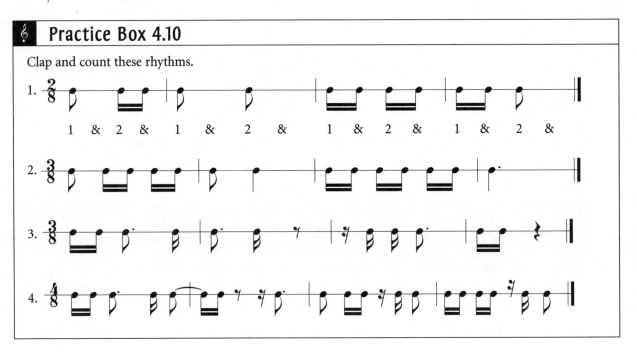

Additional Rhythms

For extra practice, clap and count these exercises.

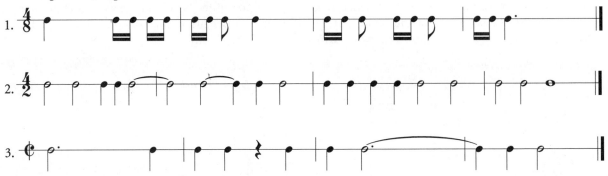

Dictation

You will hear a variety of major and minor scales. All versions of the minor scale will be used. Circle the type of scale you hear for each example below.

1.   major   natural minor   harmonic minor   melodic minor
2.   major   natural minor   harmonic minor   melodic minor
3.   major   natural minor   harmonic minor   melodic minor
4.   major   natural minor   harmonic minor   melodic minor
5.   major   natural minor   harmonic minor   melodic minor
6.   major   natural minor   harmonic minor   melodic minor
7.   major   natural minor   harmonic minor   melodic minor
8.   major   natural minor   harmonic minor   melodic minor
9.   major   natural minor   harmonic minor   melodic minor
10. major   natural minor   harmonic minor   melodic minor

Notate the rhythms that you hear. The time signature and number of measures are provided for you in each exercise. You will hear each exercise several times. It may be helpful to write the counts for each measure before you begin. There will be divisions of the beat.

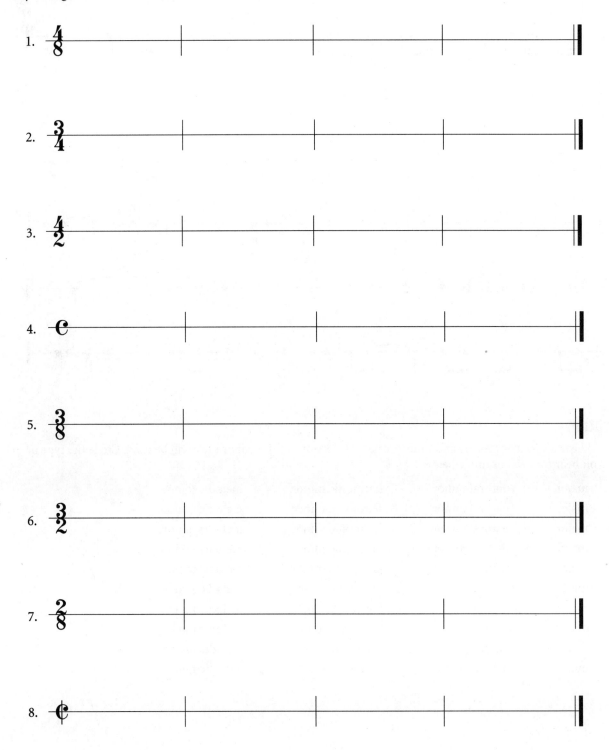

KEYBOARD APPLICATIONS

Play this new group of major scales using a tetrachord exercise similar to the one you learned in chapter 3.

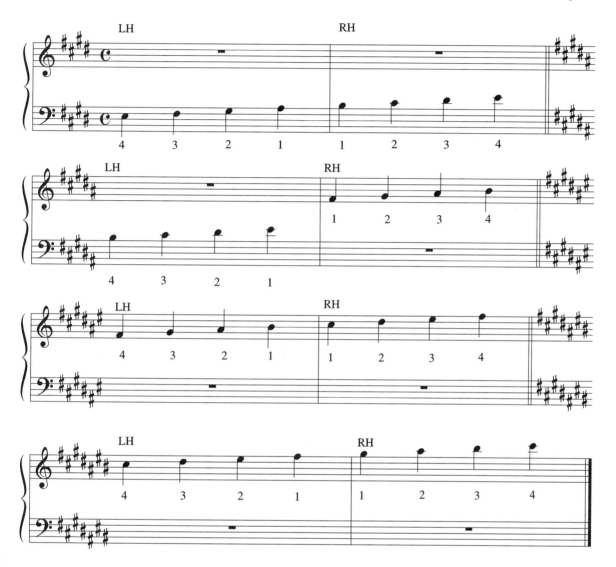

chapter 5 Triads and Figured Bass

THEORETICAL SKILLS

Chords and Triads

We have already defined a chord as a combination of three or more pitches associated together in some way. Often the word is used with a prefix that designates the chord as having a specific number of component pitches. Therefore a hexachord is a collection of six notes, a pentachord is five notes, a tetrachord is four notes, and a trichord is a group of three notes. (Remember that a collection of only two notes is usually called an interval. Occasionally it is referred to as a dyad.)

Chords are usually thought of as a group of notes heard simultaneously, but that requirement is not actually part of the definition (think of the pentachords that you played on the keyboard in chapter 2). However, as we study chords in this chapter we will deal with them in their traditional vertical formation, with the notes stacked one on top of another on the staff. The vertical chord structure is called "harmonic," as opposed to a melodic formation, which would involve seeing or hearing the notes of the chord played one at a time.

Chords constructed specifically of three notes form the basis for most tonal music. In Figure 5.1, you see chords constructed of three notes. These are given the name "trichord." A trichord is a general term that can refer to any collection of three pitches, such as those on the staff below.

Figure 5.1. Trichords

There is a more specific term that refers to a collection of three pitches that are stacked in intervals of thirds. That term is **triad.** Compare the chords above to the triads on the staff below. The triads are symmetrical in shape, and their sound may be considered pleasant, largely due to the fact that both of the constituent intervals are thirds.

Figure 5.2. Triads

When a triad is constructed above a given note, it is composed entirely either of line notes or space notes. A triad is named for the note that forms its foundation, or **root.** The names of the triads on the staff above are, from left to right, E, F, and B.

Practice Box 5.1

Name the root of each triad.

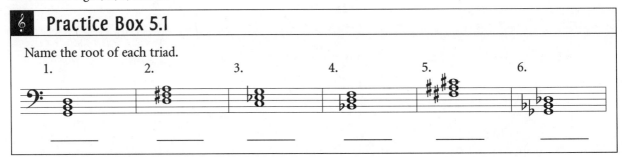

Qualities of Triads

Just as there are major, minor, diminished, and augmented intervals, there are major, minor, diminished, and augmented triads. We have also used these same words to describe pentachords and scales. If a triad is given the name "major," then it has a relationship to the major scale.

We will start with a C major triad. The notes of this chord are the first, third, and fifth scale degrees of the C major scale. The notes of the chord are known respectively as the *root*, the *third*, and the *fifth* of the triad. A triad built from the C major scale is known as a C major triad. (See Figure 5.3.)

Figure 5.3.   C major triad

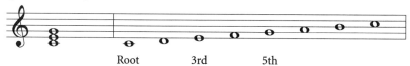

The major triad is probably the easiest of the four triad qualities to build, since its notes are drawn from major scales that should be very familiar to you by now. By thinking of the key signature of the corresponding major scale, any major triad can be created with the scale's first, third, and fifth notes.

When discussing the middle and top notes of a triad, it is typical to refer to them as the "chordal third" and the "chordal fifth," to distinguish them from the third and fifth notes of a scale and from intervals of the same size.

Practice Box 5.2

Write major triads up from each note. Think about the corresponding major scale to get the third and fifth of each chord.

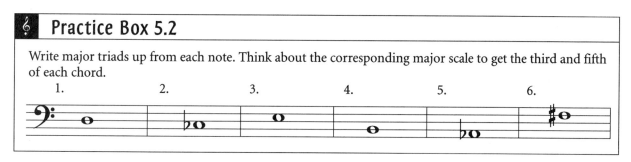

If you are called upon to build a major triad on a note such as D♯, which does not have a corresponding major scale, you can use the idea of "musical algebra," which helped you build certain intervals in chapter 3. Figure 5.4 demonstrates this principle using the D major triad as a reference point to build a D♯ major triad. The distance between D and D♯ is a chromatic half step; the only difference between them is that a sharp has been added to the first note, D, to create the second note, D♯. If you add the same accidental (a sharp) to all the notes of the D major triad, the resulting triad will also be major.

Figure 5.4.   Creating a D♯ major triad

D major triad

Each note raised by one half step
will create a
D♯ major triad

Practice Box 5.3

Build the following major triads on the given notes.

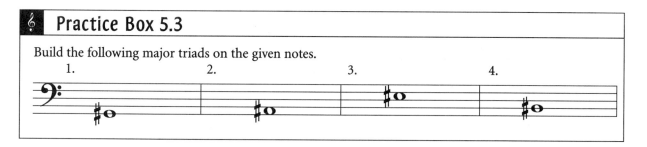

The minor triad is based on a minor scale. The notes of a minor triad are the first, third, and fifth scale degrees of a minor scale, as shown in Figure 5.5.

Figure 5.5.   A minor triad

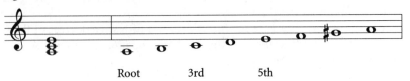

Root   3rd   5th

It is also possible to derive the minor triad from the major triad. To create a minor triad, the middle note (the third) of the major triad can be lowered a half step. The letter name of this pitch cannot be changed when it is lowered. Two examples of minor triads being created with this system are shown in Figure 5.6.

Figure 5.6.   Creating minor triads from major triads

C major   C minor   B♭ major   B♭ minor
triad   triad   triad   triad

The following rules should help when you are lowering the middle note of a major triad to form a minor triad.

1. If the third of the major triad is a natural, make it a flat in the minor triad.
2. If the third of the major triad is a sharp, make it a natural.
3. If the third of the major triad is a flat, make it a double-flat.

Practice Box 5.4

Write minor triads up from each note. These are the same roots on which you built major triads in Practice Box 5.2. You will lower the chordal third of each of those major triads.

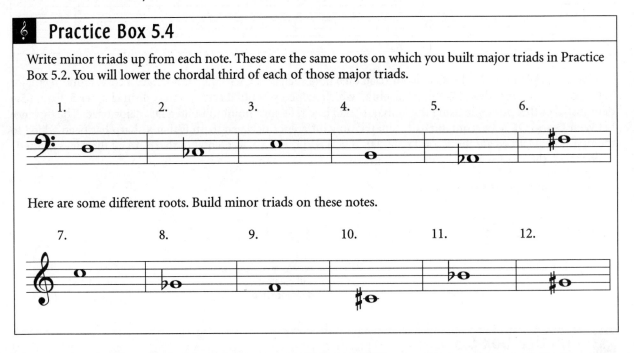

Here are some different roots. Build minor triads on these notes.

To make a diminished triad from a major triad, you must alter two notes of the chord. Both the third and fifth of the major triad must be lowered to create a diminished triad. The C major triad can be transformed into a diminished triad by adding flats to the upper two notes: C–E♭–G♭. (See Figure 5.7.) Alternatively, if you prefer to start with a minor triad (as with the A minor triad in Figure 5.7), only the fifth of a minor triad needs to be lowered in order to make it diminished.

Figure 5.7. *Creating diminished triads from major or minor triads*

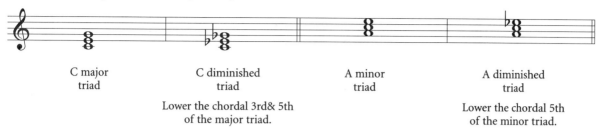

C major   C diminished   A minor   A diminished
triad   triad   triad   triad

Lower the chordal 3rd & 5th   Lower the chordal 5th
of the major triad.   of the minor triad.

Alternately, raising the root of a major triad a half step while leaving the upper two notes unchanged can create a diminished triad. This method can be helpful if the name of the diminished triad is a half step higher than a major triad that you know well, such as C♯ diminished. The C major triad can be changed into a C♯ diminished triad by raising the root: C♯–E–G. (See Figure 5.8.) Remember that you cannot change the letter name of the chord's root when you use this method. In other words, D♭–E–G is not a correct spelling of the diminished triad.

Figure 5.8. *Creating diminished triads from major triads by raising the root*

C major   C♯ diminished   F major   F♯ diminished
triad   triad   triad   triad

Practice Box 5.5

Write diminished triads up from each note. These are the same roots on which you built major triads in Practice Box 5.2. You will lower both the chordal third and chordal fifth of each of those major triads.

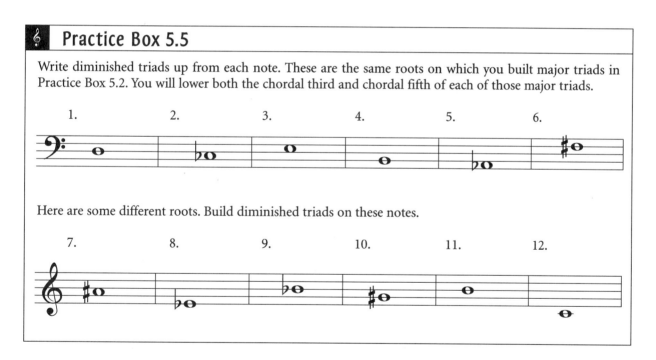

1.   2.   3.   4.   5.   6.

Here are some different roots. Build diminished triads on these notes.

7.   8.   9.   10.   11.   12.

The augmented triad is created from a major triad by raising the fifth of a major triad. (See Figure 5.9.) An augmented triad built on C would be C–E–G♯. Some augmented triads will need a double sharp on the fifth of the chord in order to raise it a half step.

Figure 5.9.   Creating augmented triads from major triads by raising the chordal 5th

| C major triad | C augmented triad | A major triad | A augmented triad | B major triad | B augmented triad |

Practice Box 5.6

Write augmented triads up from each note. These are the same roots on which you built major triads in Practice Box 5.2. You will raise the chordal fifth of each of those major triads.

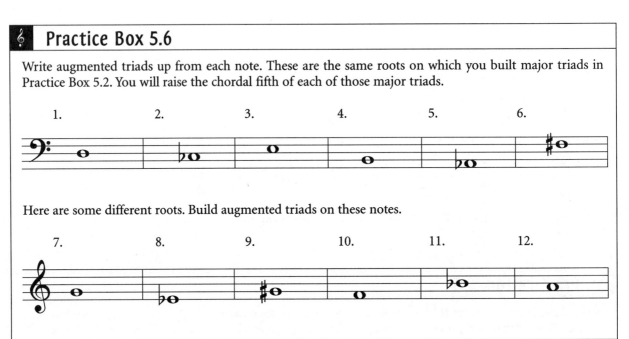

1.   2.   3.   4.   5.   6.

Here are some different roots. Build augmented triads on these notes.

7.   8.   9.   10.   11.   12.

The diminished and augmented triads are primarily categorized by their outside interval rather than by their relationship to any scale. The fifth formed between the top and bottom notes of the diminished triad is a diminished fifth, and that is the origin of the triad's name. In the case of the augmented triad, its outer interval is an augmented fifth, and that interval gives its name to the triad. (See Figure 5.10.)

Figure 5.10.   Diminished and augmented 5ths in their respective triads

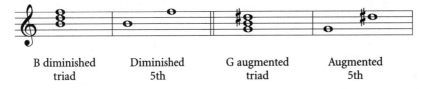

| B diminished triad | Diminished 5th | G augmented triad | Augmented 5th |

The building blocks of all triads are intervals of thirds. Thirds exist in four possible qualities—major, minor, diminished, and augmented—but it is important to note that only two of those qualities are used for building triads. All triads are built of major thirds and/or minor thirds. (Diminished and augmented thirds are never used in the construction of triads.)

Every triad has a lower third, consisting of the chord root plus the middle note of the chord, and an upper third, consisting of the middle note and the top note of the chord. There are only four ways to combine the two qualities of thirds to create triads.

Each of these combinations of thirds has a name. The name given to each combination is the quality of that triad. Table 11 shows the relationship between the four triad qualities and the qualities of their constituent intervals.

Table 11.   Triad qualities and component interval qualities

Quality	Major triad	Minor triad	Diminished triad	Augmented triad
Upper third	Minor 3rd	Major 3rd	Minor 3rd	Major 3rd
Lower third	Major 3rd	Minor 3rd	Minor 3rd	Major 3rd
Outer interval	Perfect 5th	Perfect 5th	Diminished 5th	Augmented 5th

Figure 5.11 shows how the components of a triad are arranged, demonstrating the intervals of a major triad as described in the table above.

Figure 5.11.   Component intervals in a major triad

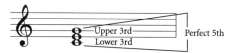

In addition to the other techniques described on the previous pages, it is also possible to build any quality of triad by constructing it up from its root in thirds. As the notes of the triad are named, you should notice that the letter names must be every other letter of the musical alphabet. Therefore, B–E♭–F♯ is not a triad, even though it sounds just like B–D♯–F♯.

For each quality of triad, use the system that makes the most sense to you.

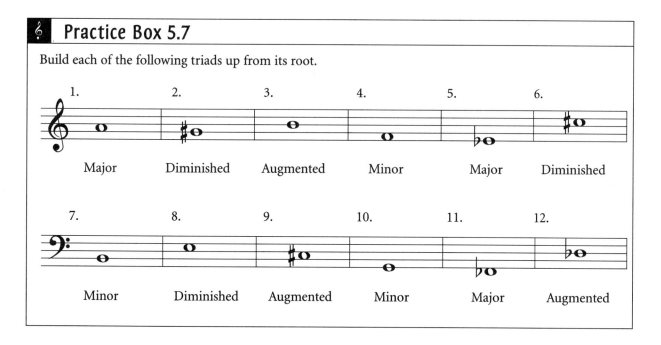

Practice Box 5.7

Build each of the following triads up from its root.

1. Major   2. Diminished   3. Augmented   4. Minor   5. Major   6. Diminished

7. Minor   8. Diminished   9. Augmented   10. Minor   11. Major   12. Augmented

Identifying Triad Qualities

When you are asked to identify the quality of a given chord, it is helpful to compare it to something that you already know, such as a major triad built on the same letter name.

In Figure 5.12, each of the chords to be identified is compared to a major triad that is similar to it.

Figure 5.12.   Identifying triads

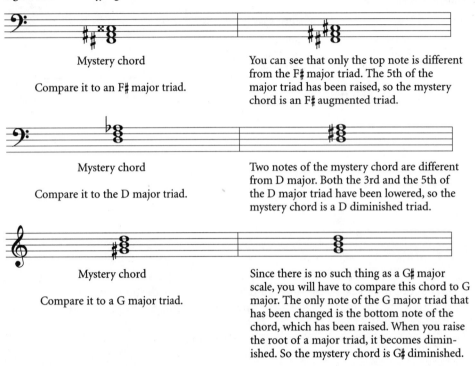

Mystery chord

Compare it to an F♯ major triad.

You can see that only the top note is different from the F♯ major triad. The 5th of the major triad has been raised, so the mystery chord is an F♯ augmented triad.

Mystery chord

Compare it to the D major triad.

Two notes of the mystery chord are different from D major. Both the 3rd and the 5th of the D major triad have been lowered, so the mystery chord is a D diminished triad.

Mystery chord

Compare it to a G major triad.

Since there is no such thing as a G♯ major scale, you will have to compare this chord to G major. The only note of the G major triad that has been changed is the bottom note of the chord, which has been raised. When you raise the root of a major triad, it becomes diminished. So the mystery chord is G♯ diminished.

♪ Practice Box 5.8

Name the quality of the following chords.

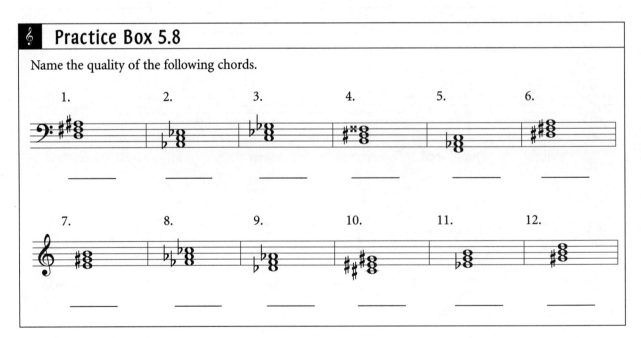

Different spacing of the notes of a triad does not alter its quality. You should be able to recognize triads even if the upper notes of the chord are arranged differently from the close spacing we have used thus far. Figure 5.13 shows several triads written with close spacing, and then rewritten with the chordal third and fifth moved away from the root in different spacings. The intervals that are formed in this open spacing are a fifth and a sixth. The sixth appears because it is the interval inversion of the upper two notes of the triad.

Figure 5.13. *Open spacing for triads*

    G major   G major   E♭ major   E♭ major   B minor   B minor

Each of these open arrangements of notes retains the identity of the closely spaced triad that precedes it. When confronted with a chord in which the notes are spread apart, you must arrange the note names in "triad order" before you can identify the quality of the chord. This process is similar to doing a type of word puzzle known as a "jumble," where you are given a group of letters and must rearrange them to spell a word. There are only seven possible letter combinations that form triads, although with the use of accidentals, it is possible to spell many more than seven triads. The possible letter combinations that can form triads are: A–C–E, B–D–F, C–E–G, D–F–A, E–G–B, F–A–C, and G–B–D. These should be memorized.

♪ Practice Box 5.9

Spell each chord above the staff in root position. Below the staff, write the quality of each chord. The first one is done for you as an example.

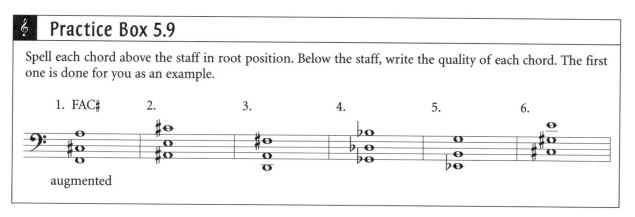

1. FAC♯   2.   3.   4.   5.   6.

augmented

Inversion of Triads

All the triads that have been discussed thus far have been written so that the root of the chord was in the lowest position. It is also possible to rearrange the notes of a triad so that the third or fifth form the lowest note. Such a chord is called an **inversion,** because the notes of the chord have been inverted or turned upside down.

When a triad is written so that its root is the lowest note, it is said to be in *root position.* When the third of the chord is the lowest note, it is said to be in *first inversion.* When the fifth of the chord is in the lowest position, it is said to be in *second inversion.* See Figure 5.14.

Figure 5.14. *Root-position, 1st-inversion, and 2nd-inversion triads*

  Root position   1st inversion   2nd inversion   Root position   1st inversion   2nd inversion

Changing the inversion of a chord does not alter its pitch content or its name and quality. In the first group above, all of the chords above are F major triads. In the second group, all are G minor triads. Only the order of the notes within the triad has been changed.

Root-position triads in close spacing are the easiest to recognize and name because of their characteristic appearance. When they appear this way, all notes of the triad are either line notes or space notes, stacked in thirds. The root is always on the bottom and can be easily identified.

Notice that in the two inversions, the notes are not equally distant. *When inverted, a triad will always contain the interval of a fourth.* In the first-inversion chord, the fourth appears as the upper interval. In the second-inversion chord, the fourth is the lower interval.

To find the root of the inverted triad, simply find the top note of the interval of the fourth. This will always be the root. Spell the triad up from this note and you will always be able to identify it, even though the notes of the chord appear in a different order.

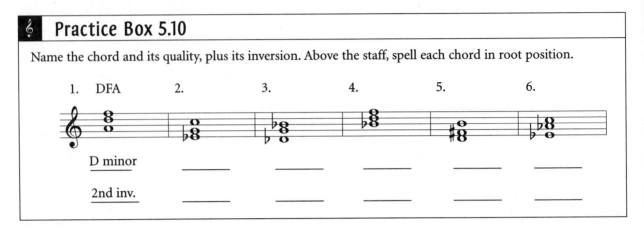

Practice Box 5.10

Name the chord and its quality, plus its inversion. Above the staff, spell each chord in root position.

1. DFA   2.   3.   4.   5.   6.

D minor   _____   _____   _____   _____   _____

2nd inv.   _____   _____   _____   _____   _____

Figured Bass

Each of the inversions studied above has a unique combination of intervals that are formed above the lowest note of the chord. These can be represented as a code that stands for a particular triad in a specific inversion. This series of numerical codes is called **figured bass.**

The word "bass" has been used before in conjunction with clef signs. The word itself means "low." This word can also be applied to the notes of a chord. When we talk about the "bass note" of a chord, we are referring to its lowest note, no matter whether this note is the root, third, or fifth of the triad. It also does not matter whether the lowest note of the chord is written in treble or bass clef. It is considered the bass as long as it is the lowest note.

Figured-bass symbols always describe the intervals that occur above the bass note, just as the name implies. It will help if you remember that "figured bass" tells you to "figure the notes above the bass." Figure 5.15 shows the way that these intervals are calculated in root position, first-inversion, and second-inversion chords. The complete figured-bass symbols for all the triads and inversions that we have studied are listed in Table 12. For most of these figured-bass combinations, abbreviated versions of the number are actually used to represent the inversions. When no number appears under a chord, it is understood that it is in root position. You should memorize the abbreviated versions.

Figure 5.15.   Intervals above the bass in root-position, 1st-inversion, and 2nd-inversion triads

Table 12.   Figured-bass symbols for triads

	Root position	1st inversion	2nd inversion
Complete version	$\frac{5}{3}$	$\frac{6}{3}$	$\frac{6}{4}$
Abbreviation		6	$\frac{6}{4}$

With these numbers plus a bass note given to you, it is possible to construct any triad in any inversion. This is demonstrated in Figure 5.16 below.

Figure 5.16.   Spelling a triad from figured-bass symbols

The figured bass tells you that the required chord is a first-inversion triad. Therefore, the bass note is the third of the chord. Two methods can be used to build the chord. First, the 6 in the figured bass is an abbreviation for 6/3. These numbers tell you exactly the intervals that need to be created above the bass note, B. The third above is D, and the sixth above is G. The bass plus upper notes are shown in the middle measure above. Once you have the three notes of the chord, you can determine its root by finding the fourth that appears between one pair of notes. You will find that the fourth is formed between D and G; therefore, the root of the chord is G.

A second method will tell you the root of the chord immediately. This method makes use of the concept of interval inversion. Remember that when you invert a sixth, the resulting interval is a third. The 6 in the figured bass is an interval *above* the bass note. Going down a third from the bass can derive the same note. Since the chord in the example above is in first inversion, the bass note is the chordal third. That means the root of the chord is exactly a third down from the given bass note. Therefore, the 6 in the figured bass identifies the root of the chord. By placing an X on the line or space that is a third down from the bass note, you will be visually identifying the root of the chord on the staff, as seen in Figure 5.17. (Think of the X as representing a "virtual" root.) It is then possible to spell the chord above the staff in root position and add the notes accordingly.

Figure 5.17.   Using an X on the staff to locate the root

When dealing with second-inversion triads, the bass note is the chordal fifth. To identify the root of the second-inversion triad or seventh chord, you must go down 2 thirds (equal to a fifth) to find the root. See Figure 5.18.

Figure 5.18.   Using 2 Xs on the staff to locate the root

🎼 Practice Box 5.11

Spell these chords above the staff from the given bass notes and figured-bass symbols. If the bass note has an accidental, you must retain that in your chord spelling.

Figured-bass symbols can also be used to represent accidentals in chords. Any number that has a slash through it should be raised a half step from the key signature. (See Figure 5.19.) The slash is a code that can be applied to any number. In order to lower a note from the key signature, a flat (or a natural if the note is sharped in the key signature) is placed in front of any number.

Figure 5.19. *Accidentals in figured bass*

In the example above, the slash through the sixth tells you to raise the root of the chord by a half step from the key signature. Since the note is C♮ in the key signature, the figured-bass symbol indicates that it should be changed to C♯. The flat beside the 5 indicates the change to that note above the bass, which is B♮ in the key signature. With the figured-bass symbol, it becomes B♭.

Another code used in figured bass is an accidental that is not accompanied by a number. Any accidental—sharp, flat, or natural—that occurs by itself automatically represents the third up from the bass note. In Figure 5.20, you see a sharp standing alone in the figured bass under the pitch E. This means the note a third up (G) would be raised from the key signature, making it G♯. In the next measure, the natural sign refers to the note a third up from F, which is A. The key signature makes this an A♭. However, the natural sign in the figured bass overrides the key signature, making the note an A♮.

Figure 5.20. *Additional accidentals in figured bass*

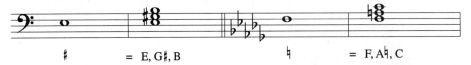

In Figure 5.20, the symbols represent chords in root position, since there is no 6 in the figured bass. Typically, a root-position triad requires no figured-bass symbols at all. However, in these examples, since the third of the chord must be altered to create the desired quality, it must be written in the figured bass. The only way to represent an inverted chord is to include the number 6 in the figured bass. If there is no 6, these triads cannot be inversions.

🎼 Practice Box 5.12

Build the following chords up from the given bass note. Use Xs on the staff to find the chord roots. Then spell the chords in root position above the staff. In the space below each chord, indicate whether it is in root position, 1st inversion, or 2nd inversion. The first one is done for you as an example.

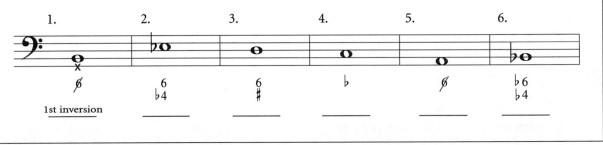

The system of musical shorthand known as figured bass was developed in the Baroque period and was found in almost all instrumental ensemble music of the period. The figures, or numbers, were written under a bass line that was performed by a low-pitched solo instrument such as the cello. The keyboard player also read the bass line and improvised an accompaniment based on the figures, which described the chords to be played above the bass. The texture created by the keyboard player was known as a keyboard **realization** of the figured bass. The ability to read figured bass and improvise was very common in the Baroque and Classical periods. The instruments whose job was to "realize" the figure bass were commonly called the **basso continuo,** or *continuo* for short.

Music for Analysis

First, determine the key of the following excerpt. Then spell the chords indicated by this figured bass line. Write a keyboard realization of this figured bass in the treble staff provided. You will be adding notes for the right hand to play. Each right hand chord should contain three notes. You may add the right hand notes in any inversion, and you should strive to make it easy to play. The first measure is done for you. All notes in the first measure of the bass represent various inversions of the same chord; therefore, a dotted half note in the treble staff is all that it needed.

Example 5.1.   Arcangelo Corelli, Sonata no. 11, Corrente, mm. 34–37

Track 5, 0:00

This excerpt, by the most prolific female composer of the Baroque period, is longer and more varied. When there are two numbers under a single bass note, construct a chord over the given note for each of those numbers. Add a right hand part to the continuo staff.

Example 5.2.   Elisabeth-Claude Jacquet de la Guerre, Céphale et Procris, scene 5, mm. 12–21

Track 5, 0:18

AURAL SKILLS

Minor Scales

Sing the following forms of the minor scale, using *do* as the tonic note of the scale. Where the pitches of the minor scales differ from those of the parallel major, note the different solfege syllables that are used.

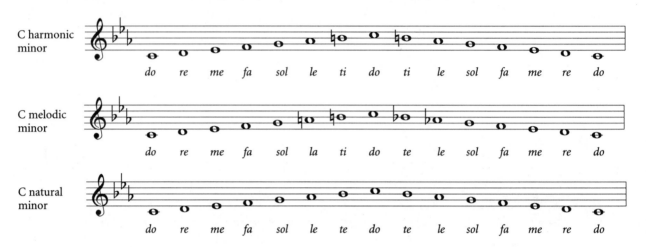

C harmonic
minor

do re me fa sol le ti do ti le sol fa me re do

C melodic
minor

do re me fa sol la ti do te le sol fa me re do

C natural
minor

do re me fa sol le te do te le sol fa me re do

Sing the following patterns in melodic minor keys.

1. Skips

2. Leaps

3. Corkscrew

Melody

For each of the following minor melodies, identify the key and the form of the scale being used. Sing each with solfege syllables.

1. Key: _____

2. Key: _____

3. Key: _____

4. Key: _____

5. Key: _____

6. Key: _____

7. Key: _____

8. Key: _____

Intervals

Practice singing the following intervals from a variety of pitches. Can you think of the name of some tunes that begin with each interval?

1. Ascending: minor 2nd   minor 3rd   augmented 4th   minor 6th   minor 7th

2. Descending: major 2nd   major 3rd   augmented 4th   major 6th   major 7th

Syncopation

The normal accent in any measure of music falls on the first beat of the measure, which is known as the "downbeat." In duple and triple meters, this is the only accented beat of the measure. In quadruple meters, there is also a secondary accent, which falls on the third beat of the measure (the beat that begins the second half of the measure). This principle of musical accents can be summed up this way: *There is an accent on the first note of any group of two or three beats.* In Figure 5.21, the arrowhead symbol, called an accent mark, represents the strongest accent of the measure, and the straight-line symbol, called a stress mark, represents the secondary accent in the measure.

Figure 5.21.   Normal accents in simple meters

Whenever anything interrupts the normal flow of accents in music, it is called **syncopation.** Syncopation is the process of stressing a beat that normally would be unaccented. There are many ways to create syncopation. The most common way is to begin the longest note of a measure on an unaccented beat. Typically, the longest note values of the measure occur on the strongest beats, 1 or 3. If a half note in $\frac{4}{4}$ time begins on beat 2, this creates syncopation. The same thing would be true if a quarter note occurred on beat 2 in $\frac{4}{8}$ time. See Figure 5.22.

Figure 5.22.   Syncopation

Practice Box 5.13

Clap and count these rhythms. Identify the syncopated rhythms.

Additional Rhythms

For extra practice, clap and count these exercises.

Dictation

Notate the rhythm of the following examples. If there is an upbeat, you will be told before you hear the rhythm the first time.

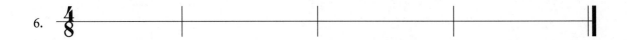

Notate the melodies that you hear. The key signature is given to you. Each melody is in a minor key and will begin on *do*. There will be some divisions of the beat in the rhythm. You will hear each melody four or five times.

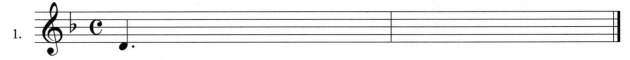

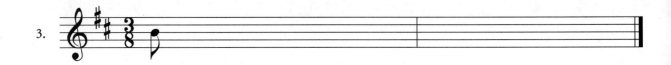

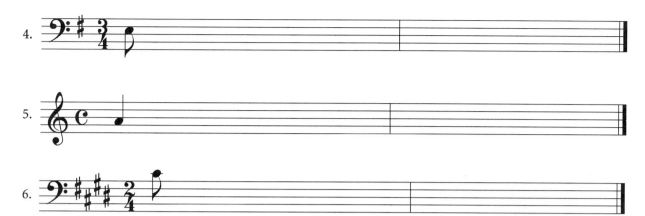

Name the following harmonic intervals by size and quality as you hear them. The choices will be major and perfect intervals.

1.   6.
2.   7.
3.   8.
4.   9.
5.   10.

The size of the interval is given to you. Name the intervals' qualities as you hear them. The choices will be major or minor.

1.	major 2nd	minor 2nd	6.	major 2nd	minor 2nd
2.	major 6th	minor 6th	7.	major 7th	minor 7th
3.	major 7th	minor 7th	8.	major 7th	minor 7th
4.	major 3rd	minor 3rd	9.	major 6th	minor 6th
5.	major 3rd	minor 3rd	10.	major 3rd	minor 3rd

The size of the interval is given to you. Name the intervals' qualities as you hear them. The choices will be perfect, augmented, or diminished.

1.	perfect 4th	diminished 4th
2.	perfect 5th	diminished 5th
3.	perfect 5th	diminished 5th
4.	perfect 4th	diminished 4th
5.	perfect 4th	diminished 4th
6.	perfect 5th	augmented 5th
7.	perfect 5th	augmented 5th
8.	perfect 4th	augmented 4th
9.	perfect 5th	augmented 5th
10.	perfect 4th	augmented 4th

Error Detection

The following rhythms contain one or more errors. There may be dots or ties missing, or the actual note values may be incorrect. Listen and correct the errors that you see. Write the corrected version under each staff.

1.

2.

3.

4.

5.

6.

KEYBOARD APPLICATIONS

Play this new group of major scales using a tetrachord exercise similar to the one you learned in chapter 3.

Looking Ahead

It is possible to use chords with more than three notes in tonal music. Although triads form the basis of the tonal system, often an extra note is added to the triad to form a *seventh chord*. A seventh chord, despite its name, is not a seven-note chord, but a four-note chord. Its name comes from the interval created by the outer notes of the chord, which is a seventh. (See Figure 5.23.)

Figure 5.23. Triad and seventh chord

triad   seventh chord

Most of the time, a seventh chord is used as a replacement for a triad built on the same pitch. Seventh chords will be studied in greater depth in chapters 20–22 of this book.

chapter 6

Melody and Counterpoint

THEORETICAL SKILLS

Characteristics of Melody

Melody is the most noticeable aspect of music. It is a musical concept that is familiar to everyone and yet can be difficult to define in specific terms. We are surrounded by music played on the radio, the television, and your home stereo, to name but a few examples. The melody of most popular songs is the feature that many of us remember. When you sing along to your favorite song, it is the melody you sing.

Good melodies share certain characteristics that can be studied, analyzed, and adapted to create newly composed melodies. Let us begin with a definition of melody. In its simplest definition, a melody is a succession of pitches. But since it is possible to create a succession of pitches so random that they have no discernible relationship to one other, we obviously need a fuller definition for the concept of melody. A more complete definition follows:

A melody is a succession of pitches that create a distinct sense of organization and a logical whole.

Most melodies are built around some recognizable shape, feature, or contour. A distinctive rhythm is frequently a component of a good melody, adding another type of organization in addition to the pitches. Unaccompanied melodies are the earliest surviving music known to man. The Gregorian chants of the Middle Ages consisted entirely of melodic lines, with no harmony and no instrumental accompaniment. The rhythm of the melody was largely determined by the pattern of the Latin texts for which the melodies were created.

The interaction of melodic lines with other melodies and harmony is known as **texture.** There are three primary types of texture:

monophonic Literally, "one sound": a melodic line that stands alone, without accompaniment. Gregorian chant is an example of this texture.

homophonic Several lines of notes moving together, creating harmony, and often using the same rhythm. A hymn is a typical example of this texture. Generally, the soprano line is considered to be the primary focus of a homophonic texture, but even if another line is given prominence, only one line at a time will be heard as the main melody.

polyphonic Several lines of melody heard at the same time, with equal importance. The melodic lines in this texture move independently from one another, although the total effect may be to produce a sense of harmony. A Bach fugue is an example of this texture. (A fugue is a type of instrumental piece based on a single melody repeated throughout several independent strands of the texture that are performed simultaneously. The lines of melody enter one at a time, like a round. Fugues were often written for a solo instrument, with the performer required to keep track of all the lines of the texture.)

Many pieces of music alternate the textures listed above. Still other pieces may be interpreted simultaneously as homophonic and polyphonic textures. They are homophonic in the sense that the individual lines of notes, often known as **voices,** move together in similar rhythms, with the soprano line generally heard as the primary melody. Even if the other voice parts are seen to function primarily as harmony, they may move with a degree of independence that makes them equally important to the soprano line. According to this point of view, even a familiar hymn can be interpreted as having a polyphonic texture.

Two important elements of melody are **range** and **tessitura**. *Range* is the span of pitches that is included within a melody—in other words, the distance from its lowest and highest notes. The term range is also used in describing the generally accepted limits that each voice part (soprano, alto, tenor, and bass) may sing. The *tessitura* of a melody describes where within the range the majority of the pitches are written. The concept of tessitura is related to range but distinct from it. The range for a bass voice is generally accepted to be from F^2 to C^4. If a melody for a bass voice were written with the bulk of the pitches from F^2 to C^3, then the tessitura would be considered to be low. If the melody were primarily written from F^3 to C^4, then the melody would have a high tessitura. Tessitura can have an impact on the level of difficulty that a particular melody may present to a performer who will sing or play it.

The intervals that comprise a melody can be described in general terms with the words **conjunct** and **disjunct**. These words refer to the prevalence of steps (intervals of a second) or leaps (intervals of a third or greater) within the melody. If a melody is primarily composed of stepwise movement, it is said to be conjunct. If leaps are more prevalent than steps, the melody is said to be disjunct. Typically, it is more common to find disjunct movement in melodies written for instruments than in music written for the voice. Examples 6.1 and 6.2 demonstrate conjunct and disjunct motion, respectively.

Example 6.1.   *Richard Rodgers and Oscar Hammerstein,* South Pacific, *"Younger than Springtime," mm. 21–27*

Track 6, 0:00

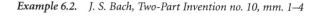

Example 6.2.   *J. S. Bach, Two-Part Invention no. 10, mm. 1–4*

Track 6, 0:31

Although the choice of whether to consider a melody good or satisfying, or even memorable, is a very personal one, certain principles of melody writing can be defined. The first of these principles involves the directional tendencies of specific scale degrees.

A study of the manner in which melody moves within its horizontal line of notes is called **voice leading.** When discussing the voice leading of a melodic line, the combination of steps, leaps, and stationary motion is taken into account, as well as the tendency of certain scale degrees to behave in a particular manner.

The second, fourth, sixth, and seventh notes of the scale have a tendency to move in certain directions. These scale degrees are considered to be *restless* and demand resolution. You have already seen this principle in action. When you write the leading tone in a melodic line, it should virtually always move to the tonic. The supertonic scale degree generally moves down to the tonic but occasionally may move upward to the mediant. The following table shows the directional tendencies of various scale degrees in a melody. The primary notes of resolution listed in Table 13 are the most common ones. Secondary notes of resolution are possible, but less common.

Table 13.   *Typical notes of resolution for active scale degrees*

	Primary resolution	Secondary resolution
Supertonic (*re*)	*do*	*mi* (or *me*)
Subdominant (*fa*)	*mi* (or *me*)	*sol*
Submediant (*la* or *le*)	*sol*	*ti*
Leading tone (*ti*)	*do*	

The secondary notes of resolution are often used when a melody moves stepwise in a specific direction. For example, if the fourth scale degree is the next to last note of a melody, it will typically move downward by step to its primary note of resolution. The following melody demonstrates an example of the fourth scale degree resolving to the third at the end of a melody.

Figure 6.1.   *Movement of fourth scale degree to primary note of resolution*

If the fourth scale degree is part of a rising pattern of melodic notes, then its movement upward to the secondary note of resolution (the fifth scale degree) will sound very logical.

Figure 6.2.   *Movement of fourth scale degree to secondary note of resolution*

The remaining scale degrees, specifically the members of the tonic triad, can be said to be at rest. They often are used to imply a sense of completion in a melody. However, these notes of the scale—the first, third, and fifth scale degrees—also have more options for movement than do the others. For example, the tonic scale degree may remain static, move up or down by step, or move by leap.

Although most examples of melodic writing demonstrate a balance between conjunct and disjunct motion, it can be said that in certain types of writing, especially for the voice, steps are preferable to leaps. A leap in one direction is often countered by a step or leap in the opposite direction. If two leaps in the same direction are used, they are usually part of the same triad. All of the principles can be seen in the examples above.

In the first measure of Figure 6.2, the leap from *re* to *fa* is followed immediately by a leap in the opposite direction from *fa* back to *re*. A similar movement happens in the second measure of Figure 6.1, with movement from *sol* to *re* and back to *sol*. After the second leap of each measure, there is stepwise movement in the opposite direction.

In Figure 6.2, the final three notes form a pattern of leaps that all move downward. These three pitches are all members of the same triad, B♭ major.

In general, a leap followed by a step is preferable to a step followed by a leap.

Certain melodic intervals are usually avoided. The melodic augmented second, found in the harmonic minor scale between the sixth and seventh scale degrees, is almost never used in melodic writing. Instead, in stepwise passages involving minor scales, it is much more common to find the melodic version of the minor scale, which does not use the augmented second. The tritone does appear occasionally in a melodic line, but it is handled with care. The diminished fifth occurs in major and minor scales between the fourth scale degree and the leading tone. With a downward leap from *fa* to *ti*, the leading tone can then resolve stepwise in the opposite direction to *do*. This voice leading is preferable to the use of the augmented fourth, *fa* to *ti*, because the leap cannot be resolved by stepwise movement in the opposite direction.

Figure 6.3.   Proper and improper resolution of a tritone

Rhythm plays an enormous role in our perception of melody. For most of us, it is usually impossible to separate the concept of melody from that of rhythm and meter. The same melodic contour can sound quite different if it is placed in two different meters and given different note values. Figure 6.4 is an example of a familiar children's tune. The pitch content is the same in both melodies, but in the second melody the meter and rhythm have changed. Notice the different character of the second version.

Figure 6.4.   Familiar tune and rhythmic variation

Mary Had a Little Lamb

Same tune with different meter and rhythm

Melodies often use repetition of elements, including pitch and rhythm, to create coherence and memorability. In the tune above, "Mary Had a Little Lamb," notice the repetition of melody and rhythm from the first half of the tune to the second half.

Even the repetition of melodic events often includes a small degree of variation. This can involve repeating a fragment of the melody starting on a different pitch. This process is known as a melodic **sequence**. The process of using a sequence is found constantly in classical styles of music, especially much of the polyphonic music written in the eighteenth century by composers such as J. S. Bach.

The following example, from the music of Bach, illustrates three melodic patterns that are sequenced. Notice that each of the three patterns has a distinctive melodic shape and a marked rhythmic pattern. The first iteration is marked for each of the three sequences. Find the repetition of each and describe its relationship to the original.

Example 6.3.   *J. S. Bach, Fugue in G Major,* The Well-Tempered Clavier, *Book I, mm. 1–4*

·Track 6, 0:49

Pattern 1   Pattern 2   Pattern 3

The leaps in measure 2 are large and abrupt, although the first leap is followed by a change of direction. The repetition of this pattern of leaps in the third measure makes its first appearance seem more deliberate. Sequences combine a sense of familiarity, from having heard the same contour more than once, with a sense of building tension as the pattern rises in pitch. These factors take precedence over the typical rules of harmonic progression.

🎼 Practice Box 6.1

Write several melodies that are approximately four measures in length on the staves provided below. Use additional staff paper if necessary.

A **phrase** is a musical sentence with a beginning, middle, and end. A phrase usually ends with a **cadence**, which is defined as a stopping place in music. Often a phrase, or a segment of it, is delineated within a musical composition by use of a phrase mark, or curved line, that is also known as a "slur." The slur mark indicates that the notes under it should be played in a smooth and connected manner. This manner of playing is also called *legato.*

The most typical length for a phrase is four measures. Using the Haydn excerpt from Example 6.4, we can see how the phrase grows out of a sequence. In this example, the phrase length is four measures.

Example 6.4. Joseph Haydn, Symphony no. 104 in D Major ("London"), 4th movement, mm. 3–6

Track 6, 1:04

Notice that the sequence that begins the phrase is not used throughout the entire four-measure segment. It is important to point out that not every note of a phrase must be related to the parts of the phrase that are sequenced.

Example 6.5 shows a phrase that is almost completely connected with a single slur mark.

Example 6.5. Beethoven, Symphony no. 5, 3rd movement, mm. 1–4

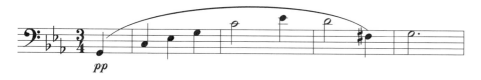

Track 6, 1:15

Although the final note is not slurred with the remaining notes, it is nevertheless part of the phrase. Notice the characteristics of the melody. The first six notes all leap in the same direction, but they are part of the same triad. What is that triad?

A phrase seldom stands on its own without another companion phrase to complement or complete it. Phrases are usually found in pairs. Two phrases that follow each other and have similar elements are called a **period**. The second phrase usually has a stronger sense of completion than the first. Look at the two phrases that form a period in Example 6.6. Would the music sound complete if it ended with the first phrase? Identify characteristics of this melody. What scale degree is used to end the first phrase? What is used at the end of the second phrase?

Example 6.6. Haydn, Symphony no. 104 in D Major ("London"), 4th movement, mm. 3–10

Track 6, 1:25

🎼 Practice Box 6.2

Write a melody that is at least eight measures in length. Try to create a period within the melody, using 2 four-measure phrases. The second phrase should sound more final than the first phrase. Try to include a sequence in your melody. Use additional staff paper if necessary.

Counterpoint

After a melody has been written, it is often desirable to add some type of accompaniment to it, so that the texture becomes something other than monophonic. In most popular styles of music that we hear today, a series of chords is added to a melody, creating homophonic texture. However, for over one thousand years in the history of Western art music, composers have chosen to put simultaneous melodic lines of equal importance together to create a texture that is often referred to as **counterpoint.** This term comes from the Latin expression *punctus contra punctum,* meaning "point against point." The single melodic line added to a given melody is known as its counterpoint. The meaning of this word is the same as "polyphonic texture." A texture that is written with this technique is called "contrapuntal."

Example 6.7.   J. S. Bach, Prelude in F Major, The Well-Tempered Clavier, *Book I, mm. 1–4*

Track 6, 1:41

A theorist by the name of Johann Joseph Fux organized the principles of counterpoint into a series of rules. Fux published his work in 1725. In it he formulated a series of five types of counterpoint, which he called "species." The first species involves note-against-note counterpoint, while the others require two or more notes against one note in the original melody. We will be looking at first-species counterpoint in this chapter.

Now that you have composed melodies of your own, we will study the process of adding contrapuntal lines to a given melody. Only first-species counterpoint will be used.

Motion between Voices

A pair of melodic lines may interact with each other in five distinct ways: by parallel, similar, oblique, contrary, and stationary motion. Two melodies, or voices, are said to *parallel* each other if they move in the same direction by the same interval (considered numerically). In Figure 6.5, the bottom voice, shown with stems pointing down, moves up by the interval of a second. The top voice, shown with stems up, also moves up by the same interval.

Figure 6.5.   *Two examples of parallel motion*

Parallel motion
Bass moves horizontally up by a major 2nd;
tenor moves up by a minor 2nd (the result is
a major 3rd followed by a minor 3rd).

Parallel motion
Both voices move horizontally up by
the interval of a major 2nd
(the result is two major 3rds).

If the two voices move in the same direction, but by different-sized intervals, the motion is said to be *similar*, as shown in Figure 6.6.

Figure 6.6.   *Similar motion*

Similar motion
Both voices move up, but by
different intervals.

Parallel and similar motion are frequently seen in counterpoint, but specific types of parallel motion are virtually always avoided. These involve harmonic intervals of parallel perfect fifths, octaves, and primes. (Parallel perfect fourths are acceptable, but uncommon.) Several types of incorrect parallels are shown in Figure 6.7. All of these examples should be avoided in contrapuntal writing.

Figure 6.7.   *Incorrect parallel motion*

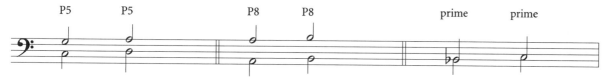

When two voices move in the opposite direction, the motion between them is said to be *contrary*. Both measures of Figure 6.8 are examples of contrary motion.

Figure 6.8.   *Contrary motion*

Contrary motion between voices is one of the most preferable ways to handle voice leading between two voices. It helps to preserve the individuality of the vocal lines and to avoid parallelism between voices.

The fourth type of motion between two voices is called *oblique*. In this type of motion, one voice remains stationary, while the other voice moves, as seen in Figure 6.9.

Figure 6.9.   *Oblique motion*

The final type of motion is actually a lack of motion. Two voices are said to be *stationary* when neither of them moves to a new note (see Figure 6.10). Although this is not seen very often in note-against-note counterpoint, this type of motion will be seen later when four-voice harmony is studied. You should not mistake this type of motion for parallelism. If the voices do not move, they cannot be parallel.

Figure 6.10.   Stationary voices

Contrapuntal Composition

Note-against-note counterpoint should consist primarily of consonant intervals. For our purposes, the following intervals are considered to be consonant: major and minor thirds, major and minor sixths, perfect fifths, and perfect octaves. The dissonant intervals are the major and minor seconds, major and minor sevenths, the perfect fourth, and the tritone (augmented fourth and diminished fifth). The minor second and major seventh are rarely a component of this style.

One voice is usually given to you as you begin a first-species counterpoint exercise. This voice is called the *cantus firmus* ("fixed voice"), and it typically is written as the lowest voice. Originally, a cantus firmus would have been a Gregorian chant melody. Using the principles of motion and voice leading discussed above, a second line is composed to function as its companion. The second line should be compatible with the cantus firmus, but should also have its own contour and independence.

Figure 6.11 is a two-voice example that demonstrates the use of consonant intervals and first-species counterpoint. The two voice parts are written on separate staves. This style of printing, called *open score,* makes it easier to see each voice as an independent melodic line. Analyze the intervals that occur between the two voices as well as the melodic characteristics of each line. Then determine the type of motion that occurs between each pair of notes. Is there any incorrect parallel motion between voices?

Other characteristics of this style include a tendency to begin and end with a perfect octave or unison. Perfect fifths are also acceptable as starting and ending intervals. Typically, first-species counterpoint is written entirely in whole notes, but the examples below use varied note values. Parallel perfect intervals should be avoided. Parallel thirds and sixths are fine, provided that no more than three are used in succession.

Finally, voices should not cross. In other words, the lower voice should always maintain its position relative to the upper voice and not cross to a note that is higher than the upper voice.

Figure 6.11.   Note-against-note counterpoint

Practice Box 6.3

Add a contrapuntal line to these melodies, using note-against-note style.

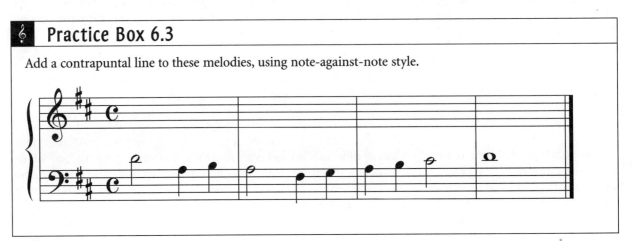

Practice Box 6.3 (continued)

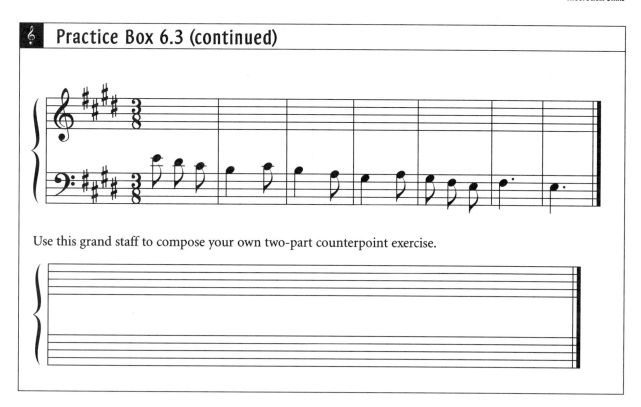

Use this grand staff to compose your own two-part counterpoint exercise.

Music for Analysis

Study the melody on the treble staff for the presence of sequences.

Track 6, 2:05

Example 6.8. *Johann Christian Bach, Sonata, op. 5, no. 1, 2nd movement (Tempo di Minuetto), mm. 37–42*

Study the following example of contrapuntal composition from the music of J. S. Bach. How does this two-voice fugue follow or depart from the rules of note-against-note counterpoint studied above?

Example 6.9. *J. S. Bach, Fugue in E Minor,* The Well-Tempered Clavier, *Book I, mm. 39–42*

Track 6, 2:24

The following fugue was written over a hundred years later than the fugue by J. S. Bach. Study it in the same manner, to determine how it follows and departs from the rules of first-species counterpoint. There are actually three voices in this fugue, although in this excerpt only two of them are active most of the time. The rests that appear in almost every measure indicate where the extra voice is not being heard.

Example 6.10.   *Clara Schumann, Fugue in D Minor, op. 16, no. 3, mm. 24–30*

Track 6, 2:39

AURAL SKILLS

Melody

Sing the following melodies in minor keys. Identify the scale used in each melody as natural, harmonic, or melodic. To understand the time signatures, study the rhythm section on the next page.

1.

2.

3.

4.

5.

6.

7.

8.

Rhythm

Remember that when the top number of a time signature is 2, 3, or 4, the meter is considered to be simple. This indicates that each beat is divided into two equal divisions. It is also possible to divide a beat into three equal parts. This kind of time signature will have as its top number a multiple of 3 that is greater than 3 itself, such as 6, 9, or 12. A time signature with any of these numbers on top is called a "compound meter." Just as with simple meters, the bottom number of the time signature does not play a role in determining whether the meter is simple or compound.

Compound meters look a little different than any of the meters than we have studied in previous chapters. Examples of compound meters are shown in Table 14, along with their characteristics.

Table 14. Compound meters

Time Signatures			Characteristics
$\frac{6}{4}$	$\frac{6}{8}$	$\frac{6}{16}$	These meters are considered to be duple compound. Duple refers to the fact that there are two beats per measure. Compound refers to the possible division of each beat into three equal parts.
$\frac{9}{4}$	$\frac{9}{8}$	$\frac{9}{16}$	These meters are considered to be triple compound. Triple refers to the fact that there are three beats per measure. Compound refers to the possible division of each beat into three equal parts.
$\frac{12}{4}$	$\frac{12}{8}$	$\frac{12}{16}$	These meters are considered to be quadruple compound. Quadruple refers to the fact that there are four beats per measure. Compound refers to the possible division of each beat into three equal parts.

In a simple meter, the unit of measurement, also known as the beat note, is divided into two equal parts and the measure is counted "one-and-two-and," and so on. In compound meters, each beat is divided into three equal parts. The top number of the time signature does not directly tell you the number of beats that occur in each measure. Instead, it tells you how many divisions of the beat occur in each measure. To determine the actual number of beats, the top number must be divided by three. Therefore, a time signature with a 6 on the top will represent two beats per measure.

Because the beat note is divisible by three, *a dotted note is always used to represent the beat in compound meters.* In order to determine the beat note for any compound meter, you must think about the type of note represented by the bottom number of the time signature and multiply that note's value by three. Figure 6.12 gives some examples.

Figure 6.12. Beats and divisions of the beat in compound meters

The musical math above shows you how to do this. If the bottom number of the time signature is an 8, it represents an eighth note. Three eighth notes added or tied together equal a dotted quarter note (this is true no matter what the time signature). The unit of measurement in $\frac{6}{8}$ time is a dotted quarter. Because there are two beats per measure, a measure of music in $\frac{6}{8}$ time can contain a maximum of two dotted quarter notes, as shown in Figure 6.13.

Figure 6.13.   *Beat notes in $\frac{6}{8}$ time*

Whenever you tie together two dotted notes, the resulting note is also dotted. In Figure 6.14, if these two dotted quarter notes are tied together to create a single note that fills the entire measure, the result is a dotted half note.

Figure 6.14.   *Dotted half note in $\frac{6}{8}$ time*

Figure 6.15 shows some examples with time signatures that have 4 and 16 as their bottom numbers. Write the counts underneath these measures.

Figure 6.15.   *Beat notes in other compound meters*

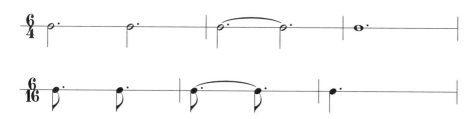

♪ Practice Box 6.4

Determine the number of beats per measure for each of these time signatures. Also, write the type of note that receives one beat.

1. $\frac{6}{8}$ _____

2. $\frac{9}{8}$ _____

3. $\frac{9}{4}$ _____

4. $\frac{6}{16}$ _____

5. $\frac{12}{8}$ _____

6. $\frac{12}{4}$ _____

When there are rests in compound meters, dots are typically used to represent beat notes. In $\frac{6}{8}$ time, a beat of silence would be represented with a dotted quarter rest. You should be aware, though, that occasionally you will see a beat of silence written as two rests, if the composer feels that it makes the rhythm of the measure more clear. In $\frac{6}{8}$ time, the beat of silence can be represented by a dotted quarter rest or quarter rest plus an eighth rest.

Practice Box 6.5

Write the counts under each line and practice these rhythms.

Additional Rhythms

For extra practice, clap and count these exercises.

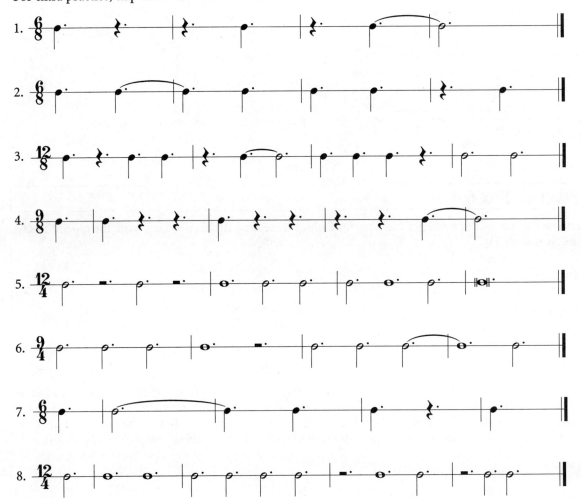

Dictation

Name the following harmonic intervals by size and quality as you hear them. The choices will be M2, mi2, M3, and mi3.

1.   6.
2.   7.
3.   8.
4.   9.
5.   10.

Name the following harmonic intervals by size and quality as you hear them. The choices will be M6, mi6, M7, and mi7.

1.   6.
2.   7.
3.   8.
4.   9.
5.   10.

Notate the melodies that you hear. Each example is in a compound meter. You will not hear any divisions of the beat. All of the notes that you write will be dotted notes. Melodies will be in minor keys only.

KEYBOARD APPLICATIONS

Practice the following exercise using all qualities of triads. Continue transposing the exercise chromatically up the keyboard, finishing with triads built on B.

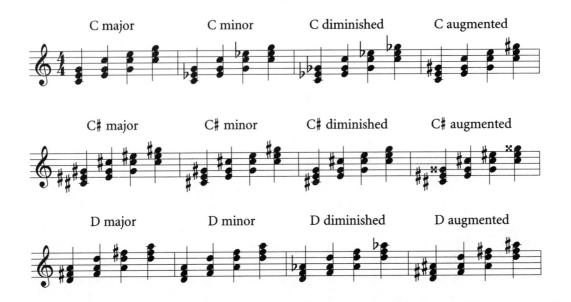

Suggested fingerings

Right hand: Root-position triads, 1-3-5
                 First-inversion triads, 1-2-5
                 Second-inversion triads, 1-3-5

Left hand: Root-position triads, 1-3-5
                 First-inversion triads, 1-3-5
                 Second-inversion triads, 1-2-5

chapter 7

The Basics of Diatonic Harmony

THEORETICAL SKILLS

Diatonic Triads in Major Keys

On each note of a major scale, it is possible to construct a triad. The triads that are constructed up from each note are called "diatonic" triads. The word "diatonic" means that the notes of the chords come from within the key signature and scale for that key.

It is also possible to build chords with notes that are not part of a key signature. Those are called *chromatic* chords and will be studied in volume 2.

For example, in the key of C major, a triad built on C would contain the notes C, E, and G. Every note of that chord is diatonic in the key of C major, meaning that they are all found in the C major scale and key signature. If an F-sharp were used in the key of C major, that note would not be diatonic. Instead, it would be a chromatic alteration to the key of C major.

When a diatonic triad is built on each note of a major scale, each chord takes the name of the scale degree on which it is formed. A triad built on the first scale degree is called the tonic triad. One built on the second scale degree is called the supertonic triad, and so on. If you need to review the scale degree names, they are in Figure 7.1 below.

Since there are no variable scale degrees in major scales (as there are in the melodic minor scale), the chord qualities of diatonic triads in a major scale are always the same, no matter what the key is. Figure 7.1 also shows the qualities of the diatonic triads in a major scale. This pattern of chord qualities should be memorized.

Figure 7.1. *Diatonic triads and scale degree names in the C major scale*

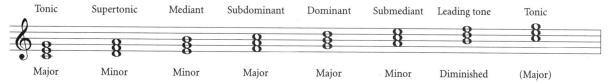

Practice Box 7.1

Construct the diatonic triads of the E major scale. The key signature has been provided. Below each chord write its scale degree name and its quality. The first one has been written in as an example.

Roman Numeral Analysis in Major Keys

There are many ways to analyze music, all dealing with different aspects of intervals, keys, scales, and rhythm. Since we are now concerned with learning about harmony and chord progressions, we will now address a kind of analysis that allows us to describe these elements. **Harmony** is the aspect of music that deals with vertical combinations of notes and the sounds they produce, just as melody deals with the horizontal aspects. A **chord progression** is a series of chords that fit together in some logical and definite manner to form a satisfying aural sensation.

Chords are defined by the scale degree on which they are built, as well as their qualities. This system of analysis gives us a way to describe both of those aspects. This type of analysis makes use of Roman numerals to describe the scale degree on which the chord is built. A chord that takes the Roman numeral I is built on the first scale degree, meaning that it is the tonic chord. This system also uses upper- and lowercase Roman numerals, such as iii and IV, to differentiate between major and minor chord qualities. A chord labeled "iii" would be a minor chord built on the mediant scale degree. Lowercase Roman numerals always refer to minor chords; uppercase Roman numerals stand for major chords.

Diminished and augmented chords are also represented by lower- and uppercase numerals respectively, but they require an additional symbol to differentiate them from major and minor chords. A diminished triad is represented with a lowercase numeral plus a small circle, such as vii°. An augmented chord is represented by an uppercase numeral with a plus sign, such as III$^+$. Figure 7.2 shows the Roman numerals for the diatonic triads of the major scale.

Figure 7.2.   Roman numerals of the major scale

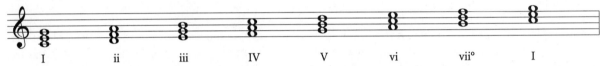

The chord symbols above describe the qualities of the diatonic triads of the major scale that you have already learned. From now on, when you compose or analyze a piece of tonal music, you will describe the harmonic language of that piece with Roman numeral analysis.

The procedure works like this: (1) look at each vertical sonority in a piece of music, (2) determine the notes that are part of each chord and spell them in root position above the chord, (3) determine the scale degree on which the chord is constructed, (4) determine the quality of the chord, (5) write a Roman numeral symbol that reflects both the scale degree and the chord quality, and (6) add the figured bass that represents the chord's inversion.

Figure 7.3 is a simple melody with a chord accompaniment, written in the style of a hymn. Notice the chords are spelled in root position above the staff (even though some of them are inverted). The name of the key is also part of the analysis and is always written to the left of the first Roman numeral. If any of the chords should appear in inversion, figured bass symbols are combined with the Roman numerals to indicate the inversion that has been used, such as ii^6.

Figure 7.3.   Chord progression in C major with Roman numeral analysis

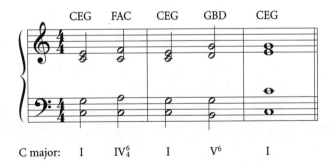

Practice Box 7.2

Spell the chords above the staff and provide a Roman numeral analysis. The Roman numeral should be written beneath each chord. In each chord, you will discover that one note is doubled, meaning that it occurs twice. You do not have to write it twice when you spell the chord.

Diatonic Triads in Minor Keys

Diatonic triads are more difficult in minor keys because there are more choices. In the melodic minor scale, there are variable scale degrees. The sixth note of the scale can appear as a note that comes directly from the key signature (used in melodic passages which descend) or it can appear as a note that is raised a half step from the key signature (used in ascending melodic passages). Exactly the same thing can be said about the seventh scale degree in melodic minor, although the leading tone is much more commonly used than the subtonic. Figure 7.4 demonstrates the triads that are commonly used in minor keys.

Figure 7.4. Commonly used chord qualities for the minor scale

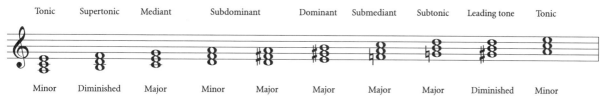

You can see that more diatonic chords are possible in the minor scale than in the major scale. By using both inflections of the sixth scale degree, it is possible to create a minor subdominant chord as well as a major subdominant. The minor subdominant is much more frequently used than its major counterpart. Since there are also two inflections of the seventh scale degree, there are two possible chords—one built on the subtonic and one built on the leading tone. These chords built on the seventh scale degrees not only have different roots, but they also have very different functions in harmonic progressions.

There are other *possible* chords in the minor scale, but most are little more than theoretical models that find little or no use in actual music. The chords in Figure 7.4 are the most commonly used of all the possible diatonic chords in a minor scale.

Occasionally, you will see a minor supertonic chord (one built using the raised sixth scale degree) and an augmented mediant chord (which uses the raised seventh scale degree). The diminished submediant triad (built on the raised sixth scale degree) is virtually unknown. The major subtonic chord is used from time to time, but not with the frequency with which the leading tone triad is seen.

Notice that in Figure 7.4, the dominant chord is major, not minor. The dominant triad is usually a major triad because the major quality will always contain the leading tone of the scale. In a minor scale, this major dominant chord will always require an accidental to create the leading tone (the raised seventh scale degree).

In tonal music, there is virtually no such thing as a minor dominant chord. Although you may occasionally encounter a minor dominant chord, it will usually be found in music from the Baroque period or earlier. The tonal system of harmonic progression, which was coming into existence during this period, was replacing an older tradition known as *modality*. Modal music did not employ the same sense of harmonic progression as the tonal music that replaced it. Even composers such as J. S. Bach, whose music is primarily considered tonal, used minor dominant chords from time to time. When you see this, you should realize that the composers of the Baroque period occasionally looked backward to the older compositional practice of modality and made use of its resources.

Practice Box 7.3

Construct the commonly used diatonic triads of the C minor scale. Add accidentals to the chords where needed. Below each chord write its scale degree name and its quality. The first one has been written in as an example.

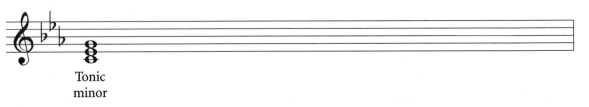

Tonic
minor

Roman Numeral Analysis in Minor Keys

The minor scale can include all possible qualities of triads—major, minor, diminished, and augmented. You should keep in mind that when you analyze the chords of a minor piece, the Roman numerals will look different than they do for the same scale degree in a major scale. See Figure 7.5.

Figure 7.5.   Roman numerals for the minor scale

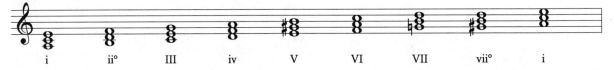

Although it is not included in Figure 7.5 because of its relative rarity, the major subdominant chord would take the Roman numeral IV. On the rare occasion that you would encounter an augmented mediant triad, its Roman numeral would be written III⁺. The "plus" sign represents the augmented quality of the triad.

As mentioned earlier, it is possible to build chords on both the subtonic and the leading tone. Notice that these two chords have very different Roman numerals, as well as differing qualities. The subtonic triad is a major chord and is written with uppercase Roman numerals (VII). The leading tone triad is a diminished triad, exactly as it appears in a major scale, and is written with the same Roman numeral as in major (vii°).

Practice Box 7.4

Spell the chords above the staff and provide a Roman numeral analysis for this example. The Roman numeral should be written beneath each chord.

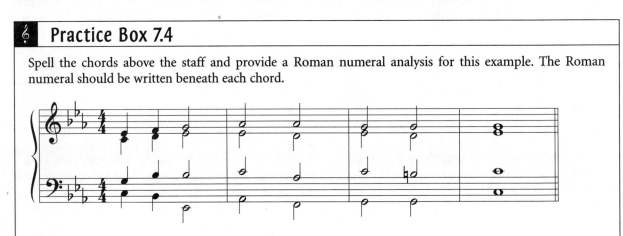

Authentic Cadences and Root Movement by Fifth

A **cadence** in music is a stopping place. The term can refer to the end of an entire composition or the end of a section of a piece. The last two chords of a piece or section form the cadence.

Cadences are extremely important because they form the model for the study of all tonal progressions. The most typical kind of cadence consists of a dominant chord followed by a tonic chord. The Roman numeral analysis for this progression is V–I in a major key or V–i in a minor key.

The dictionary definition above is a very helpful statement as we begin to look at cadences within music. When we speak most sentences (other than questions), we usually end with a falling inflection. In music, the falling inflection most often occurs in the bass line. This inflection creates a feeling of completion in music.

Remember that there is a general principle of music that states that any piece should end on the name of its key. We can now expand that principle to say that a piece of music should end on its I (or "i") chord. The tonic chord, which will usually appear in root position, is most often preceded by a dominant chord, forming the cadence.

Figure 7.6 shows an example of a musical cadence in the key of C major.

Figure 7.6.   Cadence in C major with bass movement of a 5th down

authentic cadence

C major: V   I

Any cadence that moves from a dominant chord to a tonic chord is known as an **authentic cadence**.

The idea of falling inflection can be seen in the bass line. The bass falls from G down to C, that is, from the dominant scale degree down to the tonic. This is downward movement by the interval of a perfect fifth. The principle of moving the roots of chords down by the interval of a fifth is the basis of most root movements in tonal chord progressions.

Remembering the process of interval inversion, a perfect fifth downward is equivalent to a perfect fourth moving upward. Therefore, the bass line does not always have to fall by a fifth. It is also possible to find bass lines that move upward by a fourth to create an authentic cadence, as shown in Figure 7.7.

Figure 7.7.   Cadence in C major with bass movement of a 4th up

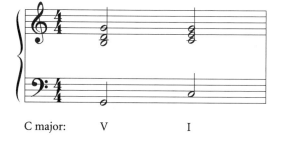

C major: V   I

This is the same progression seen in Figure 7.6, with the bass line ascending by perfect fourth. It is still an authentic cadence. Now compare the two cadences in Figure 7.8. Both are authentic cadences in C major, but the highest voice of each chord has been changed from the examples above.

Figure 7.8.   Authentic cadences

The only difference between them is the placement of the top note of the chord. The top note of the tonic chord determines the name given to the authentic cadence. When both chords are in root position and the tonic chord has *do* in the soprano, the cadence is called a *perfect authentic cadence*. If any other chord tone, such as *mi* or *sol*, is present in the top voice of the tonic chord, the cadence is called an *imperfect authentic cadence*. In imperfect authentic cadences, the chords may also appear in inversions. We will study additional imperfect authentic cadences later.

Which of the cadences in Figure 7.8 is a perfect authentic cadence?

🎼 Practice Box 7.5

Identify the keys and spell each chord above the staff. Label the chords with Roman numerals. Then name each cadence as a perfect authentic cadence or an imperfect authentic cadence. These may be abbreviated PAC and IAC.

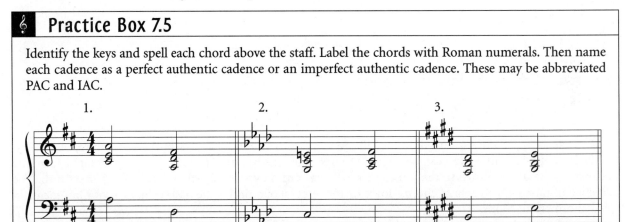

Diatonic Progressions in Major Keys

To explore the ideas behind longer chord progressions, we use the cadence as the model. We will begin with progressions in major keys and use C major. The roots of the cadence chords are related by the interval of a perfect fifth down (or a perfect fourth up).

So what is the chord that should logically precede the dominant chord in our progression? Another way to ask this question is: What is the letter name that would fall by a fifth (or rise by a fourth) to reach G? The answer is D. So a chord built on D, which would be a minor supertonic chord in the key of C major, will be the logical chord to precede the dominant in the progression. Spell the chords and label the progression in Figure 7.9 with Roman numerals.

Figure 7.9.   Progression in C major

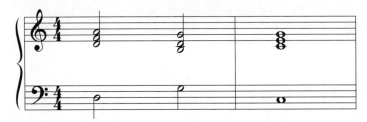

Following this idea of root movement by fifth, we can add two more chords to the progression. The letter name of the note that would fall down a fifth to the ii chord is A, which is a vi chord in C major. The letter name of the note that falls down a fifth to A is E, which is a iii chord in C major. The entire progression derived from this principle is shown in Figure 7.10.

Figure 7.10.   Chord progression based on root movement by 5th

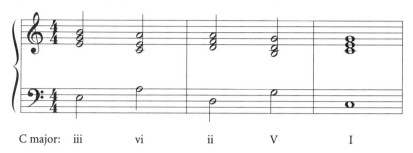

C major: iii   vi   ii   V   I

This is the most basic chord progression in any major key, and it forms the basis for all further elaboration. It is sometimes called a *circle of fifths progression.* Virtually all tonal music written in major keys is related in some way to this basic chord progression. It can be summarized this way: tonic, mediant, submediant, supertonic, dominant, tonic. Written in Roman numerals, it would be:

I–iii–vi–ii–V–I.

It is typical (although not required) to begin a progression with the tonic chord, so it has been inserted at the beginning of the progression above. You may notice that two diatonic chords from the key of C major are not included in this progression, IV and vii°. We will discuss their functions and positions in the basic chord progression in later chapters.

Any melody or chord progression that contains only notes that come directly from its scale is considered *diatonic.* In the C major progression above, all the notes in the chords are diatonic because they come from the C major scale. In a major key, diatonic harmony will not include any accidentals that are not already a part of the key signature. If one of the chords from the progression above contained an F♯, it would not be considered diatonic. Instead, it would be called a chromatic or "altered" chord. We will study chromatic harmony in Volume 2.

Diatonic Progressions in Minor Keys

Diatonic progressions are somewhat more complicated in minor keys because of the wider variety of diatonic chords that are available in a minor key. This is due to the alternate scale degrees in the melodic minor scale and the variant chord qualities that can be created within that scale.

However, the basic principles of progression by root movement of a fifth apply to all tonal music, including progressions in minor. We will start again with a cadence, this time working in the key of A minor. See Figure 7.11.

Figure 7.11.   Authentic cadence in a minor key

A minor: V   i

The authentic cadence in minor keys has one extremely important characteristic. *The dominant chord will always require an accidental in a minor key.* Remember that in minor keys, the dominant triad is usually major. In order for the dominant chord to be major, it must contain the leading tone of the key. The leading tone in minor keys always requires an accidental; it does not occur naturally in the key signature.

This is actually an easy way to distinguish major keys from minor keys at a glance. At the final cadence, if an accidental is present on the next to last chord, the key is probably minor, since an accidental is required to create the leading tone.

In minor keys, the concept of diatonic chords is expanded because of the alternate scale degrees available on the sixth and seventh notes of the scale. All of the notes of the melodic minor scale are considered diatonic in minor. Although the dominant chord requires an accidental, it is still considered diatonic.

In the key of A minor, the dominant chord is built on E. The note with the letter name that falls down a fifth to the dominant chord is B and again it is a supertonic chord. You should remember that the supertonic chord in minor is usually a diminished triad. As shown in the following example, the diminished supertonic triad often appears in first inversion, but the roots are still a fifth apart. This is illustrated in Figure 7.12.

Figure 7.12.   *Supertonic triads in minor progressions*

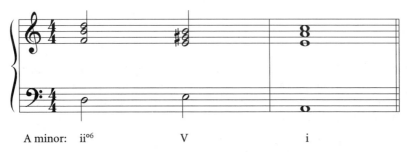

A minor: ii°⁶   V   i

As we continue to build the progression backward from the cadence, it looks very much like the basic progression for major keys: tonic, mediant, submediant, supertonic, dominant, tonic. See Figure 7.13.

Figure 7.13.   *Chord progressions in minor based on root movement by 5th*

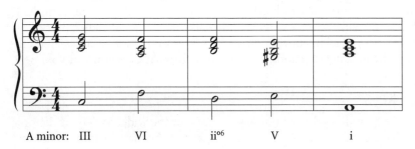

A minor: III   VI   ii°⁶   V   i

If an alternate chord quality were to be substituted into the progression, it would sit in exactly the same position in the chord progression as its counterpart. In other words, a III⁺ would sit in exactly the same place in the chord progression as the III.

Minor keys can have one additional chord inserted into the progression in addition to the ones in the example above. Since the mediant triad in this example is built on C, it is possible to precede it with a chord built on G. In the key of A minor, G is the subtonic. Subtonic triads can only exist in minor keys, since there is no subtonic scale degree in major. The function of the subtonic triad is only to precede the mediant triad in a minor progression, as in Figure 7.14.

Figure 7.14.   *Complete circle of 5ths progression in minor*

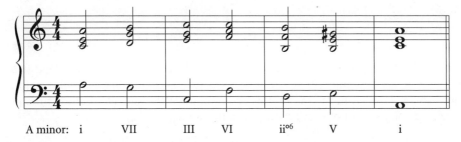

A minor: i   VII   III   VI   ii°⁶   V   i

Here is the circle of fifths progression for any minor key, and it forms the basis for all study of minor progressions. When written in Roman numerals it looks like this:

i–VII–III–VI–ii°–V–I.

Again, the subdominant and leading-tone triads have been omitted from this discussion and will be covered in a later chapter.

The tonic triad has been used to begin some of the progressions written above. The tonic triad enjoys a unique privilege in any chord progression. Unlike the other chords, the tonic triad may be followed by any chord in a progression (in major or minor keys). However, once the progression has started with a tonic triad plus one other chord, then root movement of a fifth is usually followed to the cadence. Table 15 gives some examples of progressions that demonstrate this idea.

Table 15. Circle of 5ths chord progressions

Major keys	I	V	I			
	I	ii	V	I		
	I	vi	ii	V	I	
	I	iii	vi	ii	V	I
Minor keys	i	V	i			
	i	ii°	V	i		
	i	VI	ii°	V	i	
	i	III	VI	ii°	V	i
	i	VII	III	VI	ii°	V	i

Practice Box 7.6

Spell each chord above the staff and write the Roman numerals under each of these progressions.

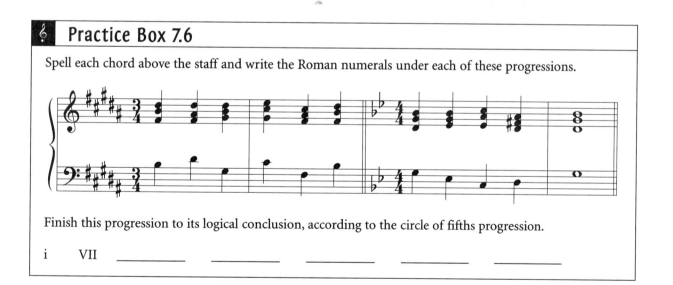

Finish this progression to its logical conclusion, according to the circle of fifths progression.

i   VII   _____   _____   _____   _____   _____

Music for Analysis

Provide a Roman numeral analysis for the following excerpts. You should spell the chords above the staff just as you have done in previous examples. Some chords may appear in inversions. For each excerpt, name the type of cadence used.

Example 7.1.   Richard Wagner, Lohengrin, "Wedding March," mm. 29–36

Track 7, 0:00

Example 7.2.   Muzio Clementi, Sonatina, op. 36, no. 1, 2nd movement, mm. 1–4

Track 7, 0:23

Example 7.3.   Friedrich Kuhlau, Sonata, op. 20, no. 2, 3rd movement, mm. 1–4

Track 7, 0:39

AURAL SKILLS

Melody

Name the key, then sing each melody using syllables.

Chords

Sing this pattern of broken chords in a variety of keys.

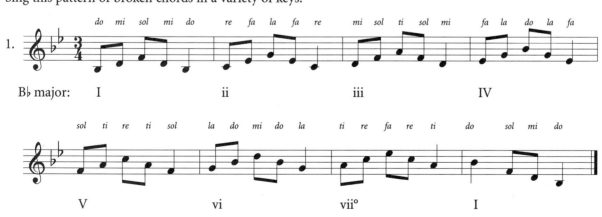

The following patterns of broken chords involve an authentic cadence in both major and minor. Sing and then transpose to other keys.

The following patterns add the supertonic chord to the progressions above.

Dynamic Markings

Certain types of markings are often found in printed music. One category of these markings is called **dynamics**, and they represent volume or loudness in music.

The terms come from the Italian language. Table 16 shows many of the most common dynamic markings, along with their abbreviations and translations.

Table 16.   Dynamic markings

forte	*f*	loud
piano	*p*	soft
mezzo	*m*	medium
fortissimo	*ff*	very loud
piannissimo	*pp*	very soft
mezzo forte	*mf*	medium loud
mezzo piano	*mp*	medium soft
crescendo	*cresc.*	gradually louder
diminuendo	*dim.*	gradually softer
sforzando	*sf, sfz*	suddenly loud, forced

Crescendo and diminuendo are often abbreviated with symbols (see Figure 7.15). The narrower end of each of these symbols represents the softer level of volume.

Figure 7.15.   Dynamic symbols

crescendo   diminuendo

The term "decrescendo" is occasionally seen and means the same as *diminuendo*. The latter, however, is a more preferable term and more commonly used in musical scores. Dynamic markings are typically written in the middle of a grand staff, and in an orchestral or ensemble score, they appear just beneath each staff of the score. In vocal music, dynamics appear above the staff.

Rhythm

In the previous examples of compound meters that we have seen, there were no divisions of the beat. As mentioned earlier, the number on the bottom of the time signature tells you the type of note that equals the division. In $\frac{6}{8}$ time, the division is an eighth note. Because each beat in a compound meter is divided into groups of threes, the eighth notes are beamed together in groups of threes, as shown in Figure 7.16.

Figure 7.16.   Divisions of the beat in $\frac{6}{8}$ time

One of the distinguishing features of compound time is that you will always see notes written in groups of threes. It is important to draw a distinction between $\frac{6}{8}$ time and $\frac{3}{4}$ time, which can contain 6 eighth notes per measure (three beats, with two divisions per beat). Compare the eighth notes in Figure 7.17 with those in Figure 7.16.

Figure 7.17.   Divisions of the beat in $\frac{3}{4}$ time

The simple meter has its divisions beamed in groups of two, while the compound meter is beamed in groups of three. It is possible to see at a glance, even without making a mental note of the time signature of each of these examples, which of them is simple and which is compound.

When you count divisions in a compound meter, a different set of words is used from the "one-and-two-and" method you used for simple meters. As shown in Figure 7.18, the first note of the group of three always takes a number, the second takes the word "la," and the third note takes the word "li" (pronounced "lee").

Figure 7.18.   Counting divisions of the beat in compound meters

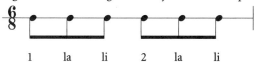

1   la   li   2   la   li

Although this may feel like a tongue twister at first, eventually you will begin to feel the swinging sensation inherent in compound meters. This combination of words for counting should help you sense that.

There is a very different combination of notes possible in compound meters that is not possible in simple meters. This combination involves two notes that are in the proportion 2:1 (two-thirds of the beat to one-third of the beat), or in the proportion 1:2. In $\frac{6}{8}$ time, this would be written as a quarter note followed by an eighth note or an eighth note followed by a quarter note. (See Figure 7.19.)

Figure 7.19.   Counting divisions of the beat in compound meters

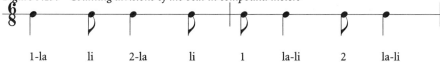

1-la   li   2-la   li   1   la-li   2   la-li

Practice Box 7.7

Write the counts under these lines, which are all in ⁶₈ time. Clap and count aloud.

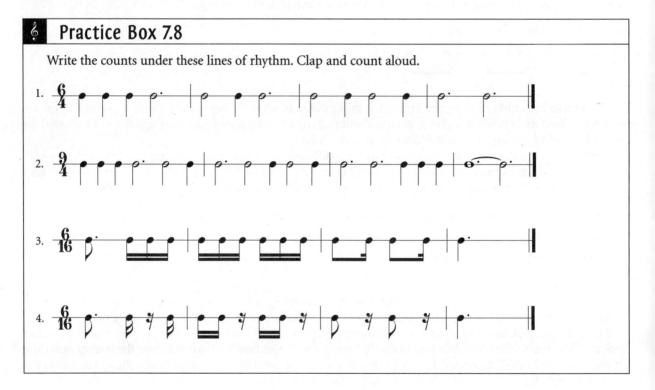

In compound meters that have 4 as their bottom number, the quarter note is the division of the beat, and the beat note is a dotted half. The challenge in this time signature comes from the fact that the groups of three divisions cannot be beamed together because they are quarter notes. This adds a slight complication to reading time signatures such as ⁶₄ or ⁹₄.

When the bottom number is 16, the division of the beat is a sixteenth note, and the beat note is a dotted eighth. In this type of meter, the groups of two notes (which are in the 2:1 proportions just described) are also beamed together.

Continue counting "one-la-li two-la-li" for all these meters.

Practice Box 7.8

Write the counts under these lines of rhythm. Clap and count aloud.

Additional Rhythms

For extra practice, clap and count these exercises.

Dictation

Notate the following rhythms in compound meters. You will hear each rhythm several times. It may be helpful to write in the counts before you begin. There will be divisions of the beat.

1. $\frac{6}{8}$

2. $\frac{9}{8}$

3. $\frac{6}{4}$

4. $\frac{12}{16}$

5. $\frac{12}{8}$

6. $\frac{9}{16}$

7. $\frac{9}{4}$

8. $\frac{6}{16}$

KEYBOARD APPLICATIONS

Play ascending diatonic triads in all keys. Examples are provided below. Play the chords with both hands together if possible. Use fingers 1-3-5 on both hands.

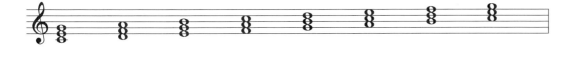

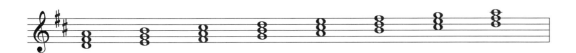

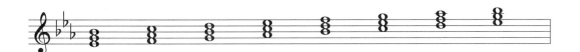

Continue transposing this exercise up by half steps until you finish all twelve positions.

chapter 8

Part Writing with Root-Position Chords

THEORETICAL SKILLS

Introduction to Four-Voice Harmony

We have covered most of the basic elements of music, including scales, key signatures, and triads. Now we can begin to explore the ways in which those elements are combined to create tonal music, which is music that is written in a key.

Most tonal music is governed by two protocols: harmonic conventions that regulate the vertical sonorities in music, and voice-leading conventions that regulate the horizontal or melodic patterns. You have already learned about diatonic chords in major and minor keys. In the next few chapters, you will study the way in which those diatonic chords can logically be combined to make good chord progressions.

The best way to study these musical conventions is in real musical compositions, such as symphonies, string quartets, piano music, vocal music, and so on. These genres, however, are not the easiest textures to study, since they usually involve reading multiple staves per system, C clefs, and transposing instruments.

Therefore, instead of using the difficult textures of actual compositions, we will use the medium of four-voice harmony to introduce each new concept and learn the rules that govern it. After writing and studying examples of each new concept in four-voice texture, we will then move on to analyze excerpts from actual compositions.

In this context, the word "voice" does not necessarily mean that the music is meant to be sung. It simply means that there are four independent melodic strands, each of which is called a *voice,* and they fit together to make up part of a larger texture. The process of creating a four-voice texture is called **part writing.**

Why do we use four-voice structures for our theoretical models? Four-voice texture is the norm for most choral music, with each horizontal line of the texture representing a section of the choir: soprano, alto, tenor, and bass. Four voices are also the standard for one of the most common types of chamber ensemble, the string quartet. Three-voice texture looks and sounds uncomplicated and does not allow for the use of complete seventh chords. And textures that are written with five voices are considerably more complicated than those using four, without providing much, if any, additional understanding of the subject matter.

Music for string quartet is typically written on open score, one voice or instrument per line, with the viola reading alto clef. Choral music, on the other hand, is often written on a grand staff. Since the grand staff is easier to read than open score, it is the notational practice we will adopt. The texture will be written with two voices per staff, with the stems for each of the two voices going in opposite directions. (See Figure 8.1.)

Figure 8.1. *Four-voice texture with voice names*

Soprano
Alto

Tenor
Bass

For the next few chapters, we will be doing part writing with diatonic triads in root position only. In later chapters, we will move on to using chords in inversion.

Doubling and Structure

To begin the discussion of four-part harmony, we will first discuss its vertical aspect. When a triad containing three notes is used in a four-voice texture, one of the three notes will have to be duplicated, or **doubled**. For now, we will be using only root position triads and the rule for doubling is easy to remember:

When writing a root position triad in four-voice harmony, the bass should be doubled.
This will be the root of the chord.

According to this rule, if you are constructing a D major triad in four-part harmony, you will have to write two Ds, one F♯, and one A. There are a few exceptions to this rule, but when we do encounter them, they will be pointed out, and the special circumstances will be discussed. Different rules of doubling apply to some inverted triads, and we will learn those rules later.

Once you understand the doubling rule for root-position chords, you must also create an aurally pleasing chord by spacing the four voices correctly. The distance that the four notes are spaced from one another is called **structure**. The structures typically used in root position chords are *open* and *close*.

The root of the chord will always be in the bass voice in a root-position chord. Any of the chord tones, root, third, or fifth, may occur in the soprano voice. If the soprano note is not already written for you, you should choose one of these chord tones and write it above the bass note in the treble clef. (The soprano note will often be given to you in your part-writing exercises.) If we go back to the D major triad mentioned above, the choices for the soprano would look like Figure 8.2.

Figure 8.2. *Various soprano notes for D major triad*

The first step in the process of adding inner voices is to make sure you know the names of all the chord tones. It is a good habit to always write the names of the chord tones above the soprano note for each chord. For the D major chord we have been discussing, you should write D–F♯–A above each chord. Do this above each measure in the example above.

To create **close structure**, always work from the soprano note down. This structure is called "close" because the upper three notes of the chord are as close together as possible below the soprano note. There should be less than an octave between the soprano and tenor voices.

For the alto note, choose the closest chord tone below the soprano note. Write the notes in the grand staff of Figure 8.2 as you read this paragraph. In the first chord above, the alto note would be A. This will be easy to see if you have spelled the chord above the staff. The tenor note must be written in the bass clef, but the closest chord tone below the alto is F♯. So this note must be written as a high ledger-line note in the bass clef. Remember that the stems of all alto notes should go down and all tenor notes should go up. In the second measure, the alto will be D, which is the closest letter name below F♯, and the tenor will take the note A. Finally, in the third chord above, the alto is F♯ and the tenor below that will be D. Now compare the chords you wrote above to the next example.

Figure 8.3. *Close-structure D major triads*

Close
structure

Remember to work from the soprano note downward. This will always result in a bass note that has been doubled in each chord. Close structure is so called because the upper three voices fit together as closely as possible. It does not matter where the bass voice is in relation to the other voices. The rules of structure apply only to the upper three voices, so you should get used to seeing the bass in a position on the staff that looks unrelated to the other three voices.

Practice Box 8.1

Spell each triad above the staff and then complete the inner voices in close structure. Use the spellings that you have written above each chord to keep track of the chord tones as you add them to the structure.

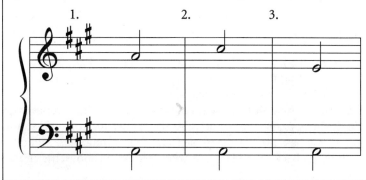

Like close structure, open structure can use any of the three chord tones as the soprano note. To create **open structure**, again start by naming the three notes of the triad. Write the names of the chord tones over the staff for each of the chords above. From the soprano note move down the staff *past* the closest chord tone to the second closest one below the soprano note. That pitch will be the alto note. The tenor note is the second closest chord tone below the alto. If the tenor is doubling the bass on the same pitch, then you simply attach an extra stem to the bass note, pointing up, which indicates that they share the same pitch. (If they are whole notes, you will write two of them side by side.) Study the open structure chords in Figure 8.4 and then compare them to Figure 8.3.

Figure 8.4.   *Open-structure D major triads*

Open
structure

The Xs represent the chord tones that
were skipped to create the open structure.

Practice Box 8.2

Spell each triad above the staff and then complete the inner voices in open structure. Use the spellings that you have written above each chord to keep track of the chord tones as you add them to the structure.

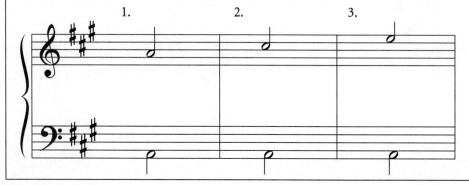

Check back through all of the chords that you have written in the two different structures to see which chord tone has been doubled in each chord. You should have the root doubled in every chord. The rules of structure and doubling go hand in hand—if you write your open or close structures from the top note down, every chord should have the root doubled.

Several things will never happen when you do open or close structure properly. Adjacent voices, such as soprano and alto, or alto and tenor, will never be separated by more than the interval of a sixth. If you see any larger intervals, such as an octave, between adjacent voices, you have not constructed the chord properly. In addition, when using good structure, you will never end up doubling the wrong note. A root-position chord with something other than the bass (root) doubled is generally incorrect. Correct structure will always circumvent this problem.

Chord structure is never random. The upper three voices must always be evenly spaced. Figure 8.5 shows incorrect chord spacing; your part writing should never look like these examples.

Figure 8.5. *Errors in spacing in four-part texture*

Identify the errors that you
see in these chords.

Vocal Ranges

The acceptable ranges of pitches for the four voice parts are shown in Figure 8.6. Usually, all notes written for each voice line— soprano, alto, tenor, and bass—should be kept within these limits.

Figure 8.6. *Acceptable ranges for the four voice parts*

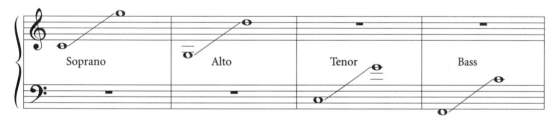

Generally, if you see a high soprano line (above the C space note in the treble clef), you should use open structure. When the soprano is high, using close structure will result in a tenor note that is too high. Conversely, a low soprano line usually demands close structure, since open structure might force the tenor note below the bass, a situation known as **crossed voices**. You should always avoid crossed voices.

Examples of crossed voices are shown in Figure 8.7. Either the alto is lower than the tenor or the tenor is lower than the bass in each. All of these part-writing examples are incorrect.

Figure 8.7. *Errors in part writing: crossed voices*

Rewrite each chord so that
the part writing is correct.

Part Writing with Repeated Chords

When writing chord progressions, each chord of the progression will have four voices, so the structure must be carefully considered on each chord. In any chord progression, no matter how many chords it contains, you should choose the structure that works the best and stick with it through the end of the chord progression. That means that if you start with open structure, you should continue with it to the end of the progression. The same is true if you start with close structure. There are only a few reasons for changing structure in the middle of a progression. One of the exceptions to the rule is:

> *You have the option of keeping the same structure or changing structure if there is a repeated chord, meaning that two chords in a row can be analyzed with the same Roman numeral.*

Usually, when there is a repeated chord in a progression, the soprano note of the chord will change on the second chord. The size of the leap in the soprano will determine whether a change of structure is appropriate. See Figure 8.8.

Figure 8.8.   *Part writing with repeated chords (C stands for close structure, O for open structure)*

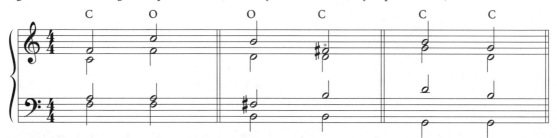

In the first two examples of Figure 8.8, the soprano leaps a fourth or a fifth. Because of this, a change of structure is appropriate. In the third example, the soprano leaps only a third, and it is possible to use the same structure on both chords. It is not a requirement that you change structure on repeated chords, but it is an option. If you intend to change structure between the chords, the chord with the higher soprano note is the most appropriate place to use open structure.

So far, we have been discussing the vertical aspect of the music, in other words the chord structure, and that is very important. Equally important is the horizontal aspect of the music, called voice leading. You are writing music in a choral texture, and each horizontal line—soprano, alto, tenor, and bass—should be written so that it would be easy to sing. The bass is the only voice of the four that will consistently use leaps. The other voices should rely primarily on stepwise movement and repeated notes, with only isolated skips in the line. If possible, it is better to avoid simultaneous leaps in the same direction between two voices.

Look again at the pairs of chords of Figure 8.8. Oblique motion, in which one voice remains stationary while another moves, is found in the first two measures. The stationary note is in the tenor in measure 1 and in the alto in measure 2. This note is called a **common tone** between the two chords.

To do the part writing yourself, you will need to follow a few precise steps, ensuring that you will always create complete chords with proper structure.

1. Identify the key of the excerpt. Write it beneath the staff followed by a colon.

2. Spell each chord above the staff, including the sharps, flats, and naturals that are in the key signature and included in the figured bass.

3. Add soprano notes for each chord, if necessary, to create a pleasing melody.

4. Determine the structure that you will use for each chord.

5. Underline the name of the soprano note within the chord spelling that you have written above that chord.

6. Add the alto note, based on the structure that you have chosen. Then underline its name in the chord spelling that you have written above that chord.

7. One chord tone will remain that has not been underlined. Add this note to the tenor voice.

8. Add the Roman numeral analysis under the staff, directly beneath its chord.

Practice Box 8.3

Spell each chord above the staff. Add inner voices to each chord, *keeping the same structure* within each pair of chords. It is not necessary to identify a key or provide a Roman numeral analysis.

Spell each chord above the staff. Add inner voices to each chord, *changing structure* within each pair of chords. If the bass note contains an accidental, duplicate it in the upper voices as shown in 4. above.

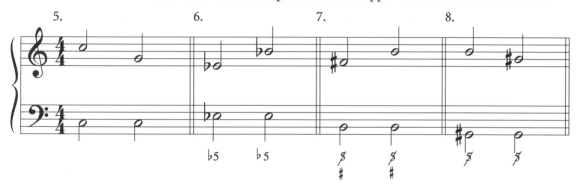

Choose different soprano notes for each chord and add inner voices, *keeping the same structure.*

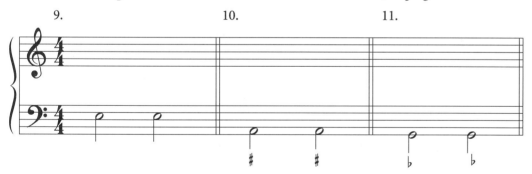

Choose different soprano notes for each chord and add inner voices, *using a change of structure.*

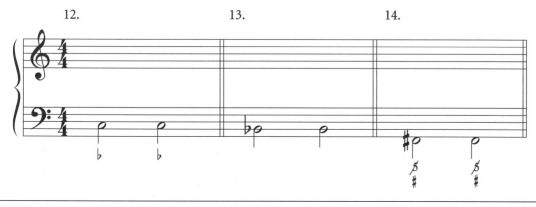

Additional Part-Writing Considerations

When two chords are found in succession that are not the same Roman numeral, many other considerations must be taken into account. Between two repeated chords, oblique and similar motion between voices may occur, but parallelism does not. You will remember that parallel motion occurs when two voices move in the same direction by the same interval. Just as in counterpoint, parallel perfect unisons, fifths, and octaves are expressly forbidden within four-part harmony. This may be summarized as a rule of part writing:

Do not write parallel perfect unisons, fifths, or octaves between any pair of voices.

You will often see many types of parallel or similar motion in part writing. The only type that is specifically forbidden is the use of perfect unisons, fifths, and octaves. Parallel thirds or fourths are fine, as long as they are not used excessively. One of the goals of four-part voice leading is independence of the individual voice parts. Although the texture appears to be vertically oriented because we study the chordal structures, four-voice harmony is inherently contrapuntal. Because they are perfect intervals, parallel fifths and octaves have a distinctive aural characteristic that destroys that independence of voice leading, making it sound as if one or more voices have dropped out of the texture.

Parallel octaves and fifths are sometimes hard to see in four-part texture, especially when they involve inner voices. The easiest way to find parallelism is to look for changes of structure. *Generally, unless you have a pair of repeated chords, the structure should not change from chord to chord.* It is essential that you learn to recognize parallelism in a four-part texture, and especially to learn the circumstances in which parallelism typically exists.

Look at Figure 8.9. Is there a change of structure? If so, can the two chords be analyzed with the same Roman numeral, which would make a change of structure acceptable? If not, there is probably parallelism between at least two voices. The diagonal lines between the notes in the bass and alto voices indicate the parallelism.

Figure 8.9.   *Parallel 8ves, because of change of structure*

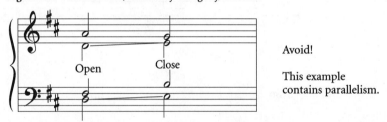

Avoid!

This example
contains parallelism.

Look at Figure 8.10. Do you have repeated chords? Is there a change of structure? Can you find the parallelism? Draw diagonal lines between the notes in each voice that creates the parallelism.

Figure 8.10.   *Parallel 5ths, because of change of structure*

Can you find and label
the parallelism?
Mark it with
diagonal lines.

It is important to understand why parallel fifths and octaves exist in Figures 8.9 and 8.10. It happens because the structure was changed between the chords. If you rewrite the second chord of each example in the same structure as the first chord, the result will be correct part writing with no parallelism.

Study Figure 8.11. You may believe at first glance that it is correct part writing with no parallelism. The interval between the bass and tenor in the first chord is a fifth. In the second chord, the interval between the same two voices is a twelfth, which is the compound equivalent of a fifth.

Figure 8.11.   *Contrary 5ths*

While this is not actually parallelism, it has the same aural effect as parallel fifths and should be avoided. This voice-leading effect can be referred to as "contrary fifths." Again, it is caused by an incorrect change of structure. The same effect can be applied to unisons and octaves and should also be avoided.

Another problematic type of voice-leading motion is called "direct fifths" and "direct octaves." This occurs only when there is a leap in the soprano voice. The leap in the soprano results in the creation of an octave or a fifth between the soprano and bass in the second chord of the pair. Figure 8.10, in addition to the parallel fifths in the bass and tenor, demonstrates a direct octave. This type of motion should be avoided.

Finally, it is possible to find a type of parallel motion that involves a diminished fifth moving to a perfect fifth, or vice versa. These are called "unequal fifths." A perfect fifth moving to a diminished fifth is always considered acceptable voice leading. A diminished fifth moving to a perfect fifth is considered acceptable provided that it does not involve the bass voice. We will encounter these in a later chapter on leading-tone triads.

𝄞 Practice Box 8.4

Find the errors in the following examples. Indicate parallel fifths and octaves with diagonal lines. There may not be errors in all of the examples.

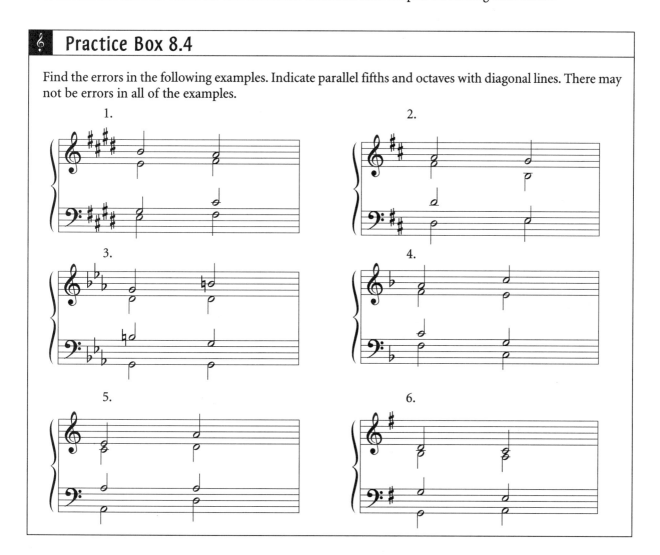

You should remember that when oblique motion is used in four-part harmony, the note that stays the same in both chords is said to be a common tone between those chords. In Figure 8.12, the pairs of notes that form common tones are marked with a line. There is one between the first and second chords, and another between the third and fourth chords. In which voice does each common tone occur? What structure is used for each chord in this example, open or close?

Figure 8.12.   Part writing with common tones marked

Oblique motion is also a very desirable form of movement between voices, because it often helps avoid unwanted parallelism. In general, when doing part writing, if it is possible to keep a common tone between two adjacent chords, you should choose to do so.

Movement to and from a unison should be handled with specific types of motion between the voices that form that interval. A unison should be approached and resolved by either contrary or oblique motion. If a unison is approached or resolved through similar motion, it creates a type of pattern called "moving crossed voices." This is similar to crossed voices in a single chord, except that the cross occurs when one voice of the texture leaps higher or lower than the adjacent voice was positioned on the first chord. Figure 8.13 demonstrates both the correct and the incorrect manner of approaching and resolving a unison.

Figure 8.13.   Approach and resolution of unisons

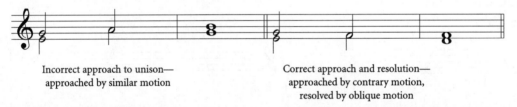

Incorrect approach to unison—
approached by similar motion

Correct approach and resolution—
approached by contrary motion,
resolved by oblique motion

You should notice the moving crossed voices in measure 1. The alto note, E, moves to a note that is higher than the soprano was on the starting chord, creating the effect of voice crossing. The final unison in Figure 8.13 is resolved correctly. What type of motion is used to resolve the unison?

Practice Box 8.5

Identify the type of motion between each pair of voices.

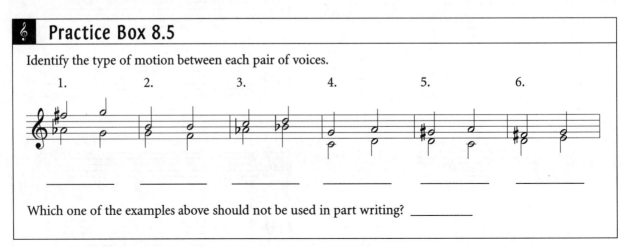

Which one of the examples above should not be used in part writing? _____

Practice Box 8.5 (continued)

Identify the common tones between chords by circling the pairs of notes that create oblique motion. The first one has been done as an example.

Name the cadence at the end of this exercise. _____

Music for Analysis

The guidelines for four-part harmony are a study of the norms that have been developed over hundreds of years. The study of the rules should always be accompanied by a study of actual music in the style under consideration. Church hymns are an excellent source of study for four-part textures. Look at the following examples and analyze them for structure (where it changes and where it remains the same), voice leading within the individual parts, motion between voices, and doubling within the chords. Name the key and add a Roman numeral analysis as well. Mark the chords that differ from the norms that have been stated in this chapter.

Example 8.1. William Kethe (attr.), "All People That on Earth Do Dwell" (Old 100th), mm. 1–6

Track 8, 0:00

Example 8.2. William Owen, "Look, Ye Saints! The Sight Is Glorious," mm. 1–4

Track 8, 0:26

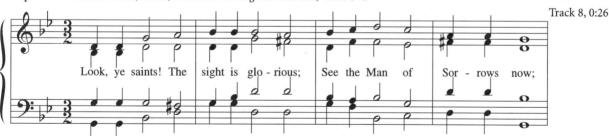

Example 8.3. William Havergal, "Lamp of Our Feet," mm. 1–4

Track 8, 0:45

AURAL SKILLS

Melody

Name the key and sing each melody with solfege syllables or scale degrees.

Chords

Sing the following patterns of broken chords.

Harmonic minor

Melodic minor

Ascending

Descending

The ascending diatonic chords of the melodic minor scale are very difficult to sing. Using the raised sixth and seventh scale degrees creates some of the chord qualities that are infrequently used in the minor scale. Notice how much easier it is to sing the descending chords. Apart from the dominant chord, which contains the raised leading tone, all the chords contain only notes that are in the key signature. This creates an interesting aural effect—your ears may tell you that you are in the key of D♭ major instead of B♭ minor. Why does this happen?

Tempo Indications

During our discussions of rhythm and meters, we have said nothing about the speed with which the music should be counted. The speed of the pulses in a composition is commonly called **tempo**. Tempo and meter are two separate ideas, although they interact during the course of counting any piece of music.

Tempo indications are generally written above a musical staff. Most compositions have tempo markings at the beginning. It is also possible to change the speed of a piece somewhere other than the beginning, and new tempo indications can appear anywhere within a composition.

Most tempo indications are written with words from foreign languages. The most common language is Italian, but sometimes you will also see French and German terms. These foreign terms are often used as titles for compositions, such as movements of larger works including symphonies, concertos, and sonatas. Table 17 provides a list of Italian terms you should learn.

Table 17. *Tempo terminology*

prestissimo	very fast	*a tempo*	at the first speed
presto	fast	*non troppo*	not too much
vivace	lively	*ma non troppo*	but not too much
allegro	cheerful	*grazioso*	graceful
allegretto	somewhat cheerful	*assai*	very
andante	at a walking speed	*con espressione*	with expression
moderato	moderately	*con spirito*	with spirit
adagio	slow	*cantabile*	singing
largo	broad, slow	*maestoso*	majestic
lento	slow	*molto*	much, very
grave	solemn, slow	*dolce*	sweet
ritardando	slowing down	*con brio*	with vigor
rallentando	slowing down	*sostenuto*	sustained
tempo primo	at the first speed		

Study the example below for the placement of dynamic markings and tempo indications. Name the notes written for the viola in alto clef.

Example 8.4.   *Ludwig van Beethoven, String Quartet, op. 18, no. 1, 1st movement, mm. 1–17*

Track 8, 1:02

Rhythm

Practice these longer rhythms in compound meters.

1.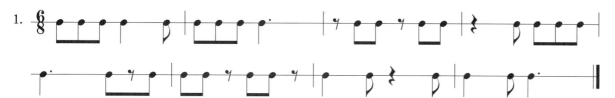

2.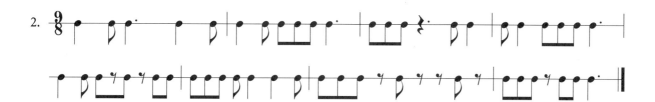

3.

4.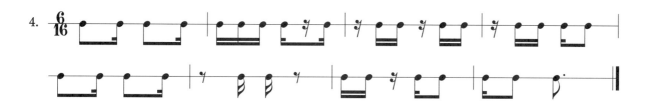

5.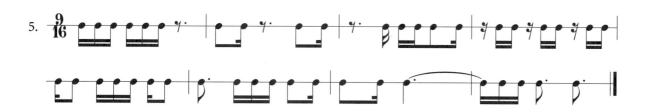

6.

Dictation

The following rhythmic dictation exercises use only compound meters and include divisions of the beat.

1.

2.

3.

4.

5.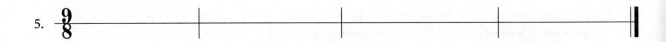

6.

The following melodic dictation exercises use compound meters. You will hear both major and minor keys and will have to determine the first note of the exercise. (Hint: the first note will be either the root, third, or fifth of the tonic triad.)

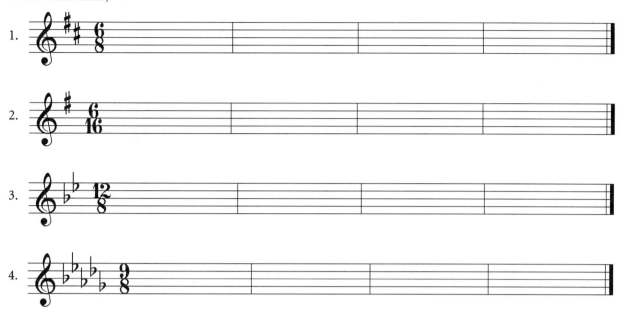

You are given the bass note for a series of major chords that are in root position. Spell each chord above the staff. You will hear the bass note alone. Sing *do–mi–sol–mi–do (do–me–sol–me–do)* or "one–three–five–three–one" above each bass note. Then listen to the chord—it will be played in close structure. You must determine the soprano note of the chord. It may be the root, the third, or the fifth of the chord. Write the soprano note on the treble staff above each bass note.

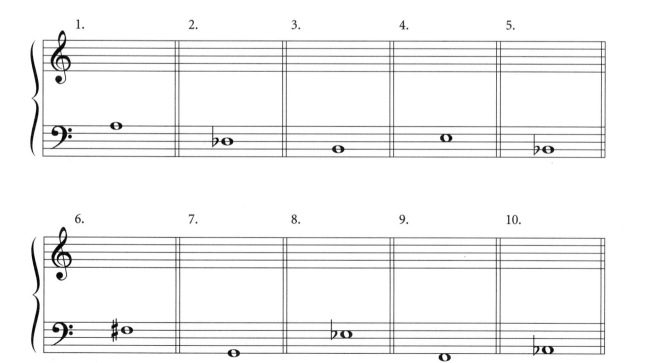

KEYBOARD APPLICATIONS

The following chords are to be played at the keyboard in close structure, with the left hand playing only the bass voice and the right hand playing the upper three voices. The symbols represent tonic triads in a variety of keys, both major and minor. The Roman numeral in the bottom half of each box represents the bass note that should be played with the left hand. It will also give you the spelling of the triad. The solfege syllable in the upper half of each box represents the soprano note. The alto and tenor voices will be played by the right hand, and each of those notes will be lower on the keyboard than the soprano note.

Use the following five-step routine to master all keyboard harmony exercises.

1. Play the soprano line alone (solfege syllables) using the right hand fifth finger.

2. Play the bass line alone, using the left hand. This is the only voice that will be played by the left hand.

3. Play the soprano and bass lines together.

4. Spell each chord as you play the soprano with the alto and tenor voices. All three voices will be played with the right hand.

5. Play all four voices together.

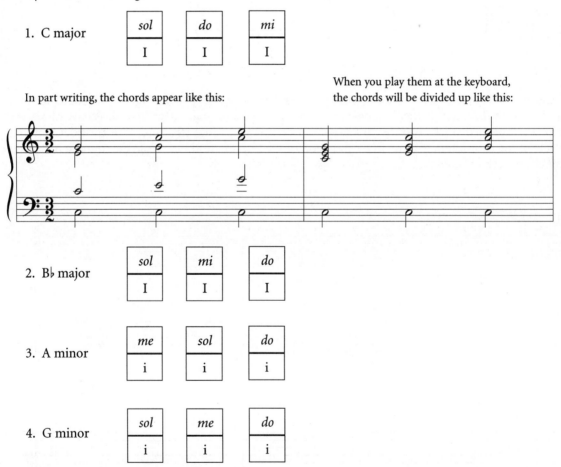

All of these exercises should be transposed to other keys.

chapter 9 Root Movement by Fifth

THEORETICAL SKILLS

Part Writing with Root Movement by Fifth

In the previous chapter, we studied part writing with repeated chords and learned that it is possible to maintain the same structure when moving between repeated chords, or to change the structure from open to close or vice versa. Now we will look at progressions related by root movement of a fifth and learn the rules of structure.

Generally, the goal in part writing is for the voices to be easy to sing. The fewer leaps that occur in individual voice lines, the easier it is to sing the part. You have already learned that the vertical aspect of part writing is known as structure. We will be using our choice of chord structures to control the voice leading of the individual parts. The main goal of good voice leading is to create individual lines that are smooth, generally with more steps than leaps. The exception to this rule is the bass line, which often will have more leaps than any other voice.

Chords with roots a fifth apart have one common tone between them. Look at the tonic and dominant chords in C major, shown in Figure 9.1.

Figure 9.1. *Common tone between tonic and dominant triads in C major*

```
I     C–E–┌G┐
V        └G┘–B–D
```

It is important to make note of this common tone, because it plays a role in part writing these progressions. The first rule, demonstrated in Figure 9.2, is:

When the roots are separated by the interval of a fifth, you should try to keep the same structure in both chords.

Figure 9.2. *Common tones in four-part harmony*

Usually a common tone will result when both chords are in the same structure. The examples above use the tonic and dominant chords in C major. In all of these examples, the same structure is maintained in both chords. The resulting common tones are circled. Look at the voice leading in the voices that do not contain the common tone. Both of the other two voices move stepwise, creating a smooth line. The bass voice leaps, but that is normal—the bass voice provides the foundation of all harmonic movement and often contains leaps. It is the upper three voices where smooth voice leading is desirable.

When the soprano notes are lower than the middle staff line, close structure is used. The last two examples have the same soprano line and chord progression. The first is done in close structure; the second is in open. Nevertheless, a common tone still appears in one voice and creates smooth voice leading in the other voices.

On each chord, you should work from the soprano downward, choosing the best structure for the chord. Then for each subsequent chord, again working from the top down, create the chord using the same structure.

Practice Box 9.1

First, spell the chords. Then name the keys and add inner voices and a Roman numeral analysis. Choose the best structure and keep that structure in both chords. Always work from the soprano down. Circle the common tones.

For each of the authentic cadences above, name the type, perfect or imperfect. You should also make it a habit to check the voice leading in each of the four parts. Occasionally you will find an example where it is not possible to maintain a common tone in any voice. A different rule applies to that situation:

> *If you cannot keep a common tone in any voice, the upper three voices*
> *should move in similar motion to the nearest chord tone.*

This will happen automatically as a result of keeping both chords in the same structure. See Figure 9.3.

Figure 9.3.   Lack of common tone in root movement by fifth

The first example above is an imperfect authentic cadence that includes a leap in the soprano. The leap is the factor that prevents the possibility of a common tone. The second example contains three chords, I–V–I. The leap in the soprano occurs between the first and second chords. Again, it is impossible to find a common tone, so the only choice is to move all three voices.

Notice that maintaining the same structure in both chords results in movement that takes all three upper voices in the same direction. Notice also that two of the upper three voices have leaps. The leaps occur in the soprano and tenor in the first measure and in the soprano and alto in the second measure. Generally, it is better to avoid simultaneous leaps in the same direction in part writing, but in these instances it is not possible to avoid them.

The leading tone is always a member of the dominant triad, whether the key is major or minor. Remember from our study of active scale degree resolutions that the leading tone should resolve upward to the first scale degree. In four-voice harmony, this is always true if the leading tone appears in the soprano or bass voice. However, if the leading tone appears in the alto or tenor voice, it may resolve to a note other than the tonic. Notice the leading tones in Figure 9.3 and observe how their placement determines resolution.

Practice Box 9.2

Add inner voices. It will not be possible to keep a common tone between every pair of chords. Identify the keys and add a Roman numeral analysis.

Here are some final examples of root movement by fifth. Look at the first measure of Figure 9.4. At first glance, it seems necessary to keep both chords in open structure and allow all three upper voices to move in the same direction, creating leaps in two voices. However, there is a way to avoid the pair of leaps.

Figure 9.4.   Avoiding leaps with change of structure

In the second measure of Figure 9.4, which has the same soprano and bass lines as the first, we go back to the idea of a common tone. If we change the second chord to maintain a common tone, the multiple leaps disappear. However, the structure has changed. This introduces another rule:

> *It is acceptable to change structure in root movement by fifth, provided that a common tone can be maintained in one voice.*

Among the upper three voices, the two leaps in the same direction, found in the first example, have now been replaced by a single leap in the tenor in the second example. In addition, the leap in the tenor creates excellent contrary motion with the bass voice, which is always desirable.

One of the most common places to change structure between chords a fifth apart is at an authentic cadence. You can take advantage of the change of structure between the V and I chords when there is a soprano line that moves from *re* to *do.*

Finally, it should be said that any change of structure that does not cause parallelism and promotes smooth voice leading is acceptable, even if it does not meet the criteria listed above. These three guidelines will help you through most progressions with root movement by fifth.

If you do change structure without a common tone, study your voice leading carefully, because parallel fifths or octaves will almost always result. In Figure 9.5, notice the parallel octaves that occur when the structure is changed with no common tones being kept. The conclusion is that you must maintain the structure used in the first chord. Rewrite the incorrect part writing on the staff provided.

Figure 9.5. *Parallel octaves because of change of structure*

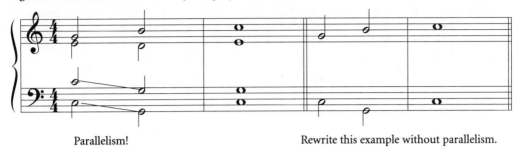

Parallelism!   Rewrite this example without parallelism.

Practice Box 9.3

Add inner voices to the following exercises. All of these exercises should change structure. Start each measure with open structure. What do these soprano lines have in common?

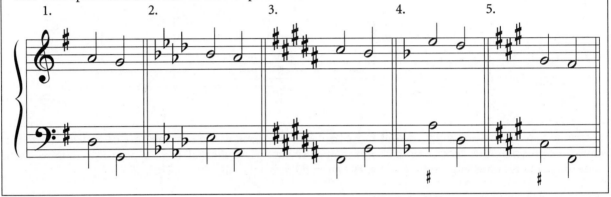

Here is a summary of the part-writing rules for chords whose roots are a fifth apart. One of these rules will always apply.

1. Keep the same structure, with a common tone if possible.

2. Keep the same structure with no common tones and move the upper three voices in the same direction.

3. Keep a common tone, with a change of structure.

Practice Box 9.4

Spell all the chords above the staff first. Determine the structure most appropriate for the first chord and add the inner voices. Move on to each successive chord in the progression and use the rules above to create the part writing. It may be possible to change structure at certain cadences. Finally, add a Roman numeral analysis.

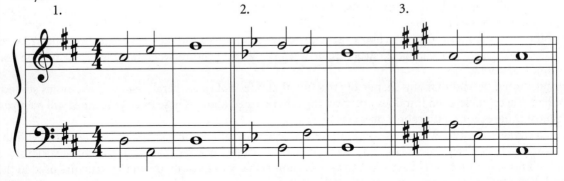

In minor keys, there will always be a figured bass symbol present at an authentic cadence. Remember that in minor, an accidental is necessary to create the dominant chord. The presence of an accidental in the figured bass, especially on the next to last chord, is an excellent hint that the key of the piece is minor.

In minor keys, another type of occurrence involves an accidental at an authentic cadence. The progression for an authentic cadence in minor should be V–i. However, any piece of music written in a minor key may end with a major tonic chord instead of the minor tonic. The major I chord is borrowed from the parallel major key. This situation is known as a **Picardy third**. (The origin of this rather obscure designation is not known.) Example 9.1 is a piece by J. S. Bach that is in a minor key, but it ends with a major tonic. Although the texture is contrapuntal, chords appear in this three-voice texture. Can you find the authentic cadence?

Example 9.1.   *J. S. Bach, Fugue in C Minor,* The Well-Tempered Clavier, *Book I, mm. 26–31*

Track 9, 0:00

Practice Box 9.5

Add inner voices for the following exercises in minor keys.

One other part-writing option is available at the final cadence. Occasionally it is desirable, owing largely to voice-leading considerations, to omit the chordal fifth from the tonic triad on the last chord of a composition. If this is done, then the root of the chord is tripled, while the fifth is omitted. Figure 9.6 demonstrates this idea in a I–V–I progression.

Figure 9.6.   *Tripled root, omitted fifth on final tonic triad*

This option is more commonly used in progressions that contain dominant seventh chords. These chords will be studied in future chapters.

Half Cadences

Thus far all the progressions we have analyzed moved from the dominant chord to the tonic chord, forming authentic cadences. It is also possible for a cadence to end with the dominant chord. That type of cadence is called a **half cadence,** and two of them are shown in Figure 9.7. For now, we will only use the tonic chord to precede the dominant in a half cadence, although other chords are possible.

Figure 9.7.   *Half cadences*

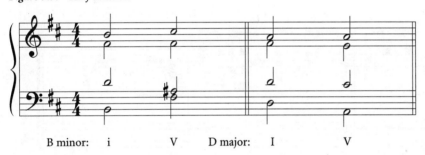

The same rules of part writing that we learned for authentic cadences apply to these half cadences, since we are still using tonic and dominant chords. A half cadence creates a sense of unrest and tension, since the aural effect is not one of completion. Typically, a half cadence is found at the end of a section of music, not at the end of a piece.

Practice Box 9.6

Name the key, provide a Roman numeral analysis, and add inner voices for the following exercises. Each exercise will contain a half cadence.

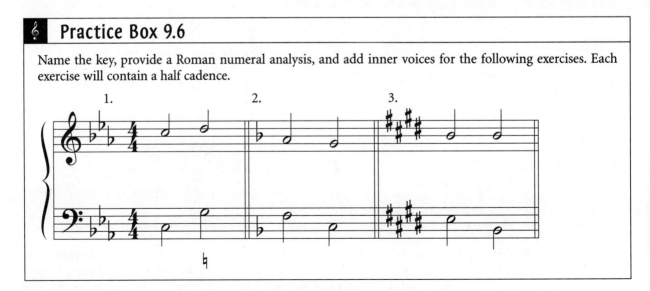

The Subdominant Chord

We will start our study of the subdominant chord with its function in a cadence. One of the most common places to hear a subdominant chord is at the end of a hymn, when the "amen" is sung. As demonstrated in Figure 9.8, the two syllables of the word "a-men" are sung on two chords, IV–I. Many hymnbooks have an "amen" at the end of every hymn. These are virtually always built on the subdominant and tonic chords.

Figure 9.8. *Amen cadence*

This progression is commonly known as a **plagal cadence.** It is also sometimes called an *amen cadence.* It is important to note that it does not replace the authentic cadence at the end of a piece, but instead expands it. The plagal cadence is always heard in music following an authentic cadence. Because of this, it is often called a **plagal extension** rather than a plagal cadence. The use of the word "extension" acknowledges the fact that the IV–I cadence cannot happen independently, but is always tied to a V–I progression.

Figure 9.9 presents the final phrase of a hymnlike tune. The perfect authentic cadence occurs first, followed by the plagal extension. The plagal extension may also occur in minor keys, where the progression usually will be iv–i, although it may be IV–i. (In minor keys, it may also include a Picardy third.)

Figure 9.9. *Plagal extension after authentic cadence*

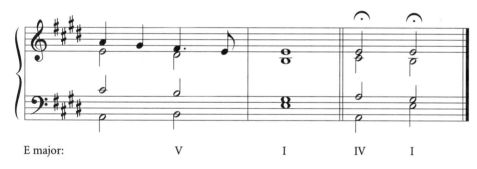

Plagal cadences can be lengthy, with the subdominant-to-tonic movement repeated numerous times. Example 9.2 shows a plagal cadence used in a vocal duet by Fanny Hensel. Try to find both the authentic cadence and the plagal extension.

Track 9, 0:28

Example 9.2. *Fanny Hensel,* Three Heine Duets, *no. 2, mm. 39–47*

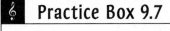

*This chord is a seventh chord. The note in parentheses is the extra chord tone, creating a V^7 chord.

When part writing a plagal cadence, the chords are handled exactly as you have already learned. We will consider roots a fourth apart to be equivalent (for part-writing purposes) to those a fifth apart.

♩ Practice Box 9.7

The following progression has an authentic cadence followed by a plagal extension. Spell the chords and add an appropriate final note for the soprano voice. (The fourth scale degree usually moves downward.) Then add inner voices and a Roman numeral analysis.

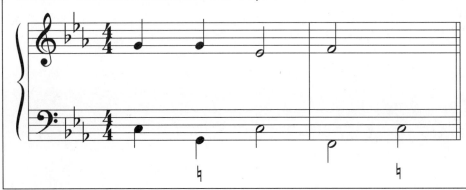

Now look at the progression in Figure 9.10. Provide a Roman numeral analysis.

Figure 9.10.   *Progression for analysis*

Here the subdominant chord occurs near the beginning of a progression, not as a cadential formula. You will remember from an earlier chapter that any chord, such as the subdominant, can follow a tonic chord. In this example, the subdominant chord then moves back to the tonic, just as it would in a plagal cadence. However, here the IV–I is not part of a cadence. When a IV–I occurs in the middle of a progression instead of as a cadence, it is called a *plagal progression.* It is typically used in the sequence found in the example above, I–IV–I–V–I. It may also occur in minor keys as i–iv–i–V–i.

Add a Roman numeral analysis to Example 9.3, which uses a plagal progression as described above.

Example 9.3.   *Robert Schumann,* Faschingsschwank aus Wien, *op. 26, 3rd movement (Scherzino), mm. 68–74*

Track 9, 1:00

🎼 Practice Box 9.8

Add inner voices and a Roman numeral analysis.

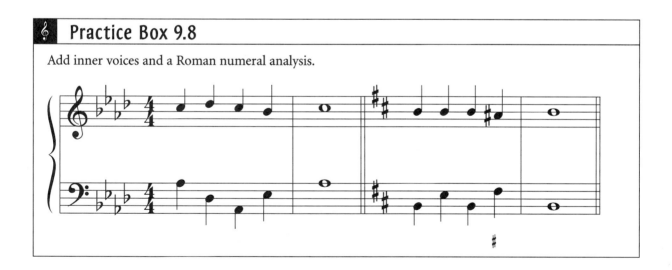

We are now ready for the final manner of using the subdominant chord. In an earlier chapter, we identified a basic chord progression that is based on the circle of fifths. The progression was:

I–iii–vi–ii–V–I.

Notice that this progression does not include the subdominant chord. Let us consider the subdominant chord and another chord that is contained in the basic progression, the supertonic. Figure 9.11 gives the spellings of these chords in the key of C major.

Figure 9.11.   *Two common tones between supertonic and subdominant chords in C major*

```
ii      D─┌F–A┐
IV        └F–A┘─C
```

Notice that these chords have two notes in common. This fact is key to understanding the position of the subdominant chord in any progression. The subdominant chord functions as an equivalent, or substitute, for the supertonic chord in any progression in major or minor keys. Their function in the progression is to precede the dominant chord. Either of these chords can be said to sit at the level of the supertonic in the basic chord progression. Table 18 demonstrates these substitutions in the circle of fifths progression.

Table 18.   *Chord substitutions in the circle of 5ths progression*

Major keys	I	iii	vi	ii	V	I
				IV		
Minor keys	i	VII	III	VI	ii°	V	i
					iv		

Each of the chords listed beneath the supertonic in the main progression can function as supertonic equivalents. Occasionally you will also see both a supertonic and a subdominant chord sitting side by side in the same progression. We will be part writing these progressions in the next chapter.

Example 9.4 uses the subdominant triad where the supertonic would typically sit in the circle of fifths progression.

Example 9.4.   *Frédéric Chopin,* Grande valse brillante, *op. 34, no. 1, mm. 17–20*

Track 9, 1:15

A♭ major: I   IV   V   I

Music for Analysis

The following excerpts contain progressions that we have studied. Some of the chords may be in inversions. Provide a Roman numeral analysis and identify the features that differ from the standard circle of fifths progression.

Example 9.5.   *J. S. Bach,* Wach' auf, mein Herz, *mm. 14–16*

Track 9, 1:28

Example 9.6.   *Johann Christoph Friedrich Bach, Variations on "Ah, vous dirai-je, Maman," mm. 1–5*

Track 9, 1:41

Example 9.7.   *Franz Schubert, Waltz, op. 9, no. 3, mm. 1–8*

Track 9, 1:55

This example contains two seventh chords (triads with an extra chord tone). Can you find them?

AURAL SKILLS

Melody

Sing the following melodies using solfege syllables or scale degree numbers.

Chords

Sing the following exercise in a variety of major keys. The progression includes an outline of the subdominant chord.

B♭ major: I   IV   V   I

Sing the following exercises in a variety of minor keys.

B♭ minor: i   iv   V   i

B♭ minor: i   IV   V   i

Rhythm

The following rhythms will involve *tapping* simultaneously with both hands. Each hand will tap a unique rhythm. The exercises all contain two staves per system. The upper staff will be tapped by the right hand and the lower staff by the left hand. In other words, the exercises are to be read as if they were music for the piano. Practice each slowly at first.

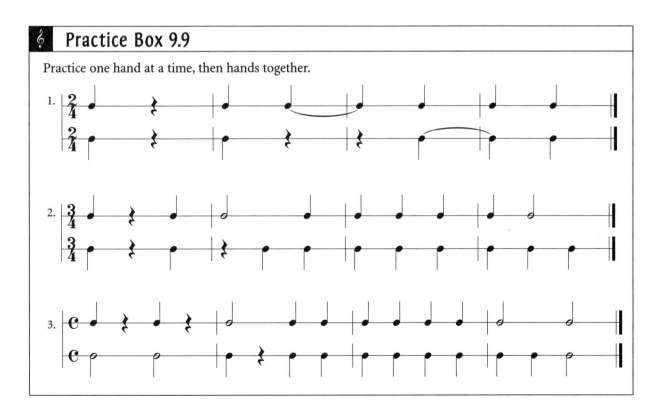

Practice Box 9.9

Practice one hand at a time, then hands together.

Additional Rhythms

For extra practice, clap and count these exercises.

1.
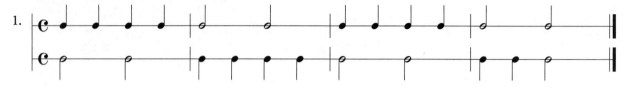

2.

3.
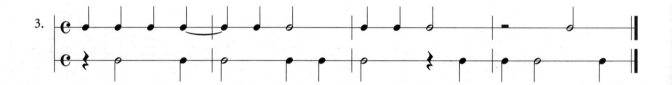

4.
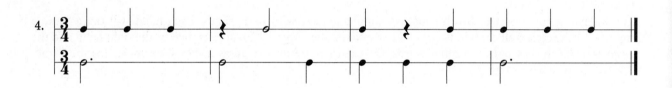

5.
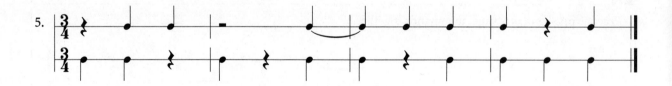

6.
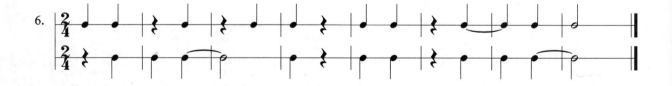

Metronome Markings

Around the year 1800, Johann Nepomuk Maelzel (1772–1826) invented a device called a *metronome*. This apparatus was based on the same principle as a wind-up clock and could be set to click a specific number of beats per minute. This invention allowed composers to specify, for the first time in the history of music, the exact speed of a composition. The first composer to use this device extensively was Ludwig van Beethoven (1770–1827).

Metronome markings are usually written above the staff, just like tempo markings. Sometimes a metronome marking exists by itself, but more often it will be accompanied by the kind of tempo indications discussed in a previous chapter. While the metronome symbol can give a definite idea of the speed required for a composition, it does not replace the other terms because they often speak to the mood of a composition in addition to its speed.

Metronome markings are usually written in this manner: m.m. = 120 or M.M. = 60. Often the beat note may be equated to a metronome speed, such as ♩ = 80. (The double Ms stand for "Maelzel's metronome.") The speeds available on a metronome vary from forty to over two hundred beats per minute. Older metronomes are pyramid shaped and made of wood. Their mechanism resembles an inverted pendulum, with an arm that moves back and forth as the device ticks. Newer models are electronic and emit a beep instead of a tick.

Dictation

You will hear several melodies. The key signature is given to you. Each melody will begin on *do*. Write all of the pitches you hear as eighth notes, quarter notes, or half notes. You will hear each melody three or four times.

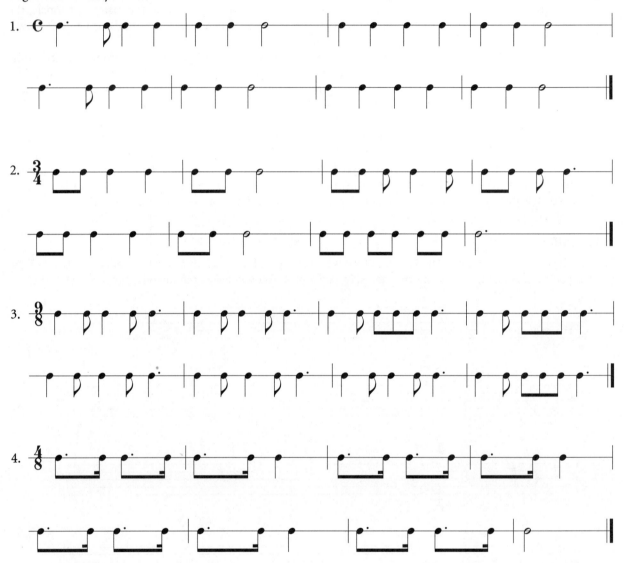162

Pitch Memory

You will hear a variety of melodies that are represented on the staves below only as rhythms. Circle the tonic scale degree whenever you hear it.

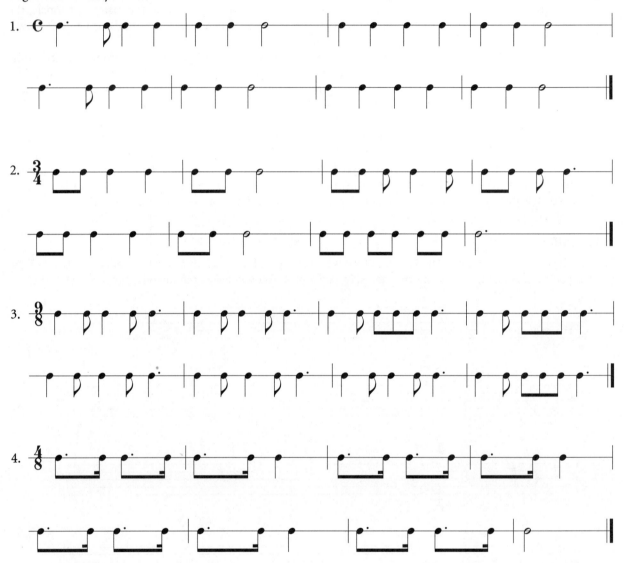

You will hear pairs of repeated chords (major and minor qualities). The bass notes are provided. Add the soprano notes. (A Roman numeral analysis is not necessary.)

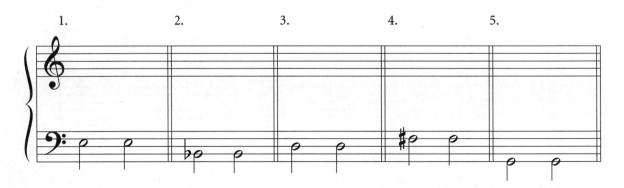

KEYBOARD APPLICATIONS

Play the following progressions in close structure. Three keys are suggested for each exercise, but they can be transposed to all other keys if desired. It is often a good idea to learn all new progressions in C major or A minor first, since those are the easiest keys.

1. C major
   G major
   Eb major

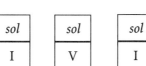

The upper 3 voices are written in the treble staff since they will be played with the right hand.

2. A minor
   B minor
   F minor

3. E major
   F major
   Bb major

4. A minor
   G minor
   D minor

Looking Ahead

Virtually any harmonic progression that you study in actual music compositions will contain notes, either in the melody or in the inner parts, that are not part of the underlying chordal structure. These notes are known as *non-harmonic tones.* These tones must be anlyzed alongside the harmonic progression for the most complete understanding of a musical composition.

Some of the simplest non-harmonic tones are those that are approached and resolved by stepwise motion. These are called *passing tones* and *neighbor tones.* Passing tones are approached and resolved by stepwise movement in the same direction, while neighbor tones involve a change of direction. These movements are demonstrated in Figures 9.12 and 9.13. The non-harmonic tones are circled.

Figure 9.12.   Passing tones

Figure 9.13.   Neighbor tones

Study the direction of the approach and the resolution for these two types of non-harmonic tones. All non-harmonic tones will be studied in greater depth in chapters 17–19 of this book.

chapter 10 Root Movement by Second

THEORETICAL SKILLS

Part Writing with Root Movement by Second

Chords whose roots are a step apart are handled quite differently than those whose roots are separated by the interval of a fifth. In Figure 10.1 you will see an example of two chords that are a second apart in the key of C major.

Figure 10.1. Chords in C major related by roots a 2nd apart

I	C–E–G
ii	D–F–A

These two chords do not have any notes in common. This is true of all chords that are separated by a second. Because of the lack of common tones, the part-writing rules are quite different than those seen in the previous chapter. First, in Figure 10.2 let us consider some possible chord progressions that include root movement by second.

Figure 10.2. Chord progressions using root movement by 2nd

⌐I ii⌐ V I   I ⌐IV V⌐ I   i ⌐iv V⌐ i

In each of these progressions, there are two chords whose roots are a step apart. They are labeled in brackets above. In the progressions containing the supertonic chords, the tonic and supertonic chords have roots a step apart. In the progressions containing the subdominant chords, the subdominants and dominants are a step apart. It should be noted that that use of the diminished supertonic triad in root position is rare, so for now, we will only be seeing the supertonic chord in major keys. Figure 10.3 shows typical bass lines for root movement by second.

Figure 10.3. Sample bass lines

C major: I   ii   V   I   I   IV   V   I

First, we will look at the proper construction of a soprano line to complement these bass lines, starting with the progression containing the supertonic. In Figure 10.4, at the point of the ascending stepwise movement in the bass, the soprano also is moving upward. This will usually result in parallelism.

Figure 10.4. Parallelism resulting from soprano moving in the same direction as bass

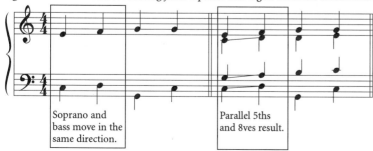

Soprano and bass move in the same direction.

Parallel 5ths and 8ves result.

This leads us to conclude that when the bass line moves stepwise, the soprano line generally should not move in the same direction. Instead, it should move in contrary motion to the bass. The two chords should then be kept in the same structure, with the alto and tenor moving in the same direction as the soprano. (See Figure 10.5.) Excellent part writing should result:

When the chord roots move by step, the soprano line should usually move in contrary motion to the bass. Keep both chords in the same structure. All three upper voices will move in similar motion.

Figure 10.5. *Soprano line moving in contrary motion to the bass*

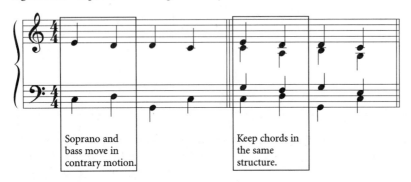

Soprano and bass move in contrary motion.

Keep chords in the same structure.

♭ Practice Box 10.1

Add the remaining notes for the soprano voice for each of these exercises, according to the rules above. Then add inner voices and a Roman numeral analysis.

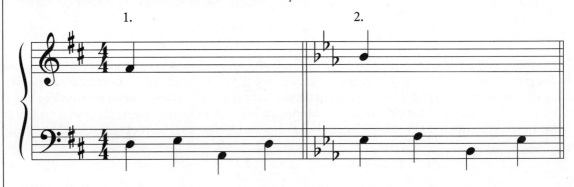

Study Example 10.1 to find the I–ii–V–I progression. Non-harmonic tones are circled.

Track 10, 0:00

Example 10.1. *Beethoven, Sonatina in D, WoO, 1st movement, mm. 1–5*

You will notice that the example above uses the supertonic chord in first inversion (measure 3). In most music, it is less common to find the supertonic chord in root position. It is more typically found in first inversion. Inverted triads will be studied in future chapters.

The progressions containing the subdominant chords are handled in exactly the same manner. The soprano line must move in contrary motion to the bass at the point of the stepwise root movement. Figure 10.6 gives examples of properly constructed soprano lines for the I–IV–V–I progression. Add inner voices and observe how the alto and tenor will also move in contrary motion to the bass.

Figure 10.6. *Soprano moving contrary to the bass at the point of root movement by 2nd*

In minor keys, the same procedure will apply. The subdominant chord will generally be minor in a minor key, although occasionally a major subdominant is found. Like the dominant chord, the major subdominant will require an accidental that will appear in the figured bass. Figure 10.7 shows examples in minor keys. Add inner voices to the second measure.

Figure 10.7. *Progressions in minor keys*

C minor: i   iv   V   i   E minor: i   IV   V   i

The Roman numeral analysis for each of the minor progressions above is provided. Notice the major subdominant chord in the second example. When you add the inner voices to the second example, don't forget to place an accidental beside the proper note in the IV chord.

In any major or minor key, the tonic, subdominant, and dominant chords are considered to be the **primary triads**. These are the most frequently used triads in any key and they are the ones most likely to appear in root position. The three primary triads form the basis for harmonizing many tunes, especially in blues, popular, and country music. You may have heard someone say, "That piece of music uses only three chords." Those three chords are the primary triads of the key.

Practice Box 10.2

Determine the key, spell the chords, write the inner voices, and provide a Roman numeral analysis. Add the soprano line where indicated. In addition, name the type of cadence in each exercise.

Practice Box 10.2 (continued)

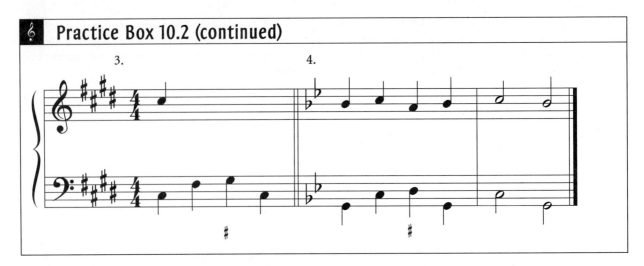

The final exercise above combined two elements that we have studied, including a progression using primary triads with an imperfect authentic cadence, and a plagal extension. Now we will look at a longer progression that combines several elements. Study the progression in Figure 10.8.

Figure 10.8.   Progression using root movement by 2nd

This progression is longer than any we have studied thus far. It combines the primary triads plus a specific type of cadence at the end. Add a Roman numeral analysis. You will see that there is a pair of repeated chords in the progression. When adding inner voices, you may take advantage of the repeated chords to change the structure. Can you name the cadence?

The half cadence may initially cause some confusion when it appears. The key signature indicates that the key is either D major or B minor. When you look at the final chord, you typically expect to see a tonic triad. However in this case, the chord is built on a root of A. You should immediately consider the spelling of the dominant triads for each of the possible keys. B minor can be ruled out, because the dominant triad would be built on F♯ and would include a leading tone, A♯. A chord built on A, however, forms the dominant triad of the key of D major. Ending on this dominant triad creates the half cadence. In the previous chapter, we only studied half cadences that moved from tonic to dominant. Here is a half cadence where the dominant triad is preceded by the subdominant.

The progression in Figure 10.9 is in F♯ minor, and there is an accidental on the final chord. The accidental affects the chordal third. Is it a half cadence or an authentic cadence? What is the name given to this type of chord?

Figure 10.9.   Progression using root movement by 2nd

The longer progresion in Figure 10.9 includes a combination of two progressions that we have learned: i–V–i and iv–V–i. The major tonic triad that ends the example is a Picardy third. Now look at Figure 10.10, which uses a different type of cadence. Can you name it?

Figure 10.10.   Progression using root movement by 2nd

Practice Box 10.3

Add a soprano line to the following bass lines. Try starting on a variety of different solfege syllables for the first chord (*do, mi* or *me, sol*). Add inner voices and Roman numerals. Name the cadence used in each exercise.

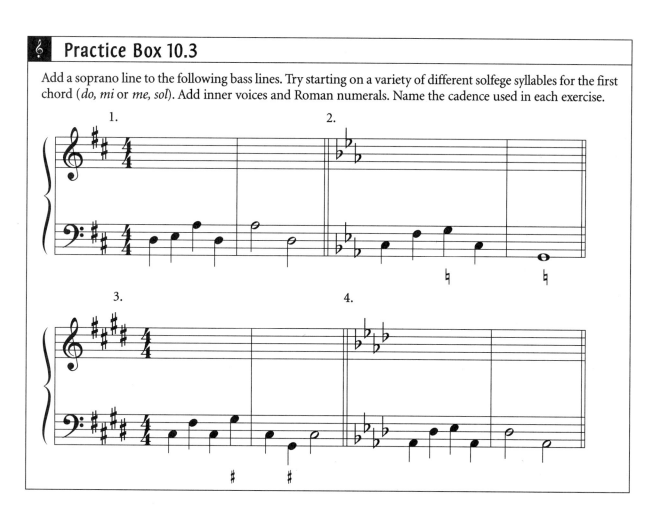

Example 10.2 is a piano piece in A minor by the romantic composer Robert Schumann. It uses the primary triads. Provide a Roman numeral analysis.

Example 10.2.   R. Schumann, Album for the Young, *"Little Romance," op. 68, no. 19, mm. 1–4*

Track 10, 0:20

Deceptive Cadences

A listener who hears an authentic cadence senses the tension of the dominant chord, which contains the leading tone. That tension then resolves when the dominant chord moves to the tonic. It is possible to redirect the resolution of a dominant chord by means of a **deceptive cadence**. In a deceptive cadence, the dominant chord is not followed by the tonic; instead, the submediant chord follows it. The submediant chord serves as a substitute for the tonic. As you can see from Figure 10.11, those two chords have two common tones.

Figure 10.11.   *Common tones between the tonic and submediant triads in C major*

I   C–E–G
vi   A–C–E

When the chords V–vi are heard at the end of a section of music, it is called a deceptive cadence. When they occur in the middle of a progression, it is called a **deceptive progression**. Figure 10.12 presents two examples in C major. Add Roman numerals to the second measure.

Figure 10.12.   *Deceptive cadences in C major*

C major: I   IV   V   vi

Just as with all root movements by second, if the soprano is moved in similar motion to the bass, parallelism will result. Notice that in each example above, there are two stepwise pairs of notes in the bass and that the soprano moves in contrary motion on each of them. Example 10.3 is from the music of Mozart. The chord in the third measure contains a B♭ that is a seventh above the bass, making it a V7 instead of a V chord. Treat it as an ordinary dominant triad in your analysis. Find the deceptive progression in this excerpt and notice the contrary motion between the outer voices.

Example 10.3.   Wolfgang Amadeus Mozart, *Piano Sonata, K. 332, 1st movement, mm. 208–213*

Track 10, 0:38

F major: IV   V⁷

Practice Box 10.4

Add inner voices and a Roman numeral analysis.

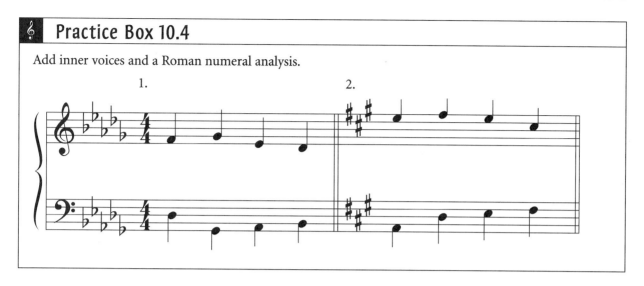

Irregular Doubling in Deceptive Cadences

It is also possible to find deceptive cadences and progressions in minor keys, where the Roman numerals will be V–VI (remember that the submediant chord is a major chord in a minor key). Figure 10.13 shows several possible deceptive cadences in a minor key, all of which contain incorrect voice leading.

Figure 10.13. *Deceptive cadences in C minor*

Avoid augmented 2nds in your voice leading.

If you use standard doubling for each of the chords in the progressions above, as shown, an augmented second occurs in one voice in each example. This interval is generally avoided in vocal lines because it is difficult to sing.

Handling the part writing for deceptive cadences in minor keys is more difficult than anything we have dealt with thus far. Study the examples in Figure 10.13 very carefully. In each measure, one voice will move the distance of an augmented second at the point of the deceptive cadence. Since this example uses all of the possible starting soprano notes for this progression, we can see that it is not possible to create good voice leading with the current rules. Whenever you encounter this progression in a minor key, you will need to create a submediant chord that uses **irregular doubling.** Instead of doubling the bass note, you will double the soprano. Typically in this progression, the soprano line will not move in contrary motion with the bass, but instead will move in similar motion. The soprano note of each chord will be the chordal third, creating parallel tenths between the outer voices. This is demonstrated in Figure 10.14.

Figure 10.14.   Deceptive cadences using irregular doubling

C minor: i   iv   V   VI

Notice the parallel motion between the soprano and bass at the point of the cadence. This parallel motion is acceptable because it is parallel major thirds, not perfect fifths or octaves. However, to offset that parallel motion between outer voices, the structure must not be the same on both chords; otherwise parallel fifths and octaves will result.

On the submediant chord, instead of doubling the bass, the structure is created another way. Working from the top down you will double the soprano note down an octave, usually in the tenor voice. (In this manner, unlike close and open structure, the chord tones are not written directly down from the top.) After filling in the tenor note, you should put the remaining chord tone (E♭) in the alto voice. If you have spelled the chord above the staff, it will be very helpful to underscore the letter names as you add them to the chord on the staff. The alto voice will take the last remaining chord tone after you have filled in the tenor note.

It is also possible to double the soprano in the alto voice, creating either a unison or an octave between these adjacent voices. The most typical soprano line for this deceptive cadence is *ti–do*.

🎼 Practice Box 10.5

Add a soprano line to these deceptive cadences, using the chordal third on both the dominant and the submediant chords. Then add inner voices and a Roman numeral analysis. Be sure to use irregular doubling on the submediant chord.

Example 10.4 shows a deceptive cadence in a minor key. Notes that are not part of the harmony are circled.

Example 10.4.   Mozart, Piano Sonata, K. 280, 2nd movement, mm. 1–4

Track 10, 0:52

Other Irregular Doubling

Any progression where there is root movement by step is a potential candidate for irregular doubling if the soprano line moves in parallel motion to the bass voice. Earlier in this chapter, we learned that the soprano typically moves in contrary motion to the bass at the point of root movement by second. This voice leading avoids the parallel fifths and octaves that will result if the two voices move in the same direction.

However, as long as the soprano note is the chordal third of both the chords, it is possible to move any soprano line in parallel motion to the bass. You have seen this in the examples above using deceptive progressions and cadences. We will now look at a few other examples in Figure 10.15.

Figure 10.15.   Root movement by second using irregular doubling

In each of the examples above, an asterisk marks the point of stepwise root movement, paralleled by movement in the soprano. As you study the inner voices, you will observe that the second chord of each pair uses irregular doubling, with the tenor voice exactly one octave lower than the soprano. This type of chord is not considered open or close structure, but because it spreads the voices farther apart than close structure, it provides an opportunity to change from close to open. In each case, the chord following the irregular doubling goes to open structure. The alto and tenor voices move in contrary motion to the bass and soprano and in so doing avoid parallelism. Add a Roman numeral analysis to the examples in Figure 10.15.

When you consider a part-writing exercise such as those in Practice Box 10.6, you should observe the root movements carefully before choosing the structure for each chord.

Practice Box 10.6

Study the bass line for types of root movement. Then add inner voices and a Roman numeral analysis. Be sure to use irregular doubling where appropriate.

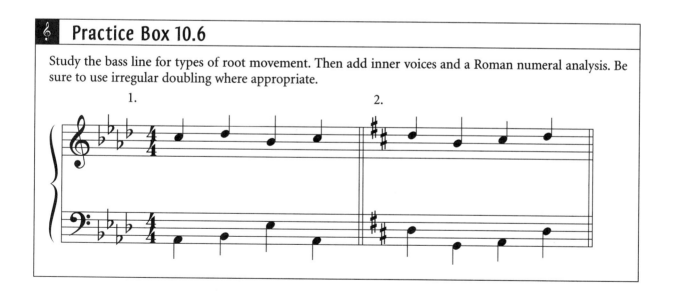

Music for Analysis

The following excerpts contain the chord progressions studied in this chapter. Identify the keys and provide a Roman numeral analysis. For each excerpt, name the type of cadence used. Notes that are circled should not be considered part of the underlying chord.

Example 10.5.　R. Schumann, Papillons, op. 2, no. 7, mm. 1–4

Track 10, 1:11

In the following excerpt, the bass note, E, is present in every measure. In some measures, however, it may not be part of the chord.

Example 10.6.　Felix Mendelssohn, Songs without Words, op. 117, no. 1, mm. 1–7

Track 10, 1:23

Example 10.7.　J. S. Bach, An Wasserflüssen Babylon, mm. 1–2

Track 10, 1:55

AURAL SKILLS

Melody

First identify the key of each of these melodies. Then sing them using solfege syllables.

1. Key: _____

2. Key: _____

3. Key: _____

4. Key: _____

5. Key: _____

6. Key: _____

7. Key: _____

8. Key: _____

Chords

Sing the following chord progressions, which involve a variety of cadences.

Rhythm

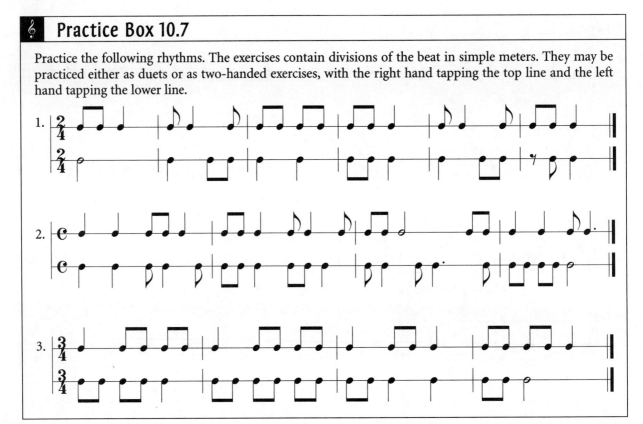

Additional Rhythms

For extra practice, clap and count these exercises.

Dictation

You will be told the name of the key before you hear each melody, and you will hear the scale on which the exercise is based. The starting pitch is not given to you, but it will be either the first, third, or fifth scale degree of the key.

1.

2.

3.

4.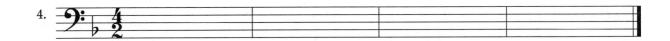

5.

6.

Circle the quality of the triads that you hear. Each chord will be played twice.

1. major	minor		6. major	minor	
2. major	minor		7. major	minor	
3. major	minor		8. major	minor	
4. major	minor		9. major	minor	
5. major	minor		10. major	minor	

1. minor	diminished		6. minor	diminished	
2. minor	diminished		7. minor	diminished	
3. minor	diminished		8. minor	diminished	
4. minor	diminished		9. minor	diminished	
5. minor	diminished		10. minor	diminished	

1. major	minor	diminished	6. major	minor	diminished
2. major	minor	diminished	7. major	minor	diminished
3. major	minor	diminished	8. major	minor	diminished
4. major	minor	diminished	9. major	minor	diminished
5. major	minor	diminished	10. major	minor	diminished

Harmonic Dictation

You will hear chord progressions in four-part harmony. The bass line is given to you. Notate the soprano line and add a Roman numeral analysis. It may help to think of the soprano in terms of scale degrees or solfege syllables as you hear the progression.

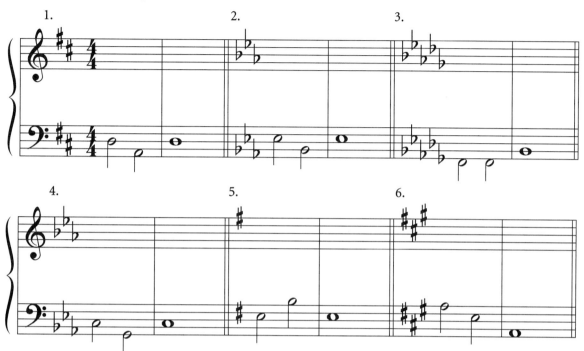

Now the soprano lines are given to you. Notate the bass lines that you hear and add a Roman numeral analysis.

KEYBOARD APPLICATIONS

Play the following progressions in close structure. Three keys are suggested for each exercise, but they can be transposed to all other keys if desired. It is often a good idea to learn all new progressions in C major or A minor first, since those are the easiest keys.

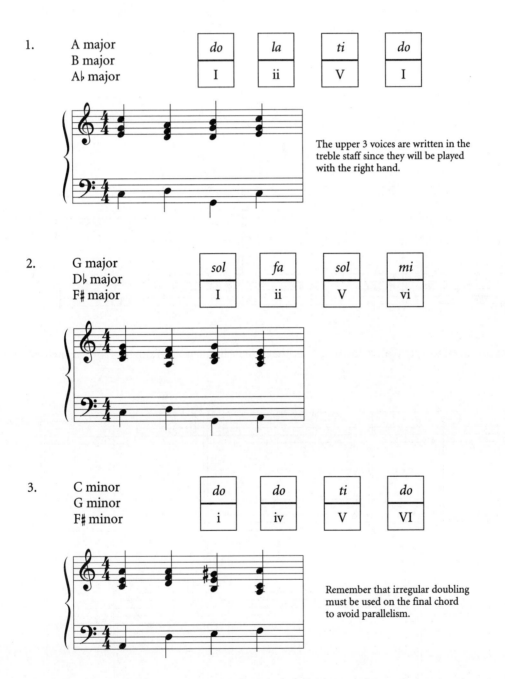

1.   A major
      B major
      A♭ major

do	la	ti	do
I	ii	V	I

The upper 3 voices are written in the treble staff since they will be played with the right hand.

2.   G major
      D♭ major
      F♯ major

sol	fa	sol	mi
I	ii	V	vi

3.   C minor
      G minor
      F♯ minor

do	do	ti	do
i	iv	V	VI

Remember that irregular doubling must be used on the final chord to avoid parallelism.

chapter 11 Root Movement by Third

THEORETICAL SKILLS

Part Writing with Root Movement by Third

The last category of root movement to be studied is that which connects chords by the interval of a third. Figure 11.1 shows how in the key of C major, the tonic chord is related to two chords by the distance of a third, the mediant and submediant.

Figure 11.1. Common tones in chords a 3rd apart in C major

```
I        C– E–G            I            C–E –G
iii          E–G –B        vi        A– C–E
```

As you can see, whenever chord roots are separated by a third, those chords will have two common tones. This plays an important role in part writing and simplifies it enormously.

When chord roots move by thirds, keep both chords in the same structure. There should be two common tones.

Typical chord progressions that use root movement by third are in Figure 11.2. Notice that the root movement by third happens directly after the tonic triad. After the progression continues, it moves by the standard distance of a fifth. Remember that the subdominant chord can be a substitute for the supertonic. If it is, then there will also be root movement of a third between the submediant and subdominant chords.

Figure 11.2. Sample progressions using root movement by 3rd

```
I    vi    ii    V    I          I    iii    vi    ii    V    I

i    VI    iv    V    i          i    III    VI    iv    V    i
```

Bass lines for these progressions are shown in Figure 11.3.

Figure 11.3. Bass lines

C major: I   vi   ii   V   I   I   iii   vi   ii   V   I

C minor: i   VI   iv   V   i   i   III   VI   iv   V   i

Figure 11.4 shows the tonic triad moving to submediant and mediant triads, with all possible soprano lines. Notice the presence of two common tones in all of the progressions.

Figure 11.4.   Two common tones when roots are a 3rd apart

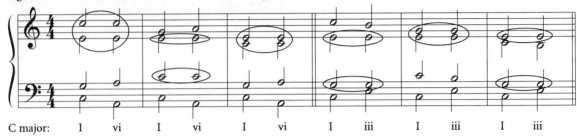

C major: I   vi   I   vi   I   vi   I   iii   I   iii   I   iii

You must take advantage of the common tones when constructing soprano lines for root movement by third. If you do not, parallelism will usually result. Figure 11.5 demonstrates the result of failure to keep the common tones. Instead of keeping the common tone in the soprano, the soprano is allowed to move upward. Parallelism results between the bass and inner voices. Remember: keep the common tones in the same voices.

Figure 11.5.   Parallelism from movement of common tones

Parallelism!

Practice Box 11.1

Add inner voices and Roman numerals. Circle the common tones and name each cadence. Add the soprano line where indicated.

Analyze Example 11.1, looking for root movement by third. The inverted chord is analyzed for you.

Example 11.1.   *Brahms, Waltz, op. 39, no. 3, mm. 14–18*

Track 11, 0:00

G♯ minor: i⁶₄

The Subtonic Triad

The subtonic scale degree exists only in minor keys. The major scale has only a single seventh scale degree, which is a leading tone because it is a half step away from the tonic. The leading tone chords will be studied in the chapters on inversions. The subtonic scale degree, which is the lowered seventh in the melodic minor scale, can have a chord built on it, also called the subtonic triad. This triad is used in a minor scale directly following the tonic triad. The following progression, in which it is followed by the III chord, is typical:

$$\text{i–VII–III–VI–ii°–V–I}$$

We have seen this progression in a previous chapter as we studied the circle of fifths progression in minor keys. The root movement from the tonic to the subtonic chord is a second, so the rules of part writing from the previous chapter should be followed. In Figure 11.6, notice the contrary motion between voices in the first measure.

Figure 11.6.   *Progression using subtonic triad*

Example 11.2 is a composition by Felix Mendelssohn that uses this progression. Add a Roman numeral analysis.

Example 11.2.   *Mendelssohn,* Venetian Boat Song, *op. 19, no. 6, mm. 1–7*

Track 11, 0:17

*The composer has written the dynamic markings above the staff to indicate that they apply only to the melodic line, not the harmonic progression.

Truncated Progressions

Although a typical progression moves by fifth, as we have learned so far, many times you will see progressions that do not follow this pattern exactly. One of the most common devices is that of the **truncated progression,** where certain chords are omitted from the circle of fifths progression. Most often only a single chord is omitted, and the most common chords to omit are the submediant and the supertonic.

When the supertonic is omitted from a progression, the result is a chord progression that looks like this:

I–vi–V–I

The omission of the supertonic allows the submediant chord to move directly to the dominant, which creates root movement by second. This progression is frequently seen in the chorale tunes of J. S. Bach. See Example 11.3.

Example 11.3.   *J. S. Bach,* Ermuntre dich, mein schwacher Geist, *mm. 1–2*

Track 11, 0:38

Other truncated progressions can also occur. In Example 11.4, the submediant chord has been omitted, creating a progression that moves from the mediant to the supertonic. Much less common are progressions that omit the dominant chord, moving from the supertonic directly to the tonic.

Example 11.4.   Brahms, Klavierstücke, op. 118, no. 2, mm. 36–38

Track 11, 0:49

A major: iii⁶   ii

Occasionally, when writing normal and truncated progressions, you will discover a soprano line with a leap of a fourth or greater. Because of the leap, it is often inappropriate to write both voices in the same structure—doing so will take one or more voices out of range. A change of structure is permitted in these circumstances.

> *When the soprano voice leaps a fourth or more, it is permissible to change structure,*
> *provided that doing so does not cause parallelism.*

Usually a change of structure will create parallelism, but occasionally when the soprano leaps a fourth, changing structure will avoid large leaps in inner voices. There are two changes of structure in the progression shown in Figure 11.7. The first occurs between the submediant and dominant chords, where the soprano leaps a fourth. The change of structure prevents the crossed voices that would result if close structure were maintained. The second occurs between the last two chords, because of the presence of a common tone in the alto.

Figure 11.7.   Change of structure with leap of 4th in soprano

C major: I   vi   V   I

Practice Box 11.2

Add inner voices and a Roman numeral analysis. Circle the two chords that form the truncated portion of the progression.

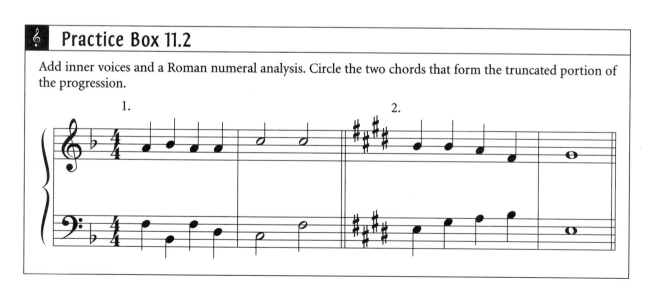

Retrogressions

Retrogressions occur when the normal order of the circle of fifths progression is reversed. The most common retrogression is movement from the dominant to the subdominant. Examples 11.5 and 11.6 are from the chorales of J. S. Bach. Some of the chords will be in inversion. As seen below, a retrogression sometimes occurs because of stepwise voice leading between repeated chords appearing in different inversions.

Example 11.5.   *J. S. Bach,* Herzlich lieb hab' ich dich, O Herr, *mm. 1–2*

Track 11, 1:01

D major: I   V   IV⁶   V⁶

Example 11.6.   *J. S. Bach,* Nun lob', mein Seel', den Herren, *mm. 1–4*

Track 11, 1:14

A major: I

Often a retrogression is combined with a truncated progression, as is seen in both of the examples above. Generally, not more than one retrogression will be used in any musical phrase.

One of the most common places to find a retrogression is in a popular musical form known as the twelve-bar blues. The **twelve-bar blues** is a harmonic pattern twelve measures in length that is based on the chord progression shown in Figure 11.8.

Figure 11.8.   *Twelve-bar blues progression*

Measure number	1	2	3	4	5	6	7	8	9	10	11	12
Roman numeral	I	I	I	I	IV	IV	I	I	V	IV	I	I

Many pieces of music in jazz, blues, and pop styles are based on the twelve-bar blues. A song that uses the chord progression is shown in Example 11.7.

Example 11.7. Ian Corbett, "Check-In To Go"

Track 11, 1:28

Copyright© 2002 Ian Corbett (ASCAP). Used by permission.

Practice Box 11.3

These exercises cover all aspects of harmony studied in this chapter. Add inner voices and Roman numeral analysis.

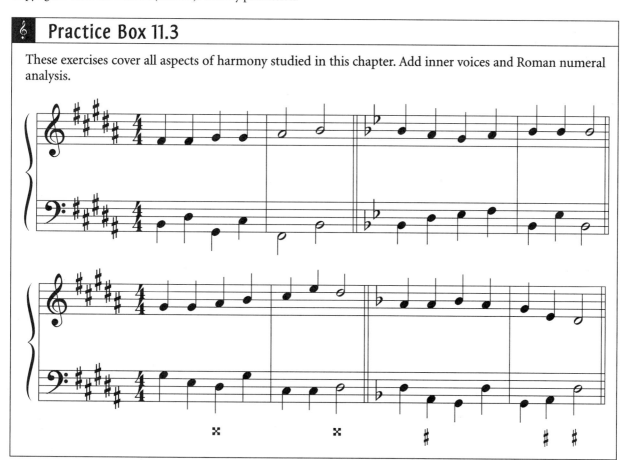

Music for Analysis

Provide a Roman numeral analysis of the following excerpts, which demonstrate the progressions studied in this chapter.

Example 11.8. R. Schumann, Album for the Young, *"Armes Waisenkind," op. 68, no. 6, mm. 1–8*

Track 11, 2:03

Example 11.9. Mozart, Piano Sonata, K. 333, 1st movement, mm. 1–4

Track 11, 2:22

Example 11.10. Richard Rodgers and Lorenz Hart, "Blue Moon," mm. 1–5

Track 11, 2:38

Example 11.11. Mozart, Piano Sonata, K. 332, 2nd movement, mm. 1–2

Track 11, 3:00

(simile)

AURAL SKILLS

Duets

Each voice part of the duet should be sung by a solo singer or a group of singers. Practice each part individually, then sing the two parts simultaneously.

1.

2.

3.

4.

Chords

Sing the following broken chord progressions in a variety of keys.

F major: I   vi   ii   V   I

F major: I   vi   IV   V   I

D major: I   iii   vi   ii   V   I

E minor: i   VII   III   VI   iv   V   i

The following group includes truncated progressions and retrogressions.

E major: I   vi   V   I

B major: I   iii   IV   V   I

B major: I   V   IV   I

Rhythm

Practice the following rhythms. They may be practiced either as duets or as two-handed exercises, with the right hand tapping the top line and the left hand tapping the lower line.

Dictation

Identify the quality of the triads that you hear. All will be in root position.

1. diminished	augmented	11. diminished	augmented
2. diminished	augmented	12. diminished	augmented
3. diminished	augmented	13. diminished	augmented
4. diminished	augmented	14. diminished	augmented
5. diminished	augmented	15. diminished	augmented
6. diminished	augmented	16. diminished	augmented
7. diminished	augmented	17. diminished	augmented
8. diminished	augmented	18. diminished	augmented
9. diminished	augmented	19. diminished	augmented
10. diminished	augmented	20. diminished	augmented

1. major	minor	diminished	augmented
2. major	minor	diminished	augmented
3. major	minor	diminished	augmented
4. major	minor	diminished	augmented
5. major	minor	diminished	augmented
6. major	minor	diminished	augmented
7. major	minor	diminished	augmented
8. major	minor	diminished	augmented
9. major	minor	diminished	augmented
10. major	minor	diminished	augmented

Circle the quality of the triads that you hear. You will hear root-position, first-inversion, and second-inversion chords. Each chord will be played twice.

1. major	minor	6. major	minor
2. major	minor	7. major	minor
3. major	minor	8. major	minor
4. major	minor	9. major	minor
5. major	minor	10. major	minor

1. major	diminished	6. major	diminished
2. major	diminished	7. major	diminished
3. major	diminished	8. major	diminished
4. major	diminished	9. major	diminished
5. major	diminished	10. major	diminished

1. minor	diminished	6. minor	diminished
2. minor	diminished	7. minor	diminished
3. minor	diminished	8. minor	diminished
4. minor	diminished	9. minor	diminished
5. minor	diminished	10. minor	diminished

1. major	minor	diminished	6. major	minor	diminished
2. major	minor	diminished	7. major	minor	diminished
3. major	minor	diminished	8. major	minor	diminished
4. major	minor	diminished	9. major	minor	diminished
5. major	minor	diminished	10. major	minor	diminished

Notate the following rhythms. Each of the rhythms is eight measures in length.

1.

2.

3.

4.

Harmonic Dictation

You will hear chord progressions that are four chords in length. The bass line is given to you. Notate the soprano line and add a Roman numeral analysis. It may help to think of the soprano in terms of scale degrees or solfege syllables.

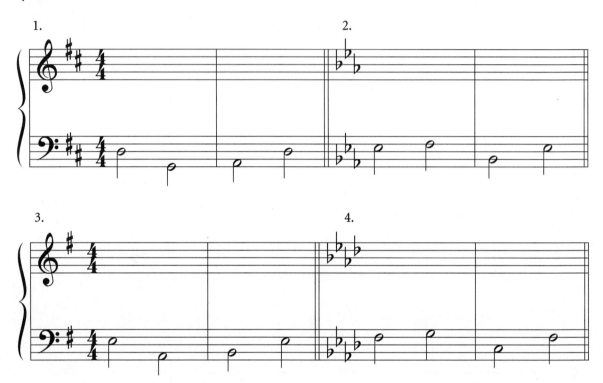

Now the soprano lines are given to you. Notate the bass lines that you hear and add a Roman numeral analysis.

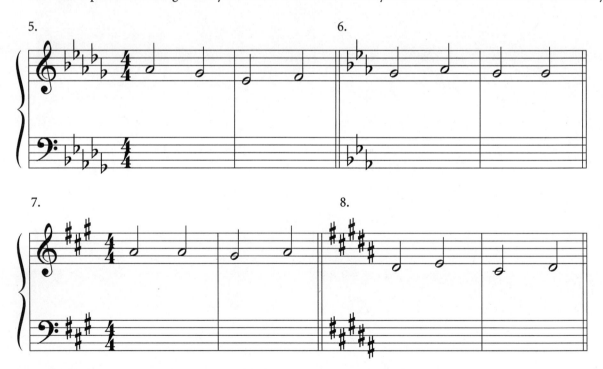

KEYBOARD APPLICATIONS

Play the following progressions in close structure. Three keys are suggested for each exercise, but they can be transposed to all other keys if desired. It is often a good idea to learn these new progressions in C major first, since that is the easiest key.

1.   A major
       D♭ major
       G♭ major

2.   F major
       E♭ major
       F♯ major

chapter 12 Review of Harmony: Root-Position Triads

REVIEW CHAPTER

Four-Part Harmony Review

Here is a summary of the rules of part writing that have been studied thus far:

1. The goal in part writing is to double the bass voice. This is accomplished with close and open structure.

2. Structure is always created working from the soprano voice downward. If the soprano is not given to you, add the soprano note first.

3. To create close structure, add the alto and tenor voices on the closest remaining chord tones beneath the soprano note.

4. To create open structure, skip a chord tone below the soprano for the alto note and skip a chord tone below the alto for the tenor note.

5. In general, the goal in part writing is to create smooth voice leading in each of the upper three voices.

6. In general, simultaneous leaps in the same direction in two or more voices are to be avoided.

7. Parallel perfect fifths and octaves between any pair of voices are to be avoided.

8. Crossed voices are to be avoided.

9. In general, you should keep the same structure throughout a part-writing exercise.

10. When the root moves by a fifth:
    a. Keep a common tone if possible.
    b. You may keep the same structure or change structure if there is a common tone.
    c. If there is no common tone, keep the same structure and move all three upper voices in the same direction.

11. When the root moves by a third, keep the same structure and keep two common tones.

12. When the root moves by a second:
    a. The soprano usually moves in contrary motion to the bass.
    b. Keep the same structure and move all three upper voices in the same direction.
    c. If the soprano moves in the same direction as the bass, you will need to use irregular doubling, usually on the second chord of the pair.

13. To create a chord with irregular doubling, double the soprano note in either the alto or tenor voice. Put the remaining chord tone in whichever voice remains open (the doubled note will be the chordal third).

14. Reasons for changing from open to close or close to open structure:
    a. Repeated chords (same Roman numerals)
    b. Leap of a fourth or greater in the soprano
    c. Root movement by fifth and a common tone in an inner voice (with *re–do* in the soprano, usually a perfect authentic cadence, one inner voice will leap a fourth)

196

Terminology Review

All of the terms below have been covered in the preceding eleven chapters. You should study them to make sure they are part of your musical vocabulary.

accent
accidental
alla breve
alto
anacrusis
analysis
augmented
authentic cadence
bar line
bass
basso continuo
cadence
chord
chord progression
chromatic scale
circle of fifths
clef
close structure
Common Practice Period
common time
common tone
compound interval
compound meter
conjunct
consonance
contour
contrary motion
counterpoint
courtesy accidental
crossed voices
cut time
deceptive cadence
deceptive progression
diatonic
diminished
disjunct
dissonance
division
dominant
dotted note
double flat
double sharp
downbeat
enharmonic
figured bass

flat
grand staff
half cadence
half step
harmonic minor
harmony
hexachords
homophonic
interval inversion
intervals
inversion
irregular doubling
key
key signature
leading tone
ledger lines
major
measure
mediant
melodic minor
meter
middle C
minor
monophonic
music theory
musical alphabet
natural
natural minor
note
oblique motion
octave
open structure
order of the flats
order of the sharps
parallel keys
parallel motion
part writing
pentachord
perfect
period
phrase
pitch
pitch class
plagal cadence
plagal extension

plagal progression
polyphonic
primary triads
prime
quality
range
realization
relative keys
rest
retrogression
root
scale
sequence
sharp
similar motion
simple meter
solfege
soprano
staff /staves
structure
subdominant
submediant
subtonic
supertonic
syncopation
system
tenor
tessitura
texture
theorist
tie
time signature
tonal music
tonic
transpose
treble
triad
tritone
truncated progression
twelve-bar blues
upbeat
vocal ranges
voice leading
voices
whole step

Practice Box 12.1

Identify the errors in the part-writing examples below. The errors will include things such as parallelism, incorrect doubling, incomplete chords, and figured-bass omissions. When you find an error, mark it with a circle or parallel lines and try to identify the reason the error occurred. These reasons may include incorrect changes of structure, omission of chord tones, improper voice leading, and incorrect chord progressions, among others.

Analysis Review

In many pieces of music that we analyze, the chords are not written vertically as they are in part writing. They are often spread out in some type of figuration, as in the piano pieces that follow. It is necessary to look at a group of notes that span one or more beats to discover the Roman numeral that should be used to analyze each chord. The rate of change of the chords is known as the *harmonic rhythm* of the piece. Usually, this rhythm is a consistent rate of change or pattern of changes. Understanding the harmonic rhythm of a piece can help you determine where and how often the chords change. Think about harmonic rhythm as you study the following examples.

There are many notes in the melody that do not form part of the harmonic structure of the composition. These are known as nonchord tones or nonharmonic tones. The harmonic structure of Example 12.1 comes primarily from the notes on the bass staff, and all chords are in root position. Determine the Roman numeral analysis of the piece, and circle any nonchord tones that you notice appearing in the upper voice.

Example 12.1.   R. Schumann, Kinderszenen, "Hansche-Mann," op. 15, no. 3, mm. 1–8

Track 12, 0:00

Example 12.2.   Mozart, Piano Sonata, K. 333, 2nd movement, mm. 5–6

Track 12, 0:20

Example 12.3.   *Mozart, Piano Sonata, K. 311, 2nd movement, mm. 1–8*

Track 12, 0:32

The following excerpt is from the ragtime music of the American composer Scott Joplin. There are a number of inverted chords, and in one place a minor iv chord is substituted for the diatonic major IV. The final chord in the next to last measure is a *secondary dominant,* a type of chord that will be studied in future chapters. (See page 347 for a "Looking Ahead" box on secondary dominant chords.)

Example 12.4.   *Scott Joplin, "The Entertainer," mm. 22–29*

Track 12, 1:03

AURAL SKILLS

Composition

Use the following blank staves to compose melodies. Your melodies should be four to eight measures long and use a variety of major and minor keys. Try to choose different time signatures for each of your melodies.

Duets

Each voice part of the duets below should be sung by a solo singer or a group of singers. Practice each part individually, then sing the two parts simultaneously as an ensemble. Use the staves in 5 and 6 to compose your own duets.

Rhythm

Practice the following rhythms. They may be practiced either as duets or as two-handed exercises, with the right hand tapping the top line and the left hand tapping the lower line.

Dictation

Identify the quality of the triads that you hear. All will be in root position.

1. major	minor	diminished	augmented
2. major	minor	diminished	augmented
3. major	minor	diminished	augmented
4. major	minor	diminished	augmented
5. major	minor	diminished	augmented
6. major	minor	diminished	augmented
7. major	minor	diminished	augmented
8. major	minor	diminished	augmented
9. major	minor	diminished	augmented
10. major	minor	diminished	augmented

Identify the quality of the triads that you hear. All inversions will be used.

1. major	minor
2. major	minor
3. major	minor
4. major	minor
5. major	minor
6. major	minor
7. major	minor
8. major	minor
9. major	minor
10. major	minor

Identify the quality of the triads that you hear. All inversions will be used.

1. minor	diminished
2. minor	diminished
3. minor	diminished
4. minor	diminished
5. minor	diminished
6. minor	diminished
7. minor	diminished
8. minor	diminished
9. minor	diminished
10. minor	diminished

Identify the quality of the triads that you hear. All inversions will be used.

1. major	minor	diminished
2. major	minor	diminished
3. major	minor	diminished
4. major	minor	diminished
5. major	minor	diminished
6. major	minor	diminished
7. major	minor	diminished
8. major	minor	diminished
9. major	minor	diminished
10. major	minor	diminished

Identify the quality of the triads that you hear. All inversions will be used.

1. major	minor	diminished	augmented
2. major	minor	diminished	augmented
3. major	minor	diminished	augmented
4. major	minor	diminished	augmented
5. major	minor	diminished	augmented
6. major	minor	diminished	augmented
7. major	minor	diminished	augmented
8. major	minor	diminished	augmented
9. major	minor	diminished	augmented
10. major	minor	diminished	augmented

Harmonic Dictation

You will hear chord progressions that are four chords in length. The bass line is given to you. Notate the soprano line and add a Roman numeral analysis. It may help to think of the soprano in terms of scale degrees or solfege syllables.

Now the soprano lines are given to you. Notate the bass lines that you hear and add a Roman numeral analysis.

KEYBOARD APPLICATIONS

Play the following progressions in close structure. Three keys are suggested for each exercise, but they can be transposed to all other keys if desired. It is often a good idea to learn these new progressions in C minor or A minor first, since those are the easiest keys.

1.   G minor
       B♭ minor
       F♯ minor

me	*me*	*me*	*fa*	*re*	*me*
i	III	VI	iv	V	i

2.   F minor
       B minor
       E♭ minor

do	*re*	*me*	*me*	*fa*	*re*	*do*
i	VII	III	VI	iv	V	i

chapter 13 The Cadential Six-Four Chord

THEORETICAL SKILLS

Cadential Six-Four Chords

At cadence points, it is common to find a specific chord inserted into the circle of fifths progression, just before the dominant triad. The chord that is typically used is a tonic triad in second inversion, often called the **cadential six-four chord**. We have already seen several pieces of music that have included the cadential six-four chord, such as the Brahms Waltz, op. 39, no. 3 (see Example 11.1), and the Mendelssohn *Venetian Boat Song*, op. 19, no. 6 (see Example 11.2).

The term *cadential* comes from the noun "cadence." A cadential six-four chord appears in a chord progression as shown in Figure 13.1, just prior to the dominant and tonic chords that form the cadence.

Figure 13.1.   Position of the cadential six-four chord

$$\text{I} \qquad \text{iii} \qquad \text{vi} \qquad \text{ii} \qquad \text{I}^6_4 \qquad \text{V} \qquad \text{I}$$
$$\text{optional}$$

The cadential six-four chord does not occur in all progressions. It can be considered an optional insertion into the traditional progression by fifths. It will only occur at an authentic cadence, either perfect or imperfect, or occasionally before a deceptive cadence. Often it occurs in a strong rhythmic position. It creates a very satisfying way to connect the supertonic or the subdominant chord to the dominant chord. Notice in Figure 13.2 how the tonic chord and the dominant chord have a single note in common. This note is the fifth of the tonic triad and the root of the dominant triad.

Figure 13.2.   Common tone between tonic six-four chord and dominant triad

C–E–G
G–B–D

Written another way, you will see that when the tonic chord is in second inversion, it has the same bass note as the dominant triad. (See Figure 13.3.) The common tone is doubled, and the upper voices of the six-four chord move stepwise downward to the corresponding notes of the dominant triad. In a sense, the tonic six-four chord can be seen as an embellishment, or ornamentation, of the dominant chord. These two chords have two voices in common, and because of the standard voice leading shown below, the remaining voices of the dominant triad are approached by stepwise movement.

Figure 13.3.   Common tones and voice leading between cadential six-four chord and dominant triad

E → D
C → B
G   G

It is this common tone that gives the cadential six-four chord its compelling aural quality. Any of the chords that typically precede the dominant chord may move to the I$^6_4$. The bass note of this chord will always be identical to the bass note of the subsequent chord, the dominant. The cadential six-four may occur in either major or minor keys.

When creating the cadential six-four in four-part harmony, the part writing will be handled in precisely the same manner as it is for a root position chord.

When creating a second-inversion chord in four-voice harmony, always double the bass.

This means you should choose open or close structure for a second-inversion chord, handling it just as if it were a root position chord. Remember that the first rule of part writing for root position chords is to double the bass. That goal is the same for all second-inversion chords. Figure 13.4 demonstrates proper doubling in the cadential six-four chord.

Figure 13.4. *Cadential six-four chord in four-part harmony*

D major: I   iii   vi   ii   I$^6_4$ V   I

In Figure 13.4, notice how the A is doubled in both the I$^6_4$ chord and the V chord. Here the doubled notes occur in the tenor and bass, but as shown in Figure 13.5, they can occur in the bass *plus* any other voice. The voices that contain the doubled notes in the six-four chord will also contain the doubled notes in the dominant chord. In other words, the dominant scale degree of the key should remain a common tone in two voices whenever a cadential six-four chord progression occurs. Add a Roman numeral analysis to these progressions and draw lines to indicate the common tones between the cadential six-four and dominant triads. Do the remaining voices move stepwise downward?

Figure 13.5. *Cadential six-four chord examples*

Here the common tones are in the bass and soprano voices.

Here the common tones are in the bass and alto voices.

Notice the characteristic bass line that is always present with a cadential six-four chord, *sol, sol, do.* This bass line will always be present with this chord progression. The repetition of the fifth scale degree may occur on the same pitch, or these notes may be separated by an octave.

Practice Box 13.1

Add inner voices and a Roman numeral analysis. All of these exercises contain cadential six-four chords. The bass voice should always be doubled.

Creating a Soprano Line

A skill the theory student must develop is the ability to create a soprano line to go with a given bass line or create a bass line for a given soprano. We have already created a few soprano lines, so now we can develop some concrete guidelines for doing this with all root position chord progressions, plus those that include cadential six-four chords. The result should be a good melody in accordance with the rules developed in chapter 6. The difference here is the necessity of following the parameters of harmony to match the given bass.

Figure 13.6 provides a sample bass line with which to work.

Figure 13.6.   *Bass line*

The procedure for creating a soprano line over a given bass should include the following steps:

1. Identify the key.

2. Identify the Roman numeral chord progression. If you see a bass line that moves *sol, sol, do* at a cadence, consider the possibility of using a cadential six-four chord.

3. Spell each chord above the staff. Each note of your soprano line must be a member of that chord.

4. Choose a starting pitch for the first chord. There will be three choices: the root, the third, and the fifth.

5. Identify the root movement between each chord. The choices will be root movement by fifth (fourth), second, or third. It is also possible to find a pair of repeated chords.

6. Root movement by fifth:
   a. If you start with a soprano note that is in both chords, keep it as a common tone.
   b. If you start with a soprano note that is *not* in both chords, move it to the nearest tone in the next chord.

7. Root movement by second:
   a. Generally you should move the soprano in contrary motion to the bass.
   b. If you write parallel motion between the bass and soprano, the soprano line should be the chordal third of each chord.

8. Root movement by third:
   a. If you start with a soprano note that is in both chords, keep it as a common tone.
   b. If you start with a soprano note that is *not* in both chords, move it to the nearest tone in the next chord.

9. Always keep in mind the principles that constitute a good melody, studied in chapter 6. These include:
   a. Using primarily conjunct motion
   b. Properly resolving the active scale degrees, such as the leading tone
   c. Following a leap with stepwise movement in the opposite direction

10. Always keep in mind the motion between voices that is created between your soprano and bass lines, including the following:
    a. Avoid parallel perfect fifths and octaves.
    b. Contrary and oblique motion are preferable to similar and parallel motion.
    c. Strive for independent voice leading for the two lines.

The beginning of the procedure is shown in Figure 13.7, with each chord spelled above the staff.

Figure 13.7.   Chord spellings for a given bass line

Each note of the melody must come from the spellings given above. Possible starting pitches for this melody are C, E, and G.

Here are some possible soprano lines that can be added to that bass line (Figure 13.8). There are many other possible soprano lines.

Figure 13.8.   Three possible soprano lines

These three soprano lines demonstrate all the possible starting pitches for the initial tonic triad, *do, mi,* and *sol.* If each soprano line is analyzed for its melodic characteristics, you should observe the following.

Melody no. 1:

a. Conjunct motion, using only steps and common tones

b. Contour moving upward from *sol* to *do*

c. *Ti* resolving to *do*

d. Independence of voice leading, with primarily contrary and oblique motion between voices, except for the similar motion between the last two chords

Melody no. 2:

a. Conjunct motion, using only steps and common tones

b. Contour moving downward from *mi* to *do*

c. *Re* resolving to *do*

d. Independence of voice leading, using only contrary and oblique motion between voices

Melody no. 3:

a. Leap countered by stepwise movement in the opposite direction

b. Contour beginning and ending on *do*

c. *Ti* resolving to *do*

d. Independence of voice leading, with primarily contrary and oblique motion between voices

Practice Box 13.2

Using the rules learned on page 212, add soprano lines to the following bass lines.

Harmonizing a Melodic Line

The process for creating a bass line for a given soprano is somewhat different. When you are given a bass line for a root position progression, you are also given the names of the chords. When you are given a soprano line, you must determine the most appropriate chords. Each note of a soprano line can be a member of three different triads. Table 19 categorizes each scale degree by the chords with which it can be harmonized.

Table 19.   *Possible Roman numerals for soprano scale degrees*

do	I	vi	IV
re	V	ii	vii°
mi	I	vi	iii
fa	IV	ii	vii°
sol	V	I	iii
la	vi	IV	ii
ti	V	vii°	iii

The first step in the procedure, as shown in Figure 13.9, is to spell all the possible chords that can be derived from each soprano note.

Figure 13.9.   *Spelling possible chords for a given soprano line*

Major key:	C E G (I)	C E G (I)	D F A (ii)	~~B D F (vii°)~~	C E G (I)
	F A C (IV)	F A C (IV)	G B D (V)	G B D (V)	~~F A C (IV)~~
	A C E (vi)	A C E (vi)	~~B D F (vii°)~~	E G B (iii)	A C E (vi)

Minor key:	A C E (i)	A C E (i)	D F A (iv)	E G♯ B (V)	A C E (i)
	C E G (III)	C E G (III)	G B D (VII)	G B D (VII)	~~C E G (III)~~
	F A C (VI)	F A C (VI)	~~B D F (ii°)~~	~~B D F (ii°)~~	F A C (VI)

For now, since we have not yet studied diminished triads, we will eliminate them from our list of possible chords. (They will be included after chords in first inversion have been studied.) Therefore, the chords spelled B–D–F have been struck through in the lists above. Other chords can logically be eliminated from the lists. The spelling of F–A–C, creating a IV chord in major keys, and C–E–G, creating a III chord in minor keys, cannot be used on the final chord of the progression, because no cadence can end on a mediant or subdominant triad. Likewise, E–G–B cannot be used on the next to last chord because no cadence uses a mediant triad as the next to last chord either. However, if we take into account that the key could also be A minor, another possible spelling for the next to last chord would be E–G♯–B.

The next step in the procedure is to create a Roman numeral chord progression that is correct according to the rules we have learned. The circle of fifths progression is the most common, but you may also use substitute chords, deceptive progressions and cadences, truncated progressions, and retrogressions. Figure 13.10 demonstrates some possible chord progressions that can be created for the soprano line above.

Figure 13.10.   *Possible chord progressions from a single soprano line*

	C major					A minor			
I	vi	ii	V	I	i	i	iv	V	i
I	iii	ii	V	I	i	i	IV	V	i
I	vi	ii	V	vi	i	III	iv	V	i
I	I	V	V	vi					

There are several other chord progressions that can be created for the soprano line above. Try creating another progression to add to the lists above. Then choose one of these progressions and add the bass line to the grand staff in Figure 13.9. Add inner voices and a Roman numeral analysis.

Practice Box 13.3

Using the rules learned above, add bass lines to the following soprano lines.

Practice Box 13.4

Use the staves below to compose chord progressions at least four chords in length that contain both a soprano and a bass line. Add a time signature and a key signature for each progression. It should be possible to write more than one progression on each grand staff. Use a variety of major and minor keys.

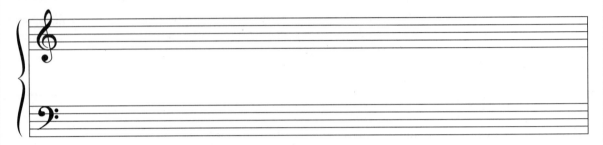

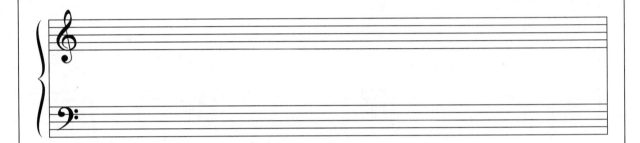

Music for Analysis

Provide a Roman numeral analysis for these examples, which may contain cadential six-four chords.

Example 13.1. *R. Schumann,* Phantasiestücke, *"Aufschwung," mm. 150–54*

Track 13, 0:00

Example 13.2. *J. C. Bach, Sonata, op. 5, no. 1, 1st movement, mm. 18–22*

Track 13, 0:15

Example 13.3. *Carl Philipp Emmanuel Bach,* Sonatina nuova, *mm. 30–33*

Track 13, 0:30

Notice the leap of an octave in the bass voice of Example 13.3. This is a common alternative to a repeated note between the tonic six-four chord and the dominant triad.

AURAL SKILLS

Melody

Sing the following melodies using solfege syllables or numbers.

Chords

Sing the following broken chord progressions in a variety of keys.

Sing each of the four lines of the following exercises separately, using solfege syllables or scale degree numbers. Pay close attention to the contour of the melody, including common tones, movement by step, and movement by leap. Then, sing as an ensemble in four-part harmony.

Rhythm

We have studied beat notes and divisions of the beat within both simple and compound meters. Now we will take up the study of subdivisions of the beat. A **subdivision** occurs when the note representing the division of the beat is itself divided into equal parts. Figure 13.11 shows an example in a simple meter.

Figure 13.11.   Subdivision example in $\frac{4}{4}$ time

A single quarter note, 2 eighth notes, or 4 sixteenth notes can represent the beat in $\frac{4}{4}$ time. Generally, all notes that occupy a single beat are beamed together as shown in Figure 13.12.

Figure 13.12.   Beaming of subdivisions

When counting subdivisions of the beat, there are two more notes per beat that must be spoken. The most typical words to use for subdivisions in simple meters are "one-e-and-a, two-e-and-a" and so on. In order to hear a steady pulse in your head, against which you can place all the rhythms that you encounter, you should count all of the subdivisions in every measure, even if not all of the beats contain subdivisions. This will create the most accurate thought process for counting any rhythm containing subdivisions. Clap and count the example in Figure 13.13.

Figure 13.13.   Example using subdivisions in common time

1 e & a   2 e & a   3 e & a 4 e   & a   1 e & a   2 e & a 3 e   & a   4 e & a

In common time, you will actually speak sixteen words in one measure. There are a variety of possible combinations of eighth notes and sixteenth notes within a single beat in common time. Figure 13.14 shows some examples using eighth and sixteenth notes in $\frac{4}{4}$ time.

Figure 13.14.   Example using subdivisions combining eighth and sixteenth notes

1 e   & a   1 e   & a   1 e &   a

If we include dotted eighth notes, there are even more possibilities. These are shown in Figure 13.15.

Figure 13.15.   Examples of subdivisions using dotted rhythms

1 e &   a   1   e & a

Practice Box 13.5

Clap and count the following rhythms.

Additional Rhythms

For extra practice, clap and count these exercises.

Error Detection

The following rhythms contain one or more errors. Listen and correct the errors that you see. Write the corrected version under the staff.

Harmonic Dictation

You will hear chord progressions that are five chords in length. You will hear each exercise several times. Notate the missing line first (soprano or bass), then listen for the quality of each chord. Using the outer voices and chord qualities you have notated, you should be able to determine a Roman numeral analysis for each progression. Some progressions may include a cadential six-four chord.

KEYBOARD APPLICATIONS

Play the following progressions in close structure. Three keys are suggested for each exercise, but they can be transposed to all other keys if desired.

1. F major
    Ab major
    D major

do	do	do	ti	do
I	IV	I$_4^6$	V	I

2. F# major
    Bb major
    E major

sol	fa	mi	re	do
I	ii	I$_4^6$	V	I

chapter 14 First-Inversion Chords

THEORETICAL SKILLS

Triads in First Inversion

First-inversion triads are occasionally used in place of their root position counterparts in a chord progression. For example, a V^6 can substitute for a V chord, and a ii^6 chord can substitute for a ii chord. A first-inversion triad is usually found in exactly the same place in a chord progression that its corresponding root position chord would be found.

First-inversion triads are often used to create a smoother bass line or to reposition the leaps in a bass line. For example, compare the two chord progressions in Figure 14.1. They are identical except for the bass line.

Figure 14.1. Comparison of ii and ii^6 in progressions

G M: I   ii   V   I   I ii^6 V   I

As you can see, the upper three voices are the same in both progressions. However, the use of the inversion in the second example makes smoother voice leading between the ii and V chords, which creates a somewhat different aural effect.

Remember that the figured-bass symbol for a first-inversion triad is 6. The number 6 is shorthand indicating the presence of both the sixth and the third above the bass. An easy way to figure out the root of a first-inversion triad is to remember that the root will be a third down from the given bass note (or if you prefer, a sixth up from the bass note). In the example above, the bass note C, with a figured-bass symbol of 6, implies that the root of the triad is down a third from C—in other words, A. In Example 14.1, the chords move according to the normal circle of fifths progression. A minor supertonic is used in place of the more standard diminished supertonic. Provide a Roman numeral analysis, paying particular attention to finding the first-inversion chords.

Example 14.1. Beethoven, Sonatina in F Minor, WoO 47/2, 3rd movement, mm. 18–25

Track 14, 0:00

Example 14.1.   *(continued)*

♪ Practice Box 14.1

Name the bass note for the V^6 chord in the following keys.

1. G major   _____   4. E minor   _____

2. B♭ major   _____   5. D♭ major   _____

3. F minor   _____   6. F♯ minor   _____

What scale degree forms the bass note for the V^6 chord in any key?   _____

Name the bass note for the ii^6 chord in the following keys.

7. E major   _____   10. E♭ minor   _____

8. B major   _____   11. A♭ major   _____

9. C minor   _____   12. C♯ minor   _____

What scale degree forms the bass note for the ii^6 chord in any key?   _____

In part writing, different rules of doubling apply to first-inversion chords. Remember that with root-position triads, the bass is virtually always doubled. In first-inversion chords, the soprano is doubled.

If possible, you should always double the soprano in first-inversion chords.

Doubling the soprano note requires a different thought process from that of doubling the bass. Close and open structures always achieve the goal of doubling the bass note of the chord. If the soprano and bass note are the same chord tone, then you may think of the chord either as having the bass note doubled or, in the case of a first-inversion chord, as having the soprano note doubled. Open and close structure are options for first-inversion triads, just as they are for root-position triads, provided that the soprano note and the bass note are the same letter name.

When part writing a first-inversion chord, you should first determine if the soprano note and bass notes are the same chord tone. If so, use open or close structure in the chord.

When open or close structure is used with first-inversion chords, all part-writing rules you have learned still apply. The surrounding chords must retain the same structure unless there is a repeated Roman numeral, a common tone in an inner voice, or a leap of a fourth or greater in the soprano, just as with root-position chords.

When doing the part writing, the first step in the process, as always, is to spell the chord. When you see a 6 in the figured bass, the bass note is not the root of the chord. Instead, it is the chordal third. Remember from chapter 5 that one of the quickest ways to identify the name of the root is to drop down a third on the staff and place an X to show the actual root of the chord. (See Figure 5.17.) The letter name represented by this X will be the first note that you write above the staff when you spell the chord. This procedure is demonstrated in Figure 14.2, with a D minor chord that has the same soprano and bass notes. Therefore, the soprano is already doubled in the bass voice, dictating either open or close structure for the chord.

Figure 14.2.   Part writing for a first-inversion chord with soprano doubled in the bass voice

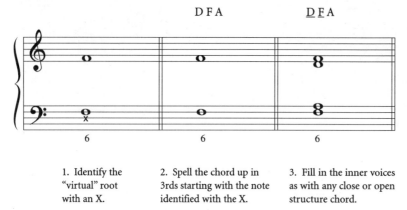

1. Identify the "virtual" root with an X.

2. Spell the chord up in 3rds starting with the note identified with the X.

3. Fill in the inner voices as with any close or open structure chord.

In the example above, the chord is in close position. The soprano note is relatively low, and there is only an octave between the soprano and bass voices, so that is the only choice. A higher soprano note might dictate open structure as a better option.

Practice Box 14.2

The following first-inversion chords all have the soprano doubled in the bass. Spell each chord. Choose open or close structure for each chord, depending upon the placement of the soprano note. Then add a Roman numeral analysis for each chord in the given key.

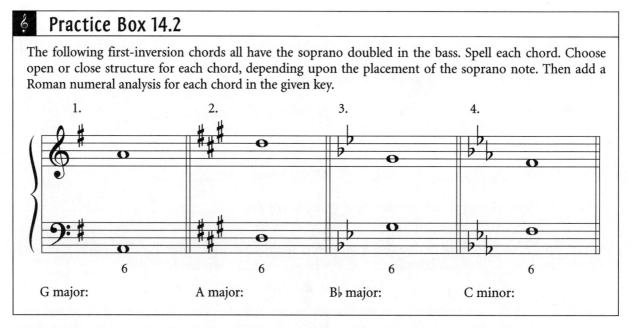

When first-inversion chords are placed in the context of a chord progression, remember that the structure of the first-inversion chord will be dictated by the prevailing structure of the chords around it. Determine the proper structure for the first-inversion chord in Figure 14.3. Spell the chord above the staff, add the inner voices, and provide the Roman numeral for the missing chord.

Figure 14.3.   Determining structure for a first-inversion chord

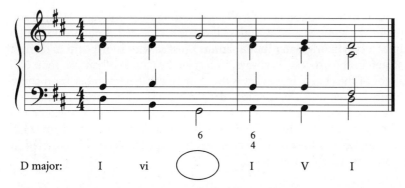

Because the soprano in the first-inversion chord in Figure 14.3 is already doubled, open and close are possible choices for structure. The prevailing structure for the remainder of the progression is close; therefore, close structure is the only choice for the chord.

Practice Box 14.3

Add inner voices and a Roman numeral analysis. Give special attention to the first-inversion chords.

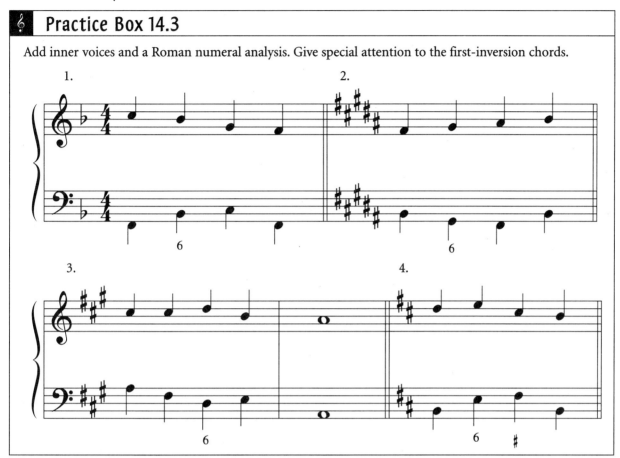

Neutral Structure

Thus far, we have only looked at first-inversion chords where the soprano and bass names are identical. Of course, it is also possible for the soprano and bass to have different letter names. Part writing for chords of this nature must be handled in another manner.

There is another type of structure that can be used with first-inversion chords, and it is known as neutral structure.* **Neutral structure** happens when the soprano note of a four-voice chord is doubled exactly one octave lower in the tenor voice. As with open and close structure, neutral structure is created by working from the top voice of the chord downward. However, the difference with neutral structure is that you must write in the tenor voice before the alto, since the tenor note is dictated by the soprano. The alto voice will take the remaining chord tone. Study the chords in Figure 14.4.

Figure 14.4.   Chords in neutral structure

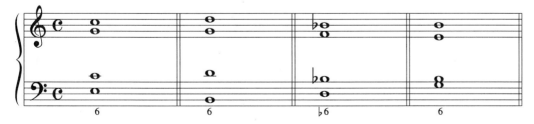

*The term "neutral structure" was also used by Dr. Stanley Shumway in his textbook *Harmony and Eartraining at the Keyboard,* 4th ed. (Dubuque, Iowa: W. C. Brown, 1984).

Each of the chords in Figure 14.4 is in neutral structure. If you check the distance in each chord between the soprano and tenor notes, you will see that it is always an octave. Now look at the distance between the soprano and alto notes. In each case, it is a fourth or a fifth. That will always be a characteristic of neutral structure.

Can you discover a relationship between the chord tone used in the soprano voice (root or fifth) and the distance between the soprano and alto voices? If the root is in the soprano, the distance between soprano and alto will be a fourth. If the chordal fifth is in the soprano, the distance will be a fifth.

If the soprano and the bass notes are the same, neutral structure cannot be used in part writing of first-inversion chords. Again, before determining the appropriate structure for a first-inversion chord, you must determine if the soprano and bass use the same letter name or different ones.

The procedure for constructing a neutral structure chord is shown in Figure 14.5. As usual, you should identify the name of the root by placing an X down a third from the bass note to show the virtual root of the chord. Then spell the chord above the staff. Underline the names of both the soprano note and the bass note. Then duplicate the soprano note down an octave in the tenor voice. One letter name of your chord will not yet have been underlined. That note will be placed in the alto voice.

Figure 14.5. *Constructing a chord in neutral structure*

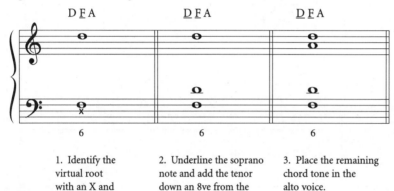

1. Identify the virtual root with an X and spell the chord.

2. Underline the soprano note and add the tenor down an 8ve from the soprano.

3. Place the remaining chord tone in the alto voice.

Practice Box 14.4

Spell each chord and complete the inner voices for each of these chords to create neutral structure. (Make sure that your chord spellings reflect the key signature.) Each is a first-inversion triad. Below the staff, name the quality of each triad.

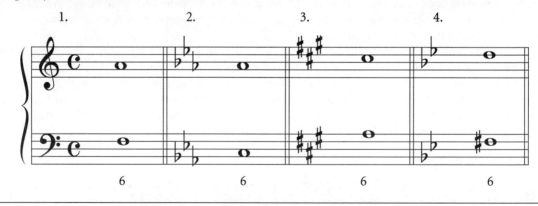

Neutral structure in part writing provides another opportunity for change of structure. When you see a 6 in the figured bass, the best choice is, if possible, to use neutral structure (unless the soprano and bass are doubled in the chord). Not only will it help you avoid parallel fifths and octaves, but neutral structure will also allow you to use either open or close structure in the chord that follows the inversion.

Either open or close structure may follow a neutral structure chord,
no matter which structure precedes it.

In Figure 14.6, a chord progression is shown with the chords labeled by their type of structure (*C, N,* or *O* written above the staff). Notice that the example begins in close structure. The third chord is in first inversion and uses neutral structure.

Figure 14.6. *Changing structure from close to open with an intervening neutral structure chord*

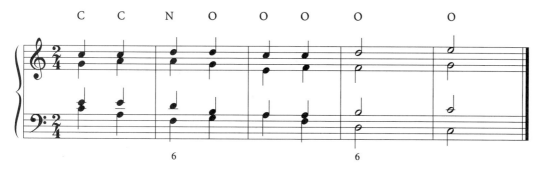

Following the neutral structure chord, the structure changes to open and remains open to the end. Why is neutral structure not used on the next to last chord, which is also a first inversion?

Practice Box 14.5

Choose open, close, or neutral structure and provide inner voices and a Roman numeral analysis for the following chords. It is possible to analyze all but one of these chords in more than one key.

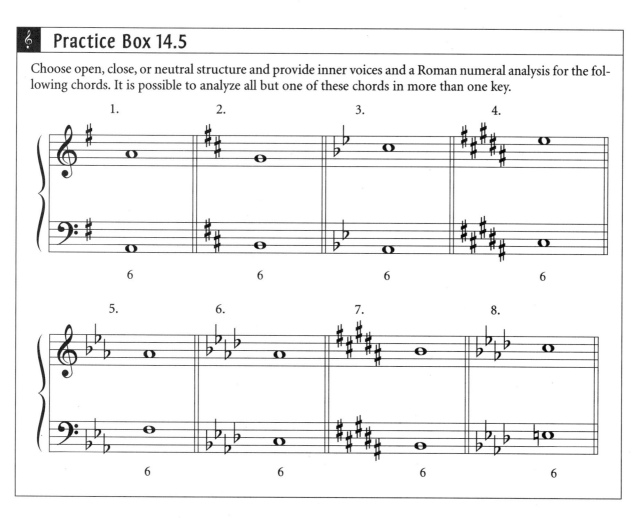

In Figure 14.7, the inner voices are not complete for the first-inversion chord. Provide the appropriate structure on the missing chord that will allow you to change from close to open. Add a Roman numeral analysis.

Figure 14.7.   Changing structure from close to open

Practice Box 14.6

Add inner voices and a Roman numeral analysis. There is an opportunity to change structure in each exercise.

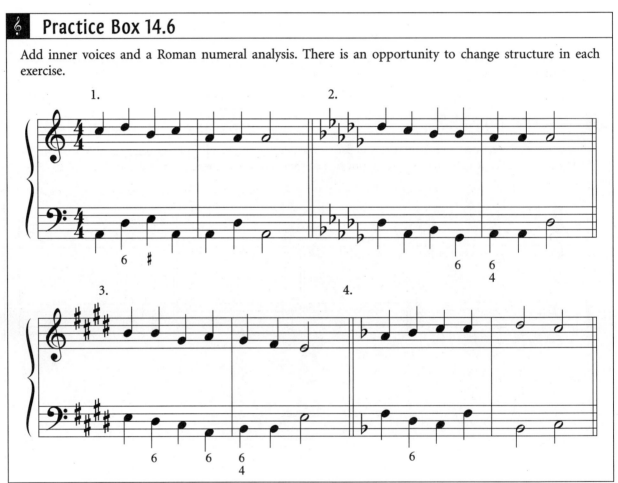

Other Structures

The soprano note of a first-inversion chord can be doubled in two more ways. These techniques are appropriate for special situations involving very high or very low soprano notes and do not appear in part writing as commonly as neutral structure.

If the soprano note is very high, generally above d^5 on the treble staff, the soprano note can be doubled in the alto voice, creating an octave between the soprano and alto. This type of structure will be referred to as "octave doubling" or "octave structure."

Conversely, if the soprano note is very low, generally f⁴ or below, the soprano can be doubled in the alto voice on exactly the same pitch. This structure will be referred to as "unison doubling" or "unison structure." Remember that unisons may be approached and resolved only by contrary or oblique motion. Just as with neutral structure, these doublings are only appropriate when the soprano and bass notes are different pitch classes. These two structures are shown in Figure 14.8. You should also be aware that adjacent voices are never separated by a distance greater than an octave in any four-voice harmonic structure.

Figure 14.8.   Octave structure and unison structure

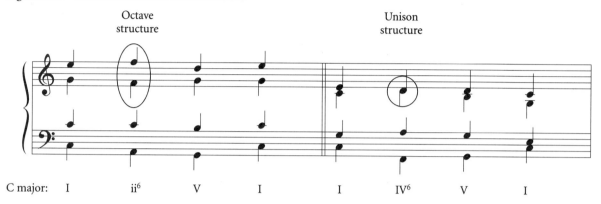

Here is a series of questions that you should ask yourself when confronted with a first-inversion triad. These questions will help you determine the proper structure and method of doubling.

Is the soprano already doubled in the bass voice?
> If yes: Use open or close structure.
> If no: See the next question.

Is the soprano located in the middle range of the treble staff?
> If yes: Use neutral structure.
> If no: See the next question.

Is the soprano extremely high on the treble staff?
> If yes: Double the soprano down an octave in the alto voice.
> If no: See the next question.

Is the soprano extremely low on the treble staff?
> If yes: Double the soprano and alto on exactly the same note.

Practice Box 14.7

Add inner voices and a Roman numeral analysis.

Music for Analysis

Provide a Roman numeral analysis of the following harmonies, paying particular attention to the first-inversion triads.

Example 14.2.   *Mozart, Piano Sonata, K. 284, 3rd movement, mm. 1–5*

Track 14, 0:22

Example 14.3.   *R. Schumann,* Album for the Young, *"Rundgesang," op. 68, no. 22, mm. 1–3*

Track 14, 0:37

Example 14.4.   *Chopin, Waltz, "Minute," op. 64, no. 1, mm. 5–9*

Track 14, 0:49

Example 14.5.   *George Frideric Handel,* Messiah, *"And the Glory of the Lord," mm. 11–17*

Track 14, 1:00

AURAL SKILLS

Melody

Sing the following melodies with solfege syllables or numbers.

Chords

Sing the following chord progressions, which contain inversions.

C major: I   V^6 I

E major: I   IV^6 V   I

F major: I   vi   ii^6 V   I

Sing each of the four lines of the following exercises separately, using solfege syllables or scale degree numbers. Pay close attention to the contour of the melody, including common tones, movement by step, and movement by leap. Then, sing as an ensemble in four-part harmony.

Rhythm

Practice the following rhythms.

Dictation

You will hear each rhythm several times. All rhythms will contain subdivisions of the beat. Notate these rhythms in the meters indicated.

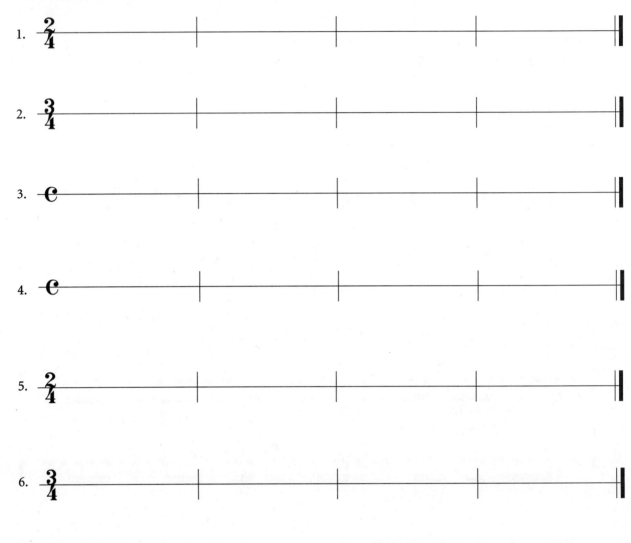

Harmonic Dictation

Notate the missing voice and Roman numeral analysis to the following bass lines. These progressions contain first-inversion chords.

Only the soprano and bass notes of the first chord are given to you. Notate the remaining soprano and bass notes, inner voices, and provide a Roman numeral analysis. All chords are in root position.

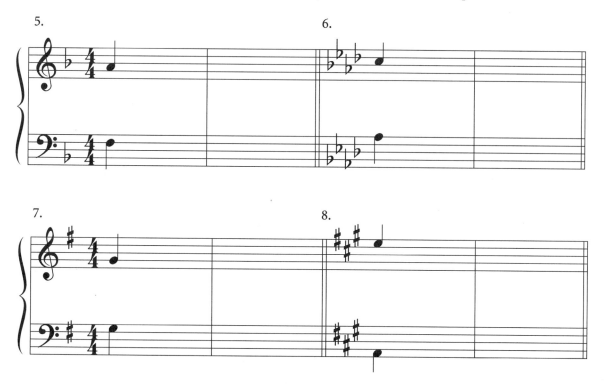

KEYBOARD APPLICATIONS

Play the following chord progressions. The first-inversion chord should be played in neutral structure in this exercise. In your right hand, you will span an octave.

1. E major
    F major
    D♭ major

In this exercise, the first inversion chord should be played in close structure because the soprano and bass are doubled.

2. D minor
    B minor
    C♯ minor

chapter 15 The Leading-Tone Triad and Other First-Inversion Practices

THEORETICAL SKILLS

The Leading-Tone Triad

The leading-tone triad is the only diatonic triad that has not yet been discussed. In a major key, the leading-tone triad is the only diminished triad to occur diatonically. In a minor key, the leading tone is created by raising the seventh scale degree a half step from the key signature; therefore, the leading-tone triad in minor will always contain an accidental.

As we saw when we studied the use of the subdominant triad, some diatonic chords can function as substitutes for others within a chord progression. This is true of the vii° chord. Its normal purpose within a chord progression is to serve as a substitute for the dominant triad. These spellings are presented in Figure 15.1 in the key of C major.

Figure 15.1. *Two common tones between the V and vii° triads in C major*

V   G–[B–D]
vii°   [B–D]–F

The dominant triad and the leading-tone triad have two notes in common. Because of this, and because of the fact that they both contain the leading-tone scale degree, the leading-tone triad is a legitimate substitute for the dominant triad in almost any chord progression. In fact, both of these chords can be considered dominant-type chords, since the function of the dominant is to move to the tonic. The primary difference between them is in the nature of the resolution of their roots. The root of the dominant chord is the fifth scale degree, so in order to resolve to the tonic, the root must move up a perfect fourth or down a perfect fifth. The root of the leading-tone triad is the seventh scale degree, so it will resolve up a half step to the tonic scale degree.

The leading-tone triad must be handled very carefully in part writing in order to avoid parallelism. Think about the normal doubling in root-position chords. The bass, or root, of the chord is doubled. If the leading-tone triad is presented in root position and the bass is doubled, two leading tones will be present in the chord. Each of those leading tones will have a tendency to resolve upward to the tonic scale degree. As shown in Figure 15.2, parallel octaves will result.

Figure 15.2. *Parallelism as a result of doubling the leading tone*

Here is an important part-writing rule:

The leading-tone scale degree should not be doubled in part writing.

239

This rule applies to both major and minor keys and affects the dominant triad and the leading-tone triad, both of which contain the leading-tone scale degree. There is a solid reason behind this rule. It prevents the parallelism that usually results when the leading tone is doubled.

Placing the leading-tone triad in first inversion will prevent the doubling of the bass, or root, of the triad. If the third of the leading-tone triad is in the bass voice, it is much easier to avoid parallelism. Notice that in Figure 15.3, the B in the leading-tone triad is in an inner voice and is not doubled. However, as is typical for first-inversion chords, the soprano has been doubled.

Figure 15.3.   Leading-tone triad in first inversion

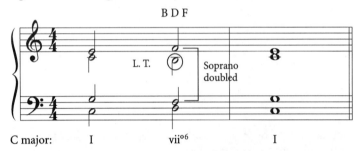

This brings us to another important principle of part writing.

Leading-tone triads should always be used in first inversion.

With this rule in mind, we can look at the three potential soprano notes that can be used with the vii°6 chord. Each chord tone, whether root, third, or fifth, appearing in the soprano of a leading-tone triad presents a special set of circumstances. As we see in the example above, when the chordal fifth is used in the soprano voice, neutral structure, unison structure, or octave structure will work fine. If the chordal third appears in the soprano, then the soprano and bass voices are already doubled; therefore, open or close structure should be used. This is demonstrated in Figure 15.4.

Figure 15.4.   Open and close structure in leading-tone triads

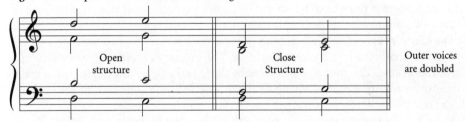

A problematic situation arises when the root of the chord, which is the leading tone, appears in the soprano of a vii°6 triad. The normal way to handle a first-inversion chord is to double the soprano. However, if the soprano is a leading tone, it cannot be doubled. In this case, a different voice must be doubled. The only other logical choice is to double the bass. Observe in Figure 15.5 how doubling the soprano creates a doubled leading tone. Irregular doubling, in this case doubling the bass voice, is a better choice.

Figure 15.5.   Irregular doubling to avoid doubled leading tone

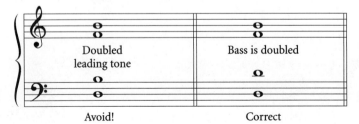

This situation creates irregular doubling in the first-inversion chord. The irregular doubling is necessary, however, to avoid the doubled leading tone. When you encounter a leading-tone triad in any part-writing exercise, you must observe the soprano note and remember to use irregular doubling if the leading tone appears in the soprano.

Practice Box 15.1

Add inner voices and a Roman numeral analysis. All exercises will include a vii°⁶.

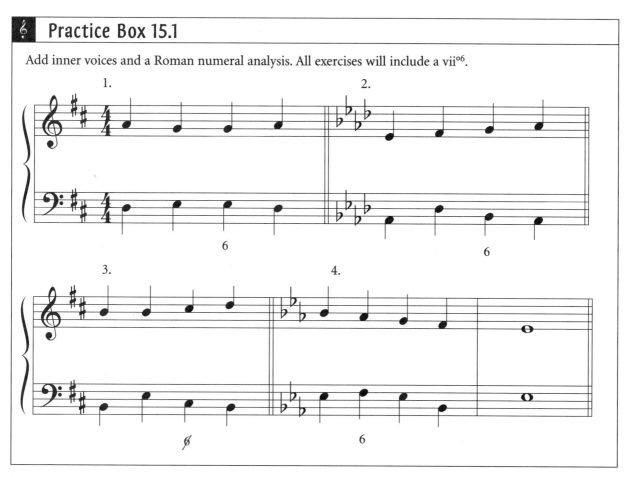

Imperfect Authentic Cadences

With the introduction of the leading-tone triad, we can now study some additional forms of the authentic cadence. As stated earlier, the vii°⁶ is a dominant-type chord; therefore, a cadence that moves from vii°⁶ to I (or i) is considered a type of authentic cadence.

To be considered a perfect authentic cadence, two conditions must be met. Both chords of the cadence must be in root position, and the tonic triad must have *do* in the soprano voice. Any other variety of dominant-to-tonic cadence is considered an imperfect authentic cadence. Figure 15.6 shows a variety of perfect and imperfect authentic cadences. The imperfect authentic cadences use first-inversion chords.

Figure 15.6.   Perfect and imperfect authentic cadences

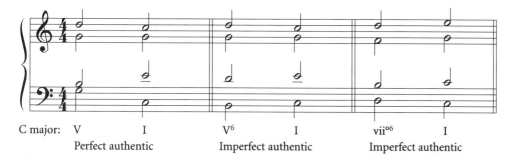

If either the V chord or the I chord is in an inversion, then the cadence is imperfect authentic. In addition, since the leading-tone triad is always found in inversion, consequently any authentic cadence involving the vii°⁶ chord is always imperfect authentic.

Practice Box 15.2

Name the following cadences. There are a total of seven cadences. Use the following abbreviations: perfect authentic cadence = PAC; imperfect authentic cadence = IAC. It is helpful to add a Roman numeral analysis before naming the cadences.

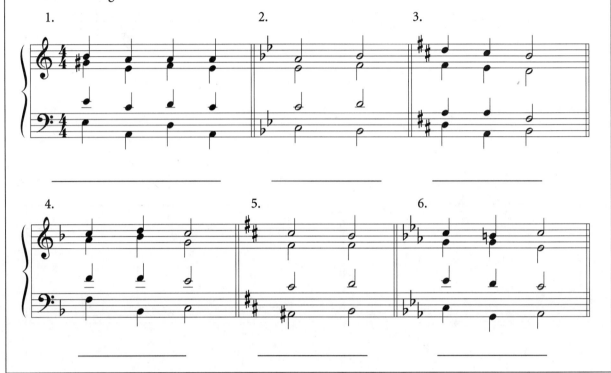

Consecutive First-Inversion Triads

If you encounter two first-inversion triads in succession in a part-writing exercise, you must be cautious in your treatment of them. If the same structure, such as neutral, is used for two successive first-inversion triads, it will almost always result in parallelism, as shown in Figure 15.7.

Figure 15.7. Parallelism resulting from use of the same structure on consecutive first-inversion triads

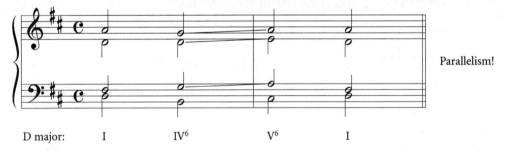

Parallelism!

D major: I   IV⁶   V⁶   I

The diagonal lines in the preceding example show the location of the parallel fifths and octaves. As you study the example above, you may realize that the stepwise movement in the same direction in both of the outer voices is causing the parallelism. As you have learned, in root-position chords, this would cause parallelism, just as it does here. However, look at Figure 15.8. You will see that the soprano voice is changed to move in contrary motion to the bass at the point of the consecutive first-inversion chords. Despite this change, the parallelism persists, although it has been reduced from three voices to two.

Figure 15.8.   *Parallelism persisting despite contrary motion*

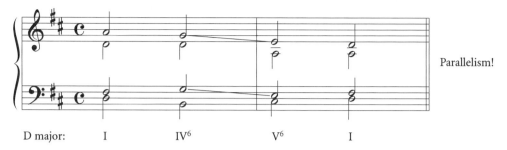

D major: I   IV⁶   V⁶   I

As you can see in the examples above, using neutral structure on consecutive first-inversion triads will usu-ally set the stage for parallel octaves. In order to avoid this, you must use something other than neutral structure on one of the first-inversion chords.

Do not use the same structure on both chords in a progression involving consecutive first-inversion triads.

This is easiest to accomplish if one of the chords already has the soprano voice doubled in the bass.

Study the first two measures of Figure 15.9 and you will notice that the final chord has the soprano already doubled in the bass voice. As you have learned, either close or open structure is an appropriate choice for this chord. Because of the relative lowness of the soprano note, close structure is the correct choice. The second chord is a vii°⁶ chord, with the chordal fifth in the soprano voice. Neutral structure will work for this chord, meaning that the consecutive first-inversion chords will use different structures. Open structure is chosen on the first chord for smooth voice leading. The inner voices are provided in the second half of Figure 15.9; study how the voice leading works to prevent parallelism.

Figure 15.9.   *Choosing structure for consecutive first-inversion triads*

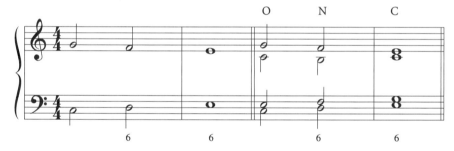

In addition, the use of the neutral structure chord has permitted us to change the structure from open on the first chord to close on the final chord.

If one of the soprano notes of the pair happens to be the leading tone, our choices will again be limited. Since the presence of the leading tone in the upper voice will prohibit the doubling of the soprano, open or close struc-ture must be the choice for that chord. This will allow the use of neutral structure on the other chord, as shown in Figure 15.10.

Figure 15.10.   *Choosing irregular doubling on leading-tone triad*

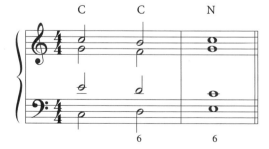

The most difficult situation arises when none of the previously-mentioned conditions are met, meaning that neither chord already has the soprano doubled in the bass and neither chord contains the leading tone in the soprano. Figure 15.11 shows a progression that has these characteristics. Neither chord has the soprano already doubled in the bass, ruling out close and open structure. The leading tone does not appear in the soprano, so irregular doubling is not automatically indicated in one chord.

Figure 15.11.   Soprano and bass lines without obvious choices for structure

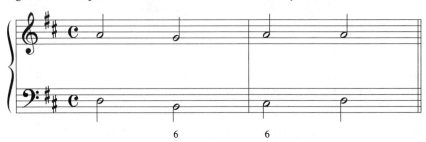

This is a scenario that typically occurs in the progression found above: IV^6–V^6. Figure 15.12 presents two possible solutions, both of which use a change of structure between the first-inversion chords. Notice that in these cases parallelism is created by either moving into or out of the first-inversion chord pair, not by moving between them. Label the types of structure used for each chord.

Figure 15.12.   Various choices for structure, resulting in parallelism

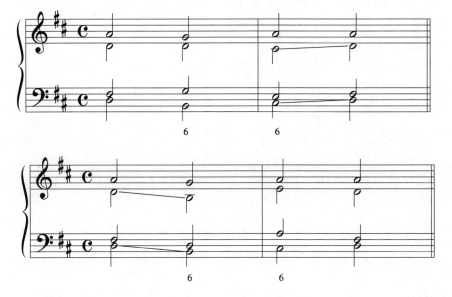

In this case, as shown in Figure 15.13, the solution comes from using a different method of doubling the soprano voice.

Figure 15.13.   Avoiding parallelism through the use of unison structure

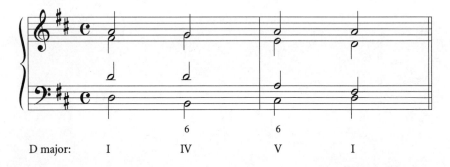

You may feel overwhelmed by the myriad of possibilities (and possible problems) that you will encounter when doing part writing with consecutive first-inversion triads. Simply think of the process as solving a puzzle. You may need to try multiple solutions before achieving a correct answer. You should carefully think through all the variables and be prepared to erase your answers several times on the path to a correct solution. The following three-step procedure may help you navigate through the options.

1. Look to see if the soprano is already doubled in the bass voice of one of the pair of chords. If so, use open or close on that chord and try neutral with the other chord (or any other structure that doubles the soprano).

2. Look to see if there is a leading tone in the soprano or bass of one chord.

    a. If the leading tone is in the soprano, use open or close structure on that chord and try neutral in the other chord (or any other structure that doubles the soprano).

    b. If the leading tone is in the bass, double the soprano in that chord. For the other chord, use the structure that creates the smoothest voice leading.

3. If the soprano is not doubled in the bass of either chord, choose neutral structure for one chord and try to double the soprano using octave or unison structure in the other. If that is not possible, use irregular doubling.

One final rule of part writing that will become increasingly important is this:

Never double an altered tone.

Altered tones are created by the use of accidentals that are not in the key signature. These tones must never be doubled in four-voice harmony. Typical altered tones would include the raised sixth and seventh scale degrees of the melodic minor scale. You already know that leading tones in minor keys are the most common altered tones found in tonal music. However, in the exercises that follow, you will also encounter the raised sixth scale degree used to create a major subdominant chord in minor. That altered sixth scale degree must not be doubled.

Interestingly enough, the practice of using the leading-tone triad in first inversion is not relegated only to part-writing exercises. In most music of the Common Practice Period, the leading-tone triad is usually found in first inversion. Here are some examples. Find the leading-tone triad in Example 15.1 and identify the inversion in which it is used.

Example 15.1. R. Schumann, Album for the Young, "Sizilianisch," op. 68, no. 11, mm. 1–4

Track 15, 0:00

Find the irregular doubling that is used in Example 15.2. Apart from the irregular doubling, what traditional rule of part writing is contravened in this Bach excerpt?

Example 15.2. J. S. Bach, Erhalt' uns, Herr, bei deinem Wort, mm. 1–2

Track 15, 0:15

Practice Box 15.3

Add inner voices and a Roman numeral analysis.

Music for Analysis

Provide a Roman numeral analysis for these excerpts. Each example will contain at least one leading-tone triad. Make sure that your analysis indicates the inversion of all triads.

Example 15.3.   Mozart, Piano Sonata, K. 280, 1st movement, mm. 131–38

Track 15, 0:30

Example 15.4.   Haydn, Piano Sonata no. 39, Hob. XVI/24, 2nd movement, mm. 1–5

Track 15, 0:54

AURAL SKILLS

Melody

Sing the following melodies using solfege or numbers.

Chords

Sing the following chord progressions, which contain diminished triads in first inversion.

C major: I   vii°6   I

C major: I   ii   vii°⁶   I

C minor: i⁶   iv   vii°⁶   i

F minor: i   VI   ii°⁶   V   i

Harmony

Sing the following progressions in four-part harmony. All progressions contain diminished triads.

Rhythm

Practice the following rhythms, which use subdivisions in a variety of simple meters. Before clapping the rhythms, identify the types of note that form the beat, the division of the beat, and the subdivision of the beat. It may be helpful to write in the counts.

Dictation

Notate the following melodies in rhythm. Each exercise contains subdivisions of the beat.

Harmonic Dictation

Notate the following progressions in four-voice harmony. You will provide the soprano line, bass line, and Roman numeral progression. All exercises will contain diminished triads.

KEYBOARD APPLICATIONS

Play the following chord progressions. When you encounter a pair of first-inversion chords, pay close attention to which one of the pair should be played in neutral structure. When you play neutral chords, your right hand will span an octave.

1. E major   G♭ major   C♯ major

2. G major   D♭ major   B major

3. B minor   F♯ minor   A♭ minor

chapter 16 Additional Six-Four Chords

THEORETICAL SKILLS

Second-Inversion Chords

Thus far, the only use of the second-inversion chord that has been studied is that of the cadential six-four chord, which is a tonic chord in second inversion that is found directly preceding an authentic cadence. Second-inversion chords can be used in three other typical manners. Here is a complete list of the types of six-four chords:

1. cadential six-four chord
2. passing six-four chord
3. arpeggiated six-four chord
4. pedal six-four chord

In part writing, each of these is handled in exactly the same manner. The chordal fifth always appears in the bass voice, and the bass voice is always doubled. This means that open and close structure are the only appropriate structures for handling any second-inversion chord, no matter what its type or classification.

Passing Six-Four Chords

The term "passing" refers to any stepwise motion that connects two chords or two melodic notes separated by the interval of a third. In the case of a **passing six-four chord,** the stepwise motion will be found in the bass voice. The passing six-four chord often connects two diatonic chords with the same Roman numeral but in different inversions, as seen in Figure 16.1.

Figure 16.1. *The passing six-four chord*

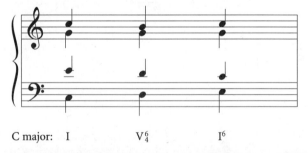

C major: I   V$^6_4$ I^6

Several characteristics of voice leading will usually appear with the passing six-four chord. All can be observed in the example above. As the bass voice moves stepwise, one other voice will also move stepwise, but in the opposite direction. In this example, that movement is in the tenor voice. In addition, one of the voices will maintain a common tone throughout the three-chord progression. This is found in the alto voice in this example.

The most commonly used passing six-four chord is the V$^6_4$, and it is typically used to connect different inversions of the tonic chord, as seen in Example 16.1. Another common progression involving a passing six-four chord is IV–I$^6_4$–IV^6.

Example 16.1. *Beethoven, Piano Sonata, op. 2, no. 3, 3rd movement, mm. 66–68*

A minor: i   V$_4^6$ i^6

Practice Box 16.1

Add inner voices and a Roman numeral analysis. These examples contain passing six-four chords.

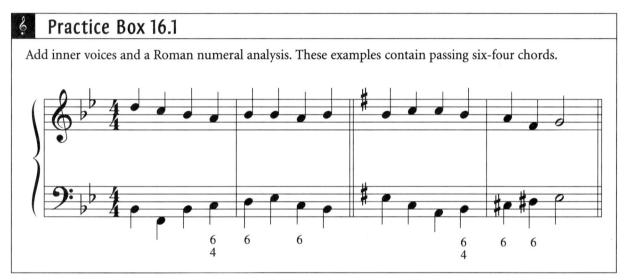

Pedal Six-Four Chords

The term "pedal" comes from organ terminology and refers to a technique found in many examples from organ literature. The organist sustains a single note on the pedal board while the hands play a variety of chord changes on the organ manuals. In any kind of music, a pedal tone is an unchanging bass note that is held during a number of chord changes.

The **pedal six-four chord** will always have a bass note in common with the chords that surround it. It can exist in many different chord progressions, but the most common is a plagal progression or plagal extension surrounded by root-position tonic triads. In this case, the bass note, which is the tonic scale degree, does not move.

There are several important characteristics of the voice leading in a pedal six-four progression, all shown in Figure 16.2. Notice that the process of doubling the bass in each chord results in the same octave notes being present in each chord (in this case, they are Cs). The other voices in the texture move stepwise in the same direction, resulting in a neighbor-tone figure that leaves and returns to the same pitch.

Figure 16.2. *The pedal six-four chord*

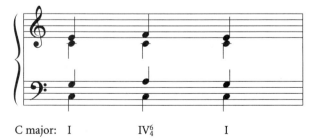

C major: I   IV$_4^6$ I

Example 16.2 shows a pedal six-four chord from the music of J. S. Bach.

Example 16.2.   J. S. Bach, Partita V in G Major, Praeambulum, mm. 1–4

Track 16, 0:15

Practice Box 16.2

Add inner voices and a Roman numeral analysis. Add a soprano line in the second exercise. These examples contain pedal six-four chords.

Arpeggiated Six-Four Chords

The word "arpeggio" means a broken chord that is spread apart, with the notes sounding one after the other instead of simultaneously. In the case of an **arpeggiated six-four chord,** it is the bass line that is arpeggiated. This type of chord occurs in a series of repeated chords, where a single triad is heard in more than one of its inversions. The most common appearance of the arpeggiated six-four chord includes all of its inversions—root position, first inversion, and second inversion—although not necessarily in that order. Figure 16.3 demonstrates an arpeggiated six-four chord.

Figure 16.3.   The arpeggiated six-four chord

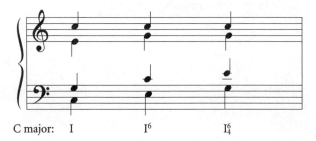

C major: I   I⁶   I⁶₄

An arpeggiated six-four chord may be used with any Roman numeral. It is far more common to find the arpeggiated six-four chord in keyboard and instrumental music than in chorale-style harmony, although its use in this style is demonstrated above.

Find the arpeggiated six-four chord in Example 16.3.

Example 16.3.   J. C. F. Bach, Menuet, mm. 1–2

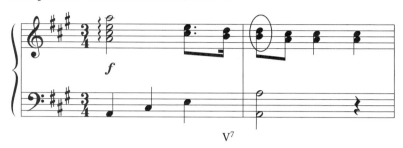

The arpeggiated six-four chord in the example above actually serves two purposes. Can you determine the other function of the chord in this context?

🎼 Practice Box 16.3

Add inner voices and a Roman numeral analysis. Add a soprano line where indicated. These examples contain arpeggiated six-four chords.

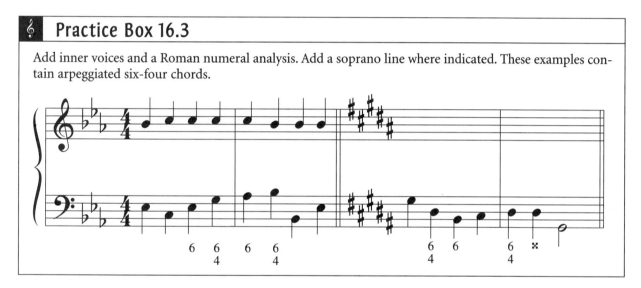

Additional Uses for Cadential Six-Four Chords

We have already studied cadential six-four chords in part writing and some musical examples. It is pertinent now while we are discussing all the types of six-four chords to look at one additional use of the cadential six-four chord.

One of the most distinctive uses of the cadential six-four chord is found in the solo concertos written during the classical and romantic periods of music history. The concerto is a musical form in which a soloist plays with an orchestra or other ensemble, with each playing alternately alone and in combination with the other. In this form, the solo instrument, often a piano or violin, plays a lengthy virtuosic solo near the end of the first movement of the concerto. This solo is called a **cadenza.** The beginning of the cadenza is usually signaled by a tonic six-four chord held by the orchestra. (This chord usually has a *fermata* or "hold" symbol over it. The symbol looks like this: ⌢.) An example of a cadenza from a Mozart flute concerto is presented in Example 16.4.

The soloist is free to play the cadenza with personalized expressiveness, and all or part of the cadenza may be improvised. The end of the cadenza is usually signaled by a trill—a rapid alternation between two pitches a step apart. This trill, which is written on the second scale degree (trilling with the note above it), plus the chord progression that precedes it, will always imply the presence of the dominant chord. The orchestra will join in with the tonic triad at the end of the trill. Therefore, the cadenza can be seen as an extended elaboration of the cadential six-four formula that we have studied (I_4^6–V–I).

Track 16, 0:37

Example 16.4.   *Mozart, Flute Concerto in D Major, K. 314, 1st movement, mm 174 ff. Cadenza by J. Donjon*

The entire cadenza is not printed in the example above. In the flute part, the symbol ∿ is used to represent the omission of several measures of the cadenza. The audio CD contains the entire cadenza.

The orchestra score is presented in this excerpt as a *piano reduction,* which means that all the instrumental parts have been condensed to a grand staff in a form playable at the piano. When the orchestra enters again after the cadenza, what chord progression is used? Does it involve a six-four chord?

Practice Box 16.4

Add inner voices and a Roman numeral analysis. A variety of types of six-four chords are used in exercises. Identify each six-four chord by its type.

Music for Analysis

Provide a Roman numeral analysis. Each excerpt contains at least one second inversion chord. Find and label them by type.

Example 16.5.   *R. Schumann,* Album for the Young, *"Wild Rider," op. 68, no. 8, mm. 1–4*

Track 16, 1:51

Example 16.6.   *Mozart, Sonata for Violin and Piano, K. 306, 2nd movement, mm. 10–13*

Track 16, 2:03

Example 16.7.   *C. Schumann, Prelude in D Minor, op. 16, no. 3, mm. 1–3*

Track 16, 2:21

Example 16.8.   R. Schumann, Faschingsschwank aus Wien, *1st movement, mm. 253–62*

Track 16, 2:33

In the next example, the key signature does not match the actual key of the excerpt. Although there is an E♭ in the key signature, it is consistently changed to E♮. Take that fact into consideration when you choose the key in which to analyze these measures.

Example 16.9.   J. C. Bach, Sonata, op. 5, no. 1, *1st movement, mm. 17–22*

Track 16, 2:53

AURAL SKILLS

Chords

Sing the following chord progressions, which contain second-inversion chord outlines.

1. B major: I   V$^6_4$ I   V^6 I

2. E♭ major: I   IV   I   V   I

3. F major: I   I$^6_4$ I^6 V   I

4. E minor: i   i$^6_4$ i^6 V   i

Harmony

Sing the following exercises in four-voice harmony.

Rhythm

You should remember that in a compound meter, the beat note is always a dotted note, and it divides into three equal parts. However, just as in simple meters, subdivisions of the beat occur when the note representing the division of the beat is divided into two equal parts. Figure 16.4 shows that there are six subdivisions in each beat in a compound meter.

Figure 16.4.   Divisions and subdivisions of the beat in ⁶⁄₈ time

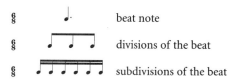

A dotted quarter note, 3 eighth notes, or 6 sixteenth notes can represent the beat in ⁶⁄₈ time. Just as in simple meters, all the notes that occupy a single beat are beamed together.

The words used for counting subdivisions in compound meters are different than those used for simple meters. Although there are several counting systems possible for compound subdivisions, the one that will be adopted here is "one-ta-la-ta-li-ta, two-ta-la-ta-li-ta," and so on. Remember that the words used for counting compound divisions were "one-la-li, two-la-li." When counting subdivisions, these same words are used, with the syllable "ta" inserted for every other note. Clap and count the rhythm in Figure 16.5. In ⁶⁄₈ time, you will speak twelve syllables in one measure.

Figure 16.5.   Subdivisions of the beat in ⁶⁄₈ time

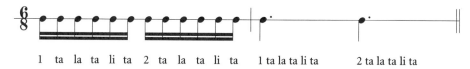

Figure 16.6 presents some of the possible combinations of eighth notes and sixteenth notes within a single beat in ⁶⁄₈ time:

Figure 16.6.   Rhythmic combinations in ⁶⁄₈ time

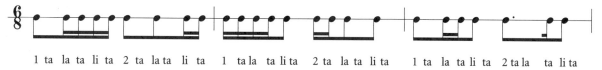

It is possible to use a dotted eighth note in ⁶⁄₈ time, but the rhythm that would be represented by the dotted note is more clearly expressed with an eighth note tied to a sixteenth note. Figure 16.7 shows both versions of this rhythm.

Figure 16.7.   Dotted rhythms in ⁶⁄₈ time

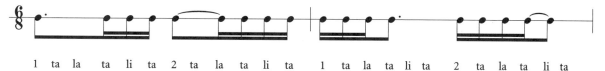

Practice Box 16.5

Clap and count the following rhythms.

Additional Rhythms

Practice these additional rhythms.

Dictation

Listen carefully to the following examples in four-part harmony. Each example contains one of the four types of six-four chords. Circle the type heard in each example. (None of the examples contains more than one six-four chord.)

1. cadential   passing   pedal   arpeggiated

2. cadential   passing   pedal   arpeggiated

3. cadential   passing   pedal   arpeggiated

4. cadential   passing   pedal   arpeggiated

5. cadential   passing   pedal   arpeggiated

Notate the rhythms that you hear. There will be subdivisions of the beat.

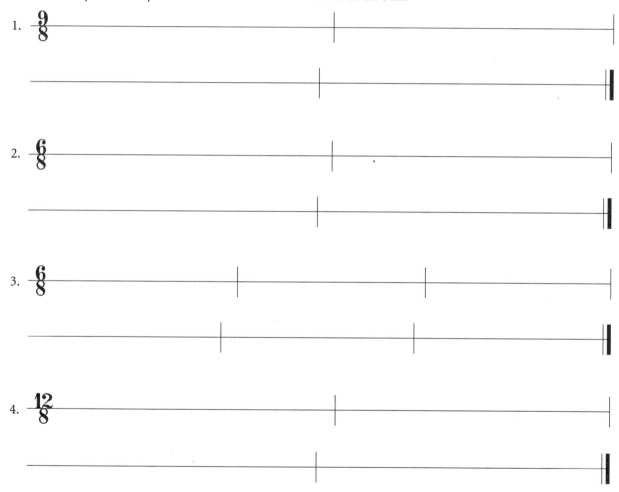

Error Detection

You will hear a rhythm that differs in some way from the examples notated below. Identify the errors and above each staff notate the correct rhythm that you have heard.

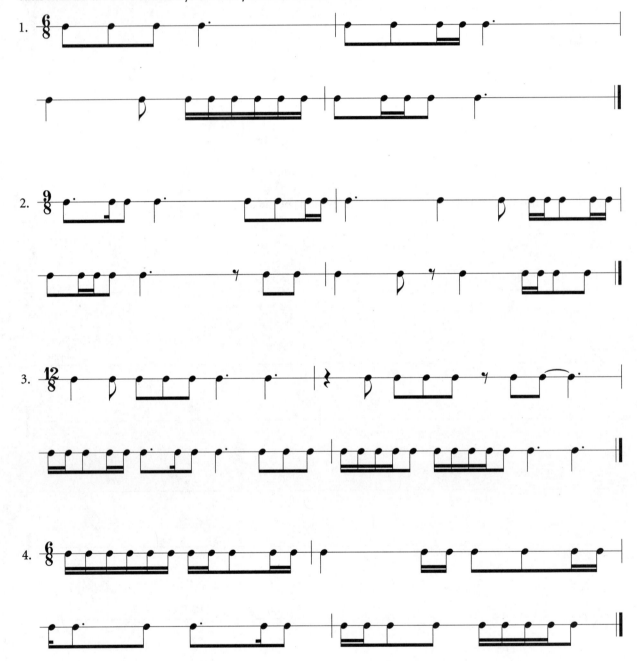

Harmonic Dictation

Notate the following exercises in four-voice harmony and add a Roman numeral analysis. Each exercise will contain one of the four types of second-inversion chords.

KEYBOARD APPLICATIONS

Play the following chord progressions. Remember to double the bass in all second-inversion chords. Name the type of six-four chord used in each exercise.

1.   G major
     B♭ major
     D♭ major

2.   A minor
     G♯ minor
     B♭ minor

3.   E♭ major
     F major
     A major

chapter 17 Introduction to Simple Non-Harmonic Tones

Non-Harmonic Tones

After analyzing the chordal structure of most compositions, you have already seen that there are often many notes that cannot be accounted for within the Roman numeral analysis. Any note of a composition that is not part of the underlying chord is called a **non-harmonic tone.** Virtually every composition contains non-harmonic tones. These are often referred to as ornaments or embellishments. Although they do not alter the Roman numeral analysis, they provide interest or decoration to the chordal backbone of a composition.

Non-harmonic tones most often appear as the middle note of a three-note pattern (or occasionally as the middle two notes of a four-note pattern). The simplest way to see non-harmonic tones in action is to think of a major scale harmonized with the tonic triad. In Figure 17.1, the circled notes are the non-harmonic tones. They are not part of the chord that provides the prevailing harmony.

Figure 17.1. Non-harmonic tones in the C major scale

C major: I   I

It is not possible to find, analyze, or understand non-harmonic tones in a composition without the context of its harmonic analysis. It is impossible to determine which notes are non-chord tones until you know which notes of the piece are a part of the harmonic structure. Therefore, the harmony of a piece must be studied before the non-harmonic tones can be analyzed.

There are nine distinct types of non-harmonic tones that will be studied in the next few chapters. They are listed in Table 20 for future reference.

Table 20. Non-harmonic tones

Non-harmonic tone	Abbreviation
Passing tone	PT
Neighbor tone	NT
Changing tone	CT
Appoggiatura	App
Escape tone	ET
Pedal tone	Ped
Suspension	Sus or Susp
Retardation	Ret
Anticipation	Ant

Each of these non-harmonic tones has a distinct pattern and manner of use. The method of showing non-harmonic tones in an analysis is to circle the notes that are not part of the chord and label them with an abbreviation. The abbreviations are listed in Table 20 next to the name of each type of non-chord tone. In addition, any types of non-harmonic tones that have not yet been studied will be labeled in the scores as NHT.

Passing Tones

A **passing tone** is used to connect two chord tones that are a third apart. Occasionally a pair of passing tones is used to connect chord tones that are a fourth apart. We already saw this kind of function when we studied the passing six-four chord.

A passing tone must occur in the middle of a group of notes that are all moving stepwise in the same direction. If there is a change of direction within the group, the non-harmonic tone cannot be analyzed as a passing tone. This stepwise movement is demonstrated on two staff lines in Figure 17.2.

Figure 17.2.   Approach and resolution of passing tones

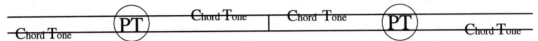

The diagram shows staff lines. The passing tones are in the center of the three-note groups, and all motion within each three-note group is stepwise in the same direction.

Passing tones may occur in any voice of a composition, including the bass voice. Here are some examples of passing tones in four-voice harmony. Before you can analyze the non-harmonic tones in any example, you must first determine the underlying harmony. Add a Roman numeral analysis to each of these examples and then label the passing tones. The chord tones that surround any non-harmonic tone do not necessarily have to be part of the same chord. For example, the second passing tone below is preceded by an F in the alto voice. The F is part of the subdominant chord, and it is followed by a D in the same voice, which is part of the dominant chord.

Figure 17.3.   Passing tones

Try writing the figured-bass symbols beneath each passing tone of the examples above. The first one is done for you. Horizontal numbers in figured bass represent the voice-leading movement of a specific part. Therefore, in the first example above, the 8 is included prior to the 7 to show that they occur in the same voice and that the 8 is moving to the 7. Notice that the 8-7 pattern continues to move downward in the same voice. This is always the proper voice leading when an 8-7 pattern appears in the figured bass.

Find the passing tones in Example 17.1. First provide a Roman numeral analysis. Be sure to determine if there are any seventh chords present, because that will affect the nature of your analysis. Circle and label all passing tones. The indication NHT in the example below indicates a type of non-harmonic tone that has not yet been studied.

Example 17.1. *Mozart, Fifth Viennese Sonatina, 2nd movement (Minuetto), mm. 70–74*

Track 17, 0:00

F major: I

In Example 17.2, the key indicated by the notes does not match the key signature. Since A♮ is used consistently, carefully determine the key of this excerpt before you begin your analysis.

Example 17.2. *Beethoven, Piano Sonata, op. 81a, "Les adieux," 2nd movement, mm. 77–81*

Track 17, 0:18

You may have noticed that almost all of the passing tones that we have analyzed thus far have been in a rhythmically weak position. That is very typical of passing tones. However, it is possible to place a passing tone on a strong beat, often a first beat in a measure. In such a case, it is called an "accented passing tone" (APT).

Example 17.3, from the music of Mozart, was also included in chapter 11 (Example 11.9) for harmonic study. Now analyze the non-harmonic tones. You will find an accented passing tone at the beginning of two measures.

Example 17.3.   *Mozart, Piano Sonata , K. 333, 1st movement, mm. 1–4*

Track 17, 0:36

B♭ major: (I)   I

Neighbor Tones

The neighbor-tone figure is very similar to the passing-tone pattern, except that it involves a change of direction. The **neighbor tone** always returns to the pitch that begins the three-note pattern, as seen in Figure 17.4.

Figure 17.4.   *Approach and resolution of neighbor tones*

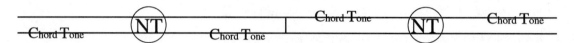

Notice in the preceding diagram that the neighbor-tone figure involves only stepwise movement. Neighbor tones always occur as the middle of a three-note figure, and the first and third notes of the figure must be the same. The pattern can move to an upper neighbor, as seen in the first measure above, or to a lower neighbor, as in the second example. If you desire, this type of non-harmonic tone can be labeled with its direction, as a UNT (upper neighbor tone) or LNT (lower neighbor tone).

Neighbor tones are demonstrated in four-voice harmony in Figure 17.5. Find the neighbor tones and label them (the first one is done for you). Another type of non-harmonic tone is also used in these measures. Can you find it? Add figured bass symbols to represent the non-harmonic tones.

Figure 17.5.   *Neighbor tones*

Find the neighbor tones in Example 17.4. Some of the triads may be incomplete.

Example 17.4.   Beethoven, Piano Sonata, op. 79, 3rd movement, mm. 1–8

Track 17, 0:53

Both passing tones and neighbor tones may occur in any voice of a composition. These figures may be represented by a variety of figured-bass symbols, including 3-2, 5-6, 6-5, and 8-7. The latter combination is often used to create a dominant seventh chord (a dominant triad plus a note that forms a seventh above the bass) at an authentic cadence. The 8-7 pattern must resolve downward; in other words, it must continue to move downward in that voice.

The important thing to learn about these figured-bass symbols is that a pair of numbers written horizontally always represents consecutive notes in the same voice. In other words, if you see a 6-5 combination, you cannot put the sixth above the bass in the alto and the fifth in the soprano. They both must occur in a single voice of the texture. Often in part writing, the pair of numbers will indicate a division of the beat, meaning that the rhythm of one voice will be different from the others in the texture. You may not be able to determine whether the numbers represent a passing tone or a neighbor tone until after you have completed the part writing. Since the 8-7 figure has a strong downward tendency through its association with seventh chords, it should always be used as a passing tone.

Practice Box 17.1

Add the non-harmonic tones that are indicated by the figured bass. Add inner voices and a Roman numeral analysis. Circle and label all non-harmonic tones, even if they appear in a voice that is given to you.

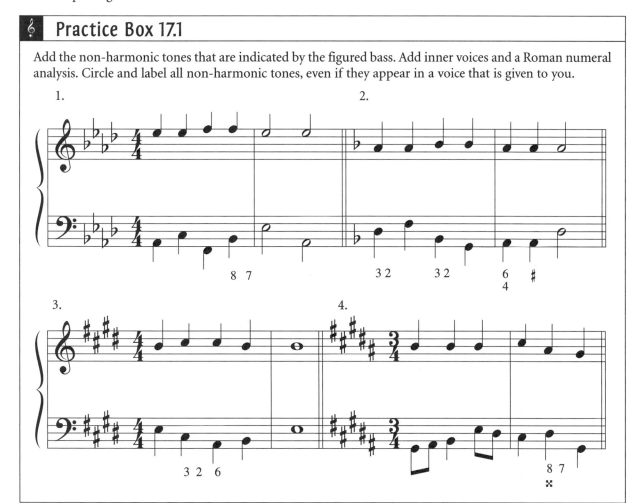

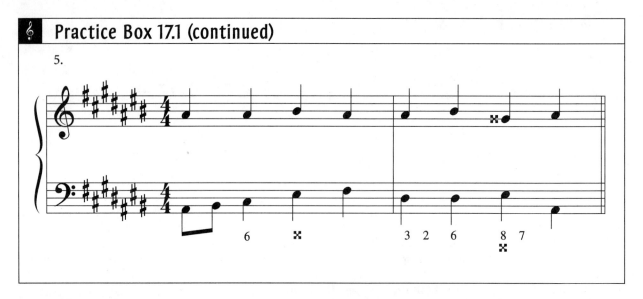

Changing Tones

The changing-tone figure can be compared to an unresolved upper- and lower-neighbor figure combined. The **changing-tone** involves a pattern of four notes, with the two in the center both being non-harmonic. A leap between the two center notes is the chief characteristic of this non-harmonic pattern. Figure 17.6 demonstrates this four-note pattern.

Figure 17.6.   Approach and resolution of changing tones

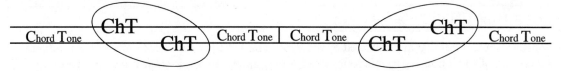

You will notice that the changing tone can start with movement in either direction from the chord tone. This figure can occur in any voice but will be found rarely in the bass. In Figure 17.7 below, there are several changing tones, but also one other type of non-harmonic tone. Can you find and name it?

Figure 17.7.   Changing tones

In a sense, the changing tone is a double-neighbor-tone figure. The first note of the neighbor-tone pair is not resolved, but instead leaps to the neighbor on the opposite side of the chord tone.

Finally, one important aspect of non-harmonic tones and voice leading involves the consideration of parallelism. It is not acceptable to insert a non-harmonic tone of any kind to attempt to avoid or obscure parallel perfect intervals. If incorrect parallelism is present between chord tones, the presence of a non-harmonic cannot disguise it.

Practice Box 17.2

Add inner voices and a Roman numeral analysis. Circle and label all non-harmonic tones. In this example, the dashes in the figured bass indicate the rhythm as well as the pitch. A variety of non-harmonic tones will be used.

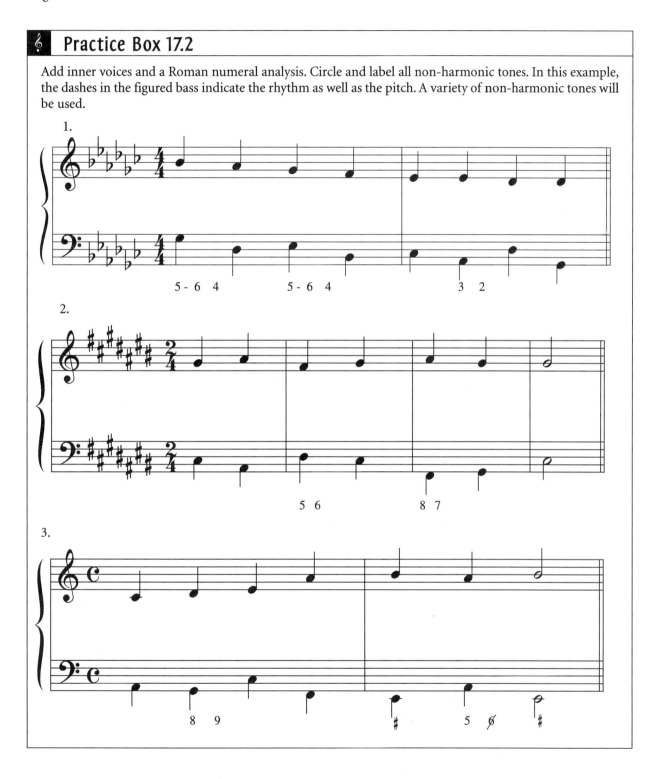

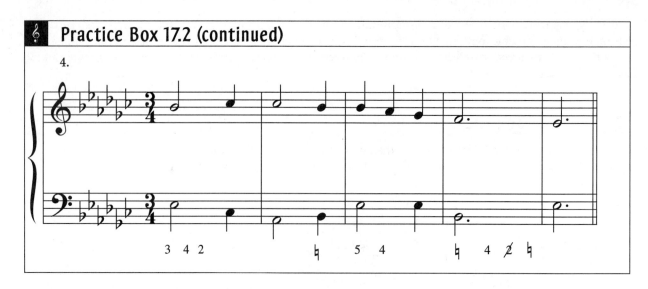

Music for Analysis

Provide a Roman numeral analysis for each example. Find and label all the passing, neighbor, and changing tones.

Example 17.5.   Mozart, Piano Sonata, K. 576, 1st movement, mm. 1–4

Track 17, 1:10

Example 17.6.   Mozart, Piano Sonata, K. 332, 3rd movement, mm. 1–6

Track 17, 1:22

Example 17.7.   Beethoven, Sonatina in C, WoO 51, 1st movement, mm. 9–13

Track 17, 1:37

Example 17.8.   Gioacchino Rossini, The Barber of Seville, *"Largo al factotum,"* mm. 1–15

Track 17, 1:56

AURAL SKILLS

Melody

Using the staves provided below, compose melodies above the chord progressions provided. Your melodies should include a variety of passing and neighbor tones. The melodies you compose will be used for sight-singing exercises in class.

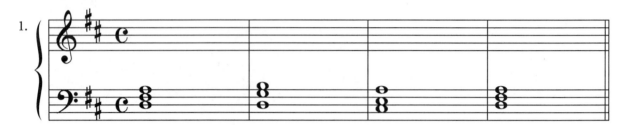

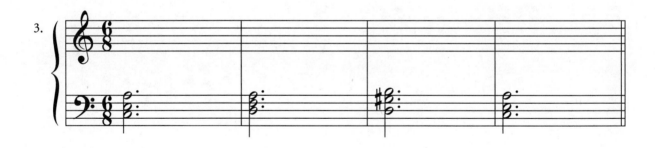

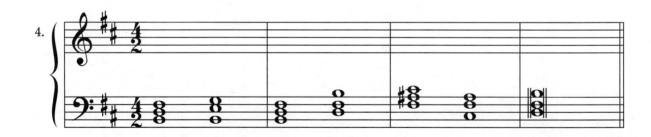

Harmony

Sing the following progressions in four-voice harmony. They contain passing tones, neighbor tones, and changing tones.

Rhythm

Practice the following compound meter rhythms containing subdivisions of the beat.

Dictation

Notate the melodies that you hear. You will hear each melody several times. Within the context of the implied harmony, there will be passing tones and neighbor tones.

3.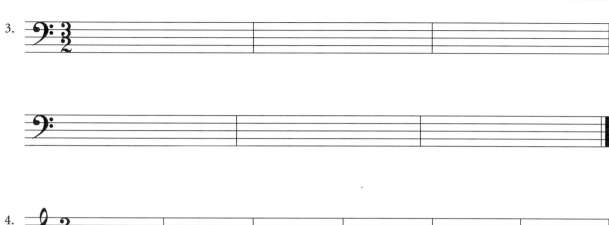

4.

You will hear simple melodies that are accompanied by triads. The rhythms below represent the melodies. Circle and label the passing tones and neighbor tones that you hear where they occur in the rhythms below.

3.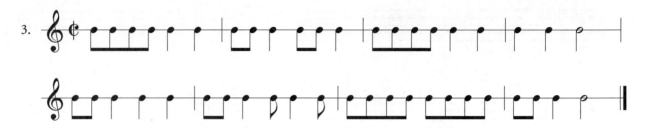

4.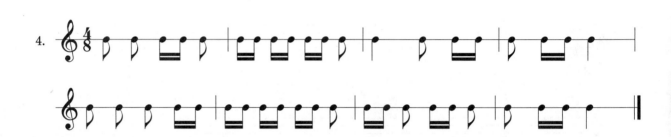

Harmonic Dictation

The following dictation exercises will contain passing tones and neighbor tones.

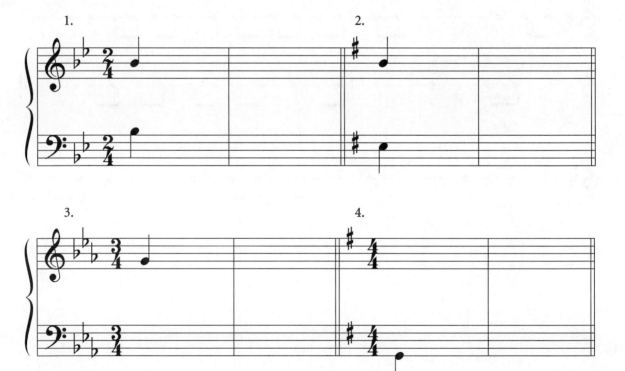

KEYBOARD APPLICATIONS

The following keyboard exercise contains at least three opportunities to insert passing tones in a variety of voices. The normal placement of a passing tone occurs between two horizontal notes that are separated by a third. (Double passing tones are an option at one point in this exercise.) The example below in C major shows the placement of one possible passing tone. Practice this exercise in the indicated keys.

1.   B major
      E♭ major
      G♭ major

mi	*mi*	*fa*	*re*	*do*
I	vi	ii⁶	V	I

The following exercise contains at least five opportunities for inserting upper or lower neighbor tones in the upper three voices. Neighbor tones can be inserted between pairs of repeated notes in any voice part. The example below in C major shows the placement of one possible neighbor tone. Practice this exercise in the keys indicated.

2.   D major
      F major
      C♯ major

sol	*sol*	*la*	*la*	*sol*	*sol*	*sol*
I	iii	vi	IV	I⁶₄	V	I

chapter 18 Appoggiaturas, Escape Tones, and Pedal Tones

THEORETICAL SKILLS

Appoggiaturas

The **appoggiatura** is the first non-harmonic tone we have studied that involves a leap (or an interval larger than a second). The term itself comes from the Italian word *appoggiare,* which means "to lean." An appoggiatura occurs as the middle note of a three-note pattern and is approached by leap and resolved by stepwise movement in the opposite direction. It is important to observe that the interval of the leap may be of any size, although most commonly it is no larger than a fourth. Usually the figure leaps upward and steps down, but it is also possible to have an appoggiatura that leaps downward and steps up. Both directions are demonstrated in Figure 18.1.

Figure 18.1. *Approach and resolution of appoggiaturas*

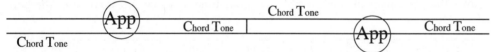

The appoggiatura may occur on either a weak or a strong beat. Figure 18.2 presents some examples in four-part harmony. The non-harmonic tones are circled.

Figure 18.2. *Appoggiaturas in four-part harmony*

Notice the manner in which the appoggiatura is written in the second example above. This style of notation was typical of the classical period. Composers such as Mozart and Haydn often used this type of non-harmonic tone. It was their practice to show the presence of appoggiaturas and other non-harmonic tones through this manner of notation. Notice that the small note is not a grace note, which would have a slash through the stem of the note. The appoggiatura will never have a slash. This note should be performed with some emphasis, indicating its status as a non-chord tone within the overall harmony. Its rhythmic value is identical to the value of the written note, in this case a sixteenth note. It is played on the beat and its value is subtracted from the value of the note that follows it. The actual performance of the passage above is written out in Figure 18.3.

Figure 18.3.   *Rhythmic interpretation of appoggiatura figure*

Appoggiaturas are frequently seen in almost all styles of music from the Common Practice Period. Here are some examples. Circle and label the appoggiaturas where you find them. Example 18.1 uses the type of notation just discussed.

Example 18.1.   *Mozart,* Piano Sonata, K. 311, 1st movement, mm. 1–4

Track 18, 0:00

Example 18.2 demonstrates an appoggiatura that descends by leap and steps upward for resolution.

Example 18.2.   *Mendelssohn,* Songs without Words, *op. 117, no. 1, mm. 7–10*

Track 18, 0:17

Example 18.3 contains a double appoggiatura. Both of the appoggiaturas are altered tones within the key of E major.

Example 18.3.   *Schubert,* Adagio und Rondo, *op. 145, mm. 23–27*

Track 18, 0:35

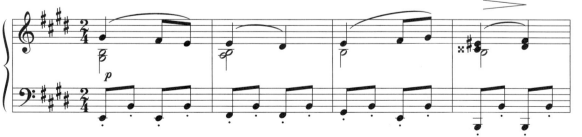

The appoggiatura in Example 18.4 occurs within the context of an irregular division of the $\frac{2}{4}$ measure into seven equal notes. Can you find the appoggiatura? Does the leap move upward or downward?

Example 18.4.   *R. Schumann,* Carnaval, *"Eusebius," mm. 1–2*

Track 18, 0:47

Escape Tones

The **escape tone** reverses the order of leap and step used in the appoggiatura. An escape tone occurs as the middle note of a three-note pattern. It is approached by step and resolved by leap in the opposite direction. Escape tones are not used as frequently as appoggiaturas. In fact, their use is somewhat rare in music of the Common Practice Period. The diagram in Figure 18.4 shows the pattern of movement of an escape tone. Notice that there must be a change of direction. The escape tone is abbreviated ET.

Figure 18.4.   *Approach and resolution of escape tones*

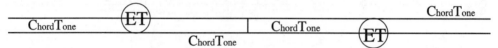

Figure 18.5 presents an escape tone in four-part harmony. The escape tone is circled.

Figure 18.5   *Escape tone used in four-part harmony*

There is an escape tone in the music by Tchaikovsky presented in Example 18.5. Can you find it? What other types of non-harmonic tones are present?

Example 18.5.   *Peter Ilich Tchaikovsky,* Album for the Young, *"Italienisches Liedchen," op. 39, no. 15, mm. 1–8*

Track 18, 0:59

♭ Practice Box 18.1

Add inner voices and a Roman numeral analysis. The following exercises contain appoggiaturas and escape tones. Circle and label all non-harmonic tones.

Pedal Tones

The **pedal tone** is the only non-harmonic tone that must occur in a specific voice: it is almost always found in the bass voice. A pedal tone is an unchanging bass note above which the harmony changes. The term comes from organ terminology. Many compositions for organ have a low bass note that is to be played on the pedals. This note is held with the foot while the chords played by the hands are free to change above this bass note. The note that is held in the bass is called a pedal tone.

Pedal tones happen frequently in all music, not just organ literature. The diagram in Figure 18.6 shows the pattern of a pedal tone.

Figure 18.6.   Approach and resolution of pedal tone

ChordTone	Ped	ChordTone

A pedal tone can be described as being approached by repetition and resolved by repetition. It is possible to have several pedal tones in a row, since a series of chords can be written above a stationary bass note. The abbreviation for the pedal tone is Ped (not PT, which is the standard abbreviation for passing tone). If a pedal tone is found in an upper voice, it can be called an "inverted pedal tone."

Figure 18.7 demonstrates a pedal tone in four-part harmony. The pedal tones are circled. Add a Roman numeral analysis to the example.

Figure 18.7.   Pedal tone in four-part harmony

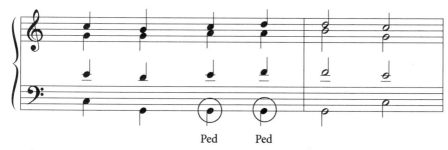

Here are two examples that contain pedal tones. Analyze the chords that occur above the pedal tones. Chord types that have not yet been studied are analyzed for you. What other kinds of non-harmonic tones are present in these examples?

Example 18.6.   Brahms, Waltz, op. 39, no. 1, mm. 1–4

Track 18, 1:13

Example 18.7.   R. Schumann, Papillons, op. 2, no. 7, mm. 1–8

Track 18, 1:25

vii°$\frac{4}{3}$/V

Practice Box 18.2

Add inner voices and a Roman numeral analysis. The unfamiliar figured-bass symbol represents a pedal tone figure.

Music for Analysis

Study the following examples for non-harmonic tones. You will find passing and neighbor tones, appoggiaturas, escape tones, and pedal tones.

Example 18.8.   Mozart, Piano Sonata, K. 330, 2nd movement, mm. 1–4

Track 18, 1:40

Example 18.9.   Mozart, Piano Sonata in A Minor, K. 310, 1st movement, mm. 33–35

Track 18, 1:57

Example 18.10.   Beethoven, Sonatina in F, WoO 50, "Andante," mm. 1–4

Track 18, 2:10

Example 18.11.   Chaminade, Danse pastorale (Air de Ballet no. 5), *op. 37, no. 5, mm. 28–33*

Track 18, 2:29

Example 18.12.   R. Schumann, Carnaval, *"Promenade," mm. 71–93*

Track 18, 2:43

AURAL SKILLS

Alto Clef

A few of the instruments of the orchestra read their music on clefs other than the bass and treble clefs that we have used thus far. In particular, music for the viola is always written on the alto clef. The alto clef places middle C on the middle line of the staff. Name the final note and then determine the key of the following examples. Then sing them using solfege or numbers. You have sung all of these exercises in previous chapters, using either treble or bass clef.

Harmony

Sing the following exercises in four-part harmony. They contain a variety of non-harmonic tones.

Rhythm

Practice the following compound-meter rhythms, which contain subdivisions of the beat.

Dictation

You will hear simple melodies accompanied by triads. The rhythms below represent the melodies. Circle and label the appoggiaturas and escape tones that you hear where they occur in the rhythms below.

Notate the following melodies that you hear. There will be a variety of non-harmonic tones within the implied harmony.

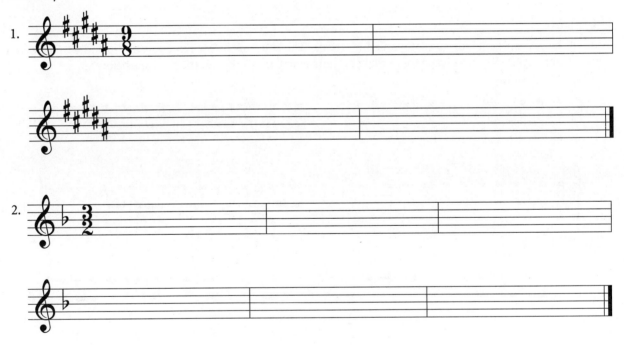

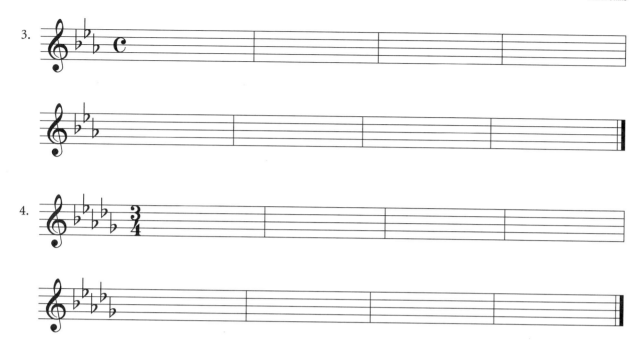

Harmonic Dictation

Add soprano and bass lines, inner voices, and a Roman numeral analysis. These progressions will contain appoggiaturas, escape tones, and pedal tones.

KEYBOARD APPLICATIONS

The following keyboard exercise contains two opportunities to insert appoggiaturas in the soprano voice. The example below in C major shows the placement of one possible appoggiatura. Practice this exercise in the indicated keys.

1. D major
    Eb major
    F# major

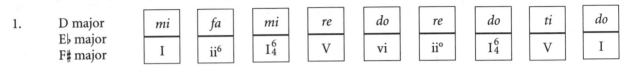

mi	fa	mi	re	do	re	do	ti	do
I	ii^6	I$^6_4$	V	vi	ii$^\circ$	I$^6_4$	V	I

In addition to the appoggiaturas, there are other opportunities in Exercise 1 to insert suspensions, passing tones, neighbor tones, and so on. Practice the exercise in keys other than those listed above and add additional non-harmonic tones.

2.   Use the following bass line to improvise a progression. Some of the repeated bass notes should be used as pedal tones. The cadence may include a cadential six-four chord. Transpose your progression into keys other than C major.

chapter 19 Suspensions, Retardations, and Anticipations

THEORETICAL SKILLS

Suspensions

The **suspension** is the most heavily governed of all the types of non-harmonic tones. It occurs very commonly in all types of music, from classical to popular to jazz, and can appear in any voice of a texture. A suspension occurs as the middle note of a three-note figure. There are three distinct parts to a suspension.

1. Preparation
2. Suspension
3. Resolution

In the diagram shown in Figure 19.1, these three parts are labeled. Notice that, like a pedal tone, this non-harmonic tone pattern involves a repeated note.

Figure 19.1. Approach and resolution of suspension

Preparation	Suspension	Resolution
~~ChordTone~~	Sus	
		ChordTone

Each of these three notes of a suspension figure is represented by one of the terms above. The preparation must be a member of the underlying chord. It usually happens on a weak beat of the measure, before the suspended note itself, which usually occurs on a strong beat. The suspended note must occur on exactly the same line or space as the preparation note, and in exactly the same voice of the texture. The suspended note must not be a part of the underlying chord. Usually the chord that occurs simultaneously with the suspension is a different chord from the one in which the preparation appeared. The chord usually stays the same between the suspension and the resolution notes. The note of resolution moves stepwise downward from the suspended note. A quick way to describe this process is to say that a suspension is prepared with a repeated note and resolves stepwise downward.

Figure 19.2. A suspension in four-part harmony

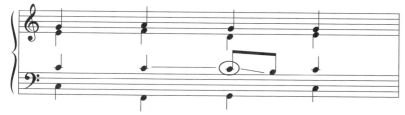

The circle in the preceding example shows the location of the suspension. It appears in the tenor voice. Notice the preparation note in the tenor, which is also on middle C, as is the suspension. Then notice the downward movement following the suspension, stepwise to B.

Now analyze the chordal structure of the piece. In C major, the example begins and ends with a tonic triad. The second chord is the subdominant triad, of which the C in the tenor is a chord tone. The chord containing the suspension is more difficult to analyze. Here we see a collection of pitches that does not make sense as a triad,

G–C–D. It does not make sense because it contains a non-chord tone that has not yet moved to the proper note of the chord; it will become a B when the suspension is resolved. In this manner, a chord containing a suspension will always be difficult to analyze, because it essentially contains a "wrong" note.

♪ Practice Box 19.1

Find the suspension figures in the following examples. Circle the suspended note and label the preparation, suspension, and resolution in each example. Add a Roman numeral analysis. Remember that the note that follows the suspended note will be the chord tone that completes the chord.

If you study the examples above to provide figured-bass symbols for the suspensions, you will find that certain pairs of numbers consistently represent the suspension figures. There are five distinct pairs of numbers that typically represent suspensions. They are listed in the table below.

Table 21.   Figured-bass symbols for suspensions

Figured bass	4-3	9-8 (or 2-1)	2-3	7-6
Normal appearance	Primarily in root-position chords	Primarily in root-position chords	Primarily in first-inversion chords	Primarily in first-inversion chords

A 9-8 suspension will involve exactly the same pitch classes as a 2-1 suspension. The only difference is register. A 2-1 suspension must resolve to a unison with the bass voice; therefore, it can occur only in the tenor. The 9-8 suspension may occur in any of the upper three voices, provided that it is at least a ninth above the bass note. The 9-8 suspension occurs much more commonly than the 2-1 suspension.

The 4-3, 9-8, and 2-1 suspensions usually will appear only in root position chords. The other two combinations usually will appear only in first inversion chords. The 2-3 suspension only appears in the bass voice, as seen in the fourth progression from Practice Box 19.1. In the 2-3 suspension, it is the bass voice that moves, not an upper voice. This set of number combinations should be memorized, as well as the position of the chords (root position or first inversion) in which they appear.

A 7-6 suspension is not an indication of a seventh chord. When found in a horizontal combination with the number 6, the 7 does not imply the presence of a chordal seventh, only the presence of a non-harmonic tone that will move downward in the voice leading.

Look at Example 19.1 and try to determine the suspension that occurs. To analyze a suspension, you should circle the non-harmonic tone and label it "susp" (or "sus"). Underneath the staff, write in the figured-bass combination that represents the intervals above the bass.

Example 19.1.   R. Schumann, Kinderszenen, *"Of Foreign Lands and People," op. 15, no. 1, mm. 19–22*

Track 19, 0:00

Two suspensions can happen at the same time; this situation is known as a double suspension. The most commonly used double suspension combines a 4-3 and a 9-8 suspension happening simultaneously, since both of these are possible in a root position chord. Example 19.2 contains two double suspensions. The first one is labeled. Can you find the second one?

Example 19.2.   J. C. F. Bach, Menuet, *mm. 1–4*

Track 19, 0:18

A major: I   I$^6_4$ V^7 I

Notice the chain of suspensions in Example 19.3. In measure 2, the resolution of each suspension becomes the note of preparation for the next suspension. Label each suspension with its figured-bass symbol and circle the suspended notes.

Example 19.3.   J. S. Bach, O wie selig seid ihr doch, ihr Frommen, *mm. 1–3*

Track 19, 0:32

F major: vi

The 4-3 suspension is often embellished, or ornamented with additional notes that occur before the resolution. These embellishments happen most often at cadences. The most typical figured-bass symbols for these ornamental figures are 4-2-3 and 4-3-2-3. Example 19.4 is an excerpt from a Bach chorale. The figured-bass symbols are written underneath the notes of the ornamented suspension.

Example 19.4.   *J. S. Bach,* Von Gott will ich nicht lassen, *mm. 3–4*

Track 19, 0:52

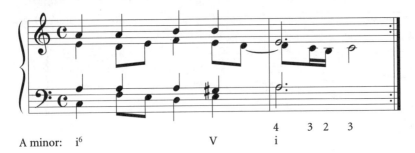

A minor: i⁶   V   i

Occasionally you will encounter musical figures that behave as if they were suspensions, with a preparation on the same note and downward resolution, but that do not involve the standard intervals that are associated with suspensions. For example, you might encounter a note that looks like a suspension but is a sixth above the bass. The figured-bass symbol for such a figure would be 6-5. Often these kinds of patterns occur in inverted chords. They should be labeled suspension-types (abbreviated "sus-type"), since they look like suspensions but do not involve one of the standard interval combinations. Another way of describing this type of suspension is to call it a consonant suspension. Most of the standard figured-bass formulas create a dissonance at the point of the suspension. In this type of suspension, the suspended note is consonant. Find the suspensions and suspension-types in Example 19.5. The first chord is a seventh chord and is spelled for you above the staff.

Example 19.5.   *R. Schumann,* Carnaval, *"Chiarina," mm. 1–8*

Track 19, 1:05

Part-writing exercises can contain suspension figures. You should make a habit of looking through the figured-bass symbols before starting the part-writing process and identifying the number combinations that represent suspensions. It can also be very helpful to name the actual pitches represented by these number combinations before beginning to spell the chord and to do the part writing. Remember that the second number of the pair represents the actual chord tone, and that letter name should be used when spelling the underlying chord. It is also helpful to remember which number combinations represent root position chords and which represent first inversion chords. When you see a 7-6 suspension, remember to treat the underlying chord just as you would any first inversion chord (finding the root down a third from the bass note). In the case of a 2-3 suspension, the actual suspension notes will be given to you in the bass voice. You will usually add a single note above the bass that will create, in sequence, the interval of a second and a third.

In addition, in minor keys it is very common to find 4-3 suspensions written as 4 ♯. Since any single accidental unaccompanied by a number represents the number 3, this figured-bass code should be read as if it were a 4-3 suspension. In terms of ornamented suspensions, the code combinations can appear quite complicated, such as 4 ♯ 2 ♯.

When adding the inner voices, remember that the suspended note must be correctly prepared. If you have named the pitches involved in the suspension, look for the same letter name as the suspended note in the preceding chord. That voice will be the correct one in which to place the suspension figure.

Practice Box 19.2

First name the pitches represented by the suspension figures. Then spell the chords and add inner voices and a Roman numeral analysis..

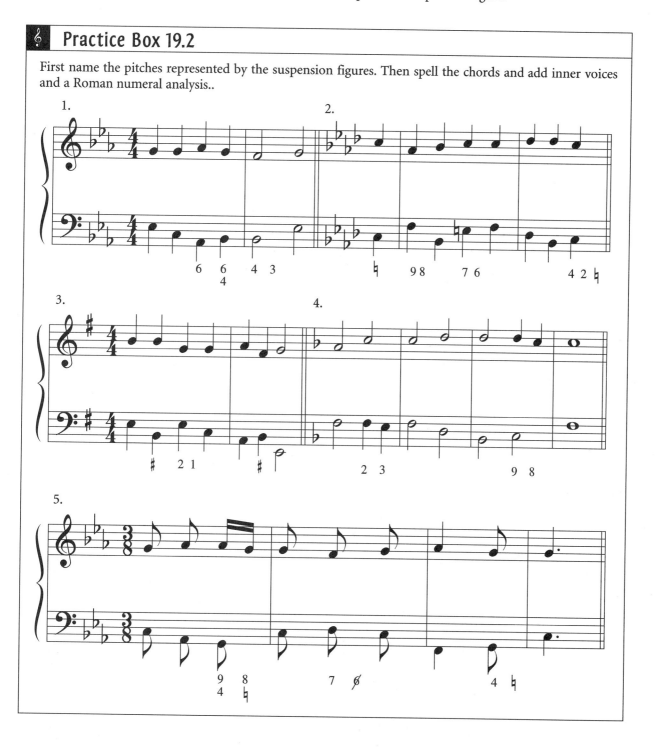

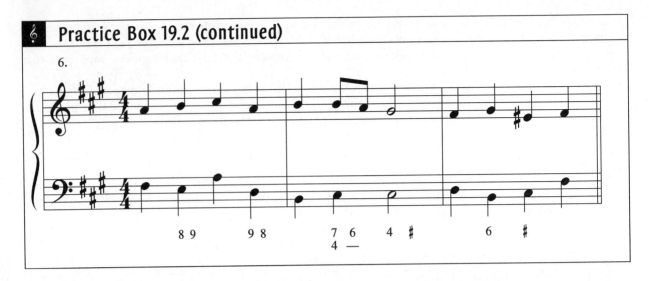

Practice Box 19.2 (continued)

Retardations

In our definition of suspensions, we have specified that the resolution of a suspension must be downward. In some theory books, the definition of a suspension considers that the resolution may be either upward or downward. More typically, though, a suspension that resolves upward is called a **retardation.**

A retardation contains the same three component parts as a suspension: preparation, suspension, and resolution. It must be prepared exactly in the same manner as a suspension, with a chord tone that does not change pitch when it becomes non-harmonic. The only difference is the direction of the resolution.

Figure 19.3. *Approach and resolution of retardation*

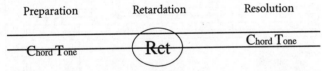

The figured-bass combinations of numbers that are associated with suspensions do not apply to retardations. In fact, there are no specific figured-bass symbols associated with retardations, probably because retardations do not occur as commonly as suspensions.

The final measure in Example 19.6 demonstrates a retardation that happens simultaneously with a suspension.

Example 19.6. *J. C. Bach, Sonata, op. 5, no. 1, 2nd movement, mm. 71–74*

Track 19, 1:24

Anticipations

When a suspension occurs, the arrival of a chord tone is delayed until after a new chord is presented in the progression. An **anticipation** occurs when a chord tone that is part of the next chord in the harmony arrives sooner than the actual chord. The anticipation is the middle note of a three-note pattern. While one chord is still sounding, one voice of the texture moves to a note that is part of the next chord in the progression. The anticipated note then does not change when the new chord arrives. Another way to say this is that the anticipation is approached by step and resolves by repetition.

Figure 19.4.   *Approach and resolution of anticipation*

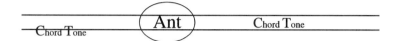

Notice that the anticipation, circled in Figure 19.5, seems to occur between the two chords. It is a chord tone of the second chord of the pair, not the first. It is, in essence, anticipating the arrival of the second chord.

Figure 19.5.   *An anticipation in four-part harmony*

Anticipations primarily occur in the more prominent upper voices of a texture, such as the soprano. Sometimes you may also see double anticipations, often appearing in the soprano and alto simultaneously. They are very prevalent in music of the Baroque period and often involve dotted rhythms, as you will see in Example 19.7.

Example 19.7.   *Handel,* Judas Maccabaeus, *Part III, no. 53, Introduction, mm. 1–7*

Track 19, 1:40

Practice Box 19.3

Add inner voices and a Roman numeral analysis. Circle and label all non-harmonic tones.

Review of Non-Harmonic Tones

Each of the nine non-harmonic tones has a distinctive pattern of approach and resolution. Here is a table to help you memorize these patterns.

Table 22.   Non-harmonic tones with their patterns of approach and resolution

Name	Pattern
Passing tone	Approached by step, resolved by step in the same direction
Neighbor tone	Approached by step, resolved by step in the opposite direction
Changing tone	Approached by step, followed by a leap in the opposite direction, resolved by step back to the original note
Appoggiatura	Approached by leap, resolved by step in the opposite direction
Escape tone	Approached by step, resolved by leap in the opposite direction
Pedal tone	Approached by repetition, resolved by repetition (in the bass voice)
Suspension	Approached by repetition, resolved by step downward
Retardation	Approached by repetition, resolved by step upward
Anticipation	Approached by step (either up or down), resolved by repetition

Music for Analysis

Study the following examples in order to identify all types of non-harmonic tones.

Example 19.8.   Mendelssohn, Songs without Words, *op. 30, no. 4, mm. 1–10*

Track 19, 2:27

Example 19.9.   Mozart, Piano Sonata, K. 311, 2nd movement, mm. 1–11

Track 19, 2:50

AURAL SKILLS

Alto Clef

Sing the following melodies. All of these melodies have been studied previously in this textbook, written in bass and treble clefs.

1.

2.

3.

4.

5.

6.

7.
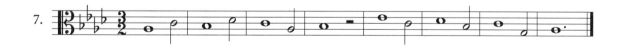

8.

Harmony

Sing the following exercises in four-part harmony. They contain suspensions and anticipations.

Rhythm

In a simple meter, the beat is normally divided into two equal parts. It is also possible to divide a beat from a simple meter into three equal parts; this is called a **borrowed division** of the beat. The term comes from the idea of borrowing the type of division that is used in compound meters, in which it is normal to divide the beat into three equal parts. When the beat note of a simple meter is divided in this way, the resulting group is called a **triplet.**

Borrowed divisions of the beat are indicated with a number that is generally placed on the stem side of the group (as opposed to the note-head side) when the notes are beamed together. The number can go over or under the group, depending on the stem direction. If the triplet group is made up of quarter notes, then the number is paired with a bracket.

Figure 19.6 shows triplet figures in both four-four time and four-two time. Notice the differences in notation.

Figure 19.6.   Borrowed divisions of the beat

The triplet figure is counted as if it were a regular division of the beat in a compound meter, using "one-la-li" to represent the group of notes. The challenge of counting borrowed divisions of the beat is to be able to easily alternate the counting schemes of regular and borrowed divisions.

Practice Box 19.4

It may be helpful to practice these rhythms with a metronome to ensure the steadiness of the beat.

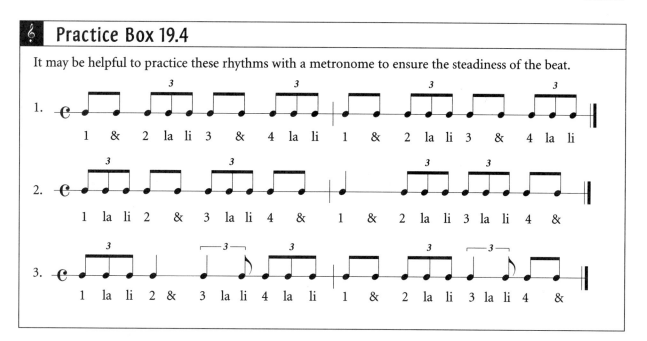

Additional Rhythms

For extra practice, clap and count these exercises.

Dual Rhythms

These rhythms should be tapped with both hands. They use simple meters and subdivisions of the beat.

Dictation

Notate the following rhythms, which use borrowed divisions of the beat.

1.

2.

3.

4.

5.

6.

You will hear simple melodies that are accompanied by triads. The rhythms below represent the melodies. Circle and label the suspensions and anticipations you hear where they occur in the rhythms below.

Notate the following melodies, which may use borrowed divisions of the beat.

Harmonic Dictation

Add soprano and bass lines, inner voices, and a Roman numeral analysis. These progressions will contain suspensions.

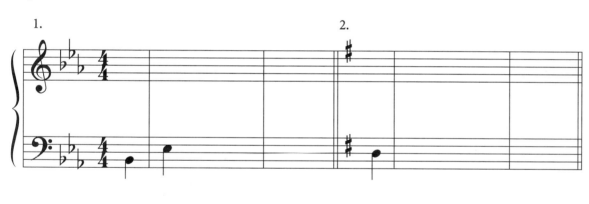

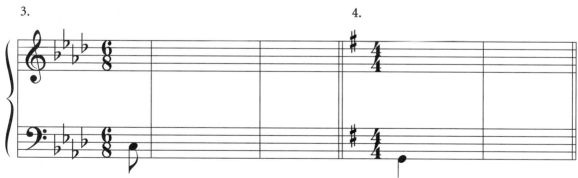

KEYBOARD APPLICATIONS

Practice the following exercises in the keys indicated. Each exercise contains at least one suspension. The figured bass for the suspension is indicated in Arabic numerals beneath the Roman numerals.

1.   G major
      B♭ major
      A major

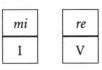

mi	*re*	*do*
I	V	I
	4 3	

2.   B minor
      C minor
      F♯ minor

sol	*me*	*me*	*fa*	*re*	*do*
V	i	VI	iv	V	i
	9 8			4 3	

chapter 20 Introduction to Seventh Chords

THEORETICAL SKILLS

Seventh Chords

Triads are three-note chords stacked in intervals of thirds. It is possible to add another note to a triad, positioned so that it is another third up from the top note of the triad. This creates a four-note chord that is still considered to be **tertian,** or based on the interval of a third, just like the triad. Figure 20.1 shows the process of adding this extra note to a triad to form a seventh chord.

Figure 20.1. Building seventh chords

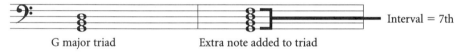

The four-note chord is called a **seventh chord.** This type of chord does not derive its name from the number of notes present, but instead from the distance between the outer two notes of the chord, as shown above. The lowest and highest notes of the chord, respectively, are G and F. They form the interval of a seventh between them. When a fourth note that is a third higher than the top note is added to any root position triad, the outer interval always will be the interval of a seventh.

The four notes of the seventh chord are shown in Figure 20.2 and are called the root, third, fifth, and seventh.

Figure 20.2. Components of a seventh chord

Because of the extra note in the chord, naming the quality of a seventh chord is more complicated than naming triads. Seventh chords have two primary distinguishing characteristics: the quality of the triad that forms the lower three notes of the chord, and the quality of the seventh that forms the outer interval of the chord.

In the chord above, the lower three notes, G, B, and D, form a G major triad. The outer interval, G to F, is a minor seventh. This triad is referred to as a "major-minor" seventh chord. Since there are four possible triad qualities and four possible qualities for the interval of the seventh, there are a total of sixteen possible seventh chords. They are demonstrated below in Figure 20.3, each built on the same root, C.

Figure 20.3. All possible qualities for seventh chords

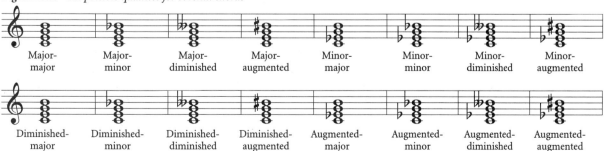

It is important to note that most of these sixteen chords are nothing more than theoretical possibilities. That means that they can be constructed using the rules that we have learned but do not generally exist in music of the Common Practice Period. The five qualities of seventh chords that are frequently used in actual music are listed below, along with their common nicknames:

1. Major-major seventh (often called a major seventh)
2. Major-minor seventh (often called a dominant seventh)
3. Minor-minor seventh (often called a minor seventh)
4. Diminished-minor seventh (often called a half-diminished seventh)
5. Diminished-diminished seventh (often called a fully diminished seventh)

These are the seventh chords that are typically used in diatonic harmony. On the preceding staves, find these five diatonic seventh chords among the sixteen theoretical possibilities and circle them.

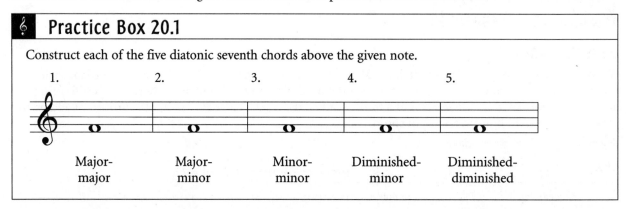

Naming seventh chords involves two familiar processes. First you must identify the quality of the triad; then you must identify the quality of the outer interval (the seventh). These chords are often referred to by the nicknames listed above. However, in order to be comprehensively named, two words should always be used to fully describe the qualities of seventh chords.

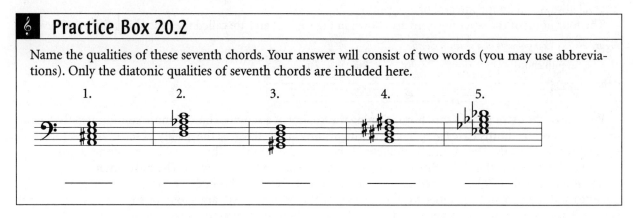

Inversion of Seventh Chords

Thus far, we have only discussed seventh chords in root position. It is also possible to rearrange the notes of a seventh chord so that it forms an inversion.

As you already know, when a triad is written so that its root is the lowest note, it is said to be in *root position.* When the third of the chord is the lowest note, it is in *first inversion,* and when the fifth of the chord is in the lowest position, it is in *second inversion.* Since there are three notes in a triad, there are three possible positions (root position and two inversions). In seventh chords, there are four possibilities (root position and three inversions).

When a seventh chord is written so that its root is the lowest note, it is said to be in *root position,* just like a triad. If the third of the chord is the lowest note, it is in *first inversion.* If the fifth of the chord is the lowest, it is in *second inversion.* Unlike triads, though, seventh chords can also appear in *third inversion,* when the chordal seventh is used as the lowest note. Figure 20.4 shows root position and all inversions of a seventh chord.

Figure 20.4. Inversions of the seventh chord

| Root position | 1st inversion | 2nd inversion | 3rd inversion |

You will notice that in all inversions of a seventh chord, *a characteristic interval of a second appears between one pair of notes.* This interval will help you identify the root of the seventh chord when it is inverted. *The top note of the interval of a second is always the root of an inverted seventh chord.* Once you know the root, you can spell the chord up in thirds to obtain its root-position identity.

Practice Box 20.3

Circle the root of each chord. If it is in an inversion, remember to look for the interval of a second. Use the name of the note you circled as the root and spell each chord in root position above the staff. Then name the quality and inversion in the blanks provided below each measure. The first chord is done for you as an example.

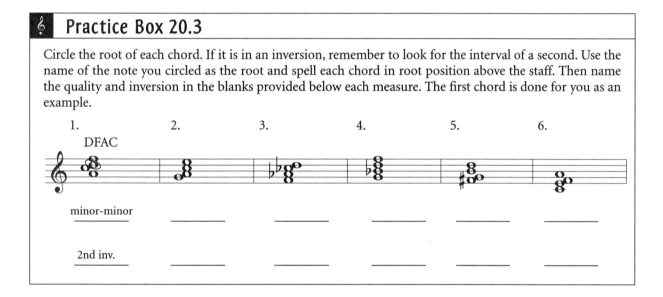

1. DFAC minor-minor 2nd inv.
2. _____ _____
3. _____ _____
4. _____ _____
5. _____ _____
6. _____ _____

Figured-bass symbols represent distances above the bass notes. Since there are three notes above each bass note in a seventh chord, a complete representation of the chord in figured bass would involve three numbers. All of the complete figured-bass symbols for seventh chords are shown in Figure 20.5.

Figure 20.5.   Figured bass for seventh chord inversions

7	6	6	6
5	5	4	4
3	3	3	2

As you can see, these sets of numbers are very similar and rather cumbersome. They are typically abbreviated in the manner shown in Table 23.

Table 23.   *Figured-bass abbreviations for 7th chords*

	Root position	1st inversion	2nd inversion	3rd inversion
Complete figured bass	7 5 3	6 5 3	6 4 3	6 4 2
Common abbreviations	7	6 5	4 3	4 2 (or 2)

For third-inversion seventh chords, the most common figured-bass abbreviation is $\frac{4}{2}$. However, occasionally you will see only the number 2 in figured bass; this also can represent a third-inversion seventh chord.

This series of abbreviations must be memorized. It is possible to learn them as if they were a phone number, 765-4342. This "number" represents, respectively, the figured-bass symbols for the root position and the first, second, and third inversions of any seventh chord.

When you see a 7 below a bass note, you are looking at the root of the chord. As shown in Figure 20.6, the chord is spelled with the bass note as the root, and three notes above it all stacked in thirds.

Figure 20.6.   *Interpreting 7 as a figured-bass symbol*

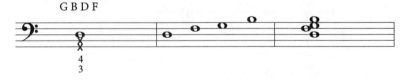

Finding $\frac{6}{5}$ in the figured bass means that the chord is in first inversion. Just as we learned with triads, the root of a seventh chord in first inversion is always a third down from the given bass note. By placing an X on the line or space that is a third down from the bass note, you will be visually identifying the root of the chord on the staff, as seen in Figure 20.7. You can then spell the chord in thirds above the root that has been identified with an X.

Figure 20.7.   *Interpreting $\frac{6}{5}$ as a figured-bass symbol*

When dealing with second-inversion seventh chords, the bass note is the chordal fifth. To identify the root of the second-inversion triad or seventh chord, you must go down 2 thirds (an interval equivalent to a fifth) to find the root. This is demonstrated in Figure 20.8.

Figure 20.8.   *Interpreting $\frac{4}{3}$ as a figured-bass symbol*

Third-inversion chords can be approached in two ways. The bass note is the chordal seventh. The root of the chord is down a seventh, or three skips. However, you should remember, when a seventh is inverted, it becomes a second. Therefore, instead of looking for the root down a seventh, you can look at a note that is up a second from the given bass note, as shown in Figure 20.9.

Figure 20.9.   Interpreting ⁴₂ as a figured-bass symbol

Practice Box 20.4

Spell the chords indicated by the figured-bass symbols. Use Xs where necessary to help you determine the root.

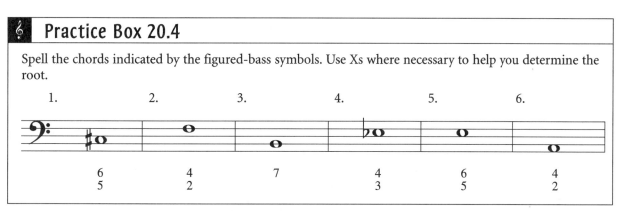

All of the other figured-bass symbols that you have learned can also apply to seventh chords. These include slashes through numbers, flat or natural signs placed beside numbers, and single accidentals unaccompanied by numbers. Some of these symbols are shown in Figure 20.10. In addition, it may be necessary to include the additional numbers that are typically omitted in abbreviations for certain inversions, if those notes above the bass require accidentals.

Figure 20.10.   Accidentals in seventh chord figured bass

In the first example above, the slash through the 6 raises that note one half step. The letter name that is a sixth above the bass is G, so it becomes G♯. In the second example, the chord is in root position. Typically, the only figured-bass symbol needed is the 7. However, the third above the bass is required to be raised, therefore, it must be represented in the figured bass as a sharp (♯).

Practice Box 20.5

Spell the chords indicated by the following figured-bass symbols.

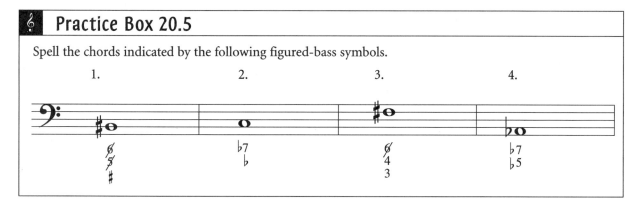

Diatonic Seventh Chords in Major Keys

Seventh chords are generally used in the same position in a chord progression in which their triadic counterparts would be found. However, seventh chords are seldom built on certain scale degrees, such as the tonic, the mediant, and the submediant.

First, we will look at all the theoretical possibilities for seventh chords that exist in a major scale. These are shown in Figure 20.11.

Figure 20.11.   Diatonic seventh chords in the major scale

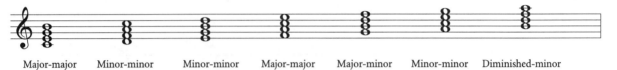

Major-major   Minor-minor   Minor-minor   Major-major   Major-minor   Minor-minor   Diminished-minor

Of the five possible diatonic seventh chord qualities, four exist in the major scale. Several of the chords on the staff above seldom appear in tonal music. The mediant seventh and submediant seventh chords are not as common as the other diatonic seventh chords and are harder to find in actual compositions.

The tonic seventh chord requires slightly more explanation. This chord is commonly heard in jazz styles where it is often used in place of the tonic triad at cadences. Dissonant chords are used with much more freedom in jazz harmony than in tonal harmony.

In music of the Common Practice Period, the tonic seventh chord is virtually never used. A seventh chord built on the tonic scale degree contains some inherent contradictions. The tonic triad is meant to provide a sense of repose in music; it can be said to form a conclusion to a musical phrase. However, a seventh chord is intrinsically unstable, since the interval of the seventh demands resolution. A seventh chord built on the tonic scale degree frustrates the ability of the tonic triad to be at rest.

In fact, if a chord appears to be a I^7, there is usually another, better explanation for it. These alternative explanations often involve a non-harmonic tone or a chromatically altered chord. Altered chords will be studied in volume 2 of *Theory Essentials*.

Figure 20.12.   Commonly used diatonic seventh chords in major keys

ii^7 IV^7 V^7 $vii^{ø7}$

The four chords above are the commonly used diatonic seventh chords in a major scale. Notice the manner in which the Roman numerals are written. With the exception of the half-diminished leading-tone seventh chord, they are the same as their triadic equivalents. The leading-tone chord uses a different symbol: a slash through the circle that represents the diminished quality of the triad. The slash shows at a glance that only one part of the chord (the triad) is diminished. (Remember that the outer interval of the chord is a minor seventh.) This slash helps to make the Roman numeral for this chord easily distinguishable from that of the fully diminished leading-tone seventh chord.

By far the most common of these four is the dominant seventh chord, which is used almost as frequently as the dominant triad. The half-diminished leading-tone seventh chord is rarely used as a substitute for the dominant seventh. The following list shows some typical diatonic chord progressions using seventh chords:

I	IV	V^7	I		
I	iii	vi	ii	V^7	I
I	ii^7	I^6_4	V	I	
I	vi	IV^7	V^7	I	
I	ii	$vii^{ø7}$	I		

Practice Box 20.6

Write the four commonly used diatonic seventh chords for the key of F major and label them with Roman numerals.

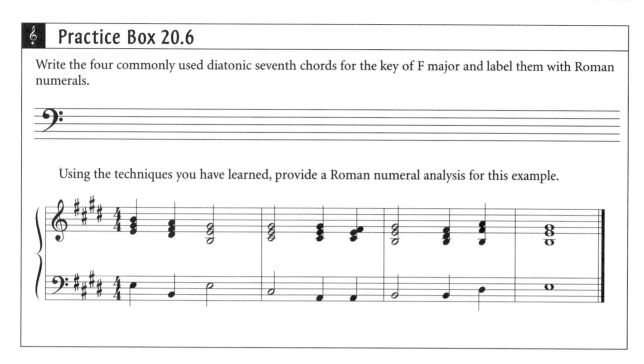

Using the techniques you have learned, provide a Roman numeral analysis for this example.

Diatonic Seventh Chords in Minor Keys

As with triads, there are many more seventh chords possible in a minor scale than in a major scale. Again, we will start by looking at all the possibilities. These are shown in Figure 20.13. If you need additional practice identifying chord qualities, name the qualities of all the chords shown in this figure.

Figure 20.13.   *Diatonic seventh chords in the minor scale*

It is almost superfluous to say that most of the chords on the staff above are nothing more than theoretical possibilities. As in major keys, the only seventh chords commonly used in minor keys are built on the supertonic, subdominant, dominant, and leading-tone scale degrees. Figure 20.14 presents those that are commonly used.

Figure 20.14.   *Commonly used seventh chords in minor keys*

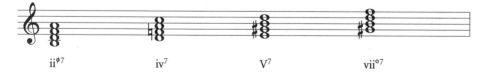

A few of the alternate chord qualities are occasionally used in minor keys. A minor-minor supertonic seventh chord is possible but is much rarer than the half-diminished seventh chord. On the leading-tone scale degree, the fully diminished chord is much more frequently used than the half diminished. And of course, in tonal music, on the dominant scale degree the chord will always require an accidental to create the major-minor chord quality.

Again as in major, the most commonly used of these chords is the dominant seventh. However, in minor keys, the fully diminished vii°7 chord is frequently used as a substitute for the dominant seventh. Notice the Roman numeral used for this chord. One circle after the triad symbol represents the fact that both components of the chord, the triad and the outer seventh, are diminished. (Some textbooks use a Roman numeral that contains two circles to represent the fully diminished seventh chord. One circle follows the triad symbol and the other follows the 7, to indicate that both components of the seventh chord are diminished.)

The following list presents some diatonic chord progressions that can be found in minor keys:

i	iv	V⁷	i			
i	VII	III	VI	ii°	V⁷	I
i	ii°⁷	i⁶₄	V	i		
i	ii°	vii°⁷	i			

🎼 Practice Box 20.7

Write the four most commonly used diatonic seventh chords for the key of B minor and label them with Roman numerals.

Provide a Roman numeral analysis for this example. Every note in the example is part of a chord.

Structure in Seventh Chords

The study of structure in part writing is designed to govern one specific aspect of four-voice texture: the issue of doubling. When using triads in four-part harmony, it is always necessary to double one chord tone.

When dealing with seventh chords, that consideration is removed. There are four chord tones in a seventh chord; therefore, generally each of them is assigned to one voice, and the issue of doubling is no longer a part of the process. That is not to say that it is not possible to double one of the tones of a seventh chord, but to do so would involve omitting one of the other chord tones. When doubling does occur, typically the root is doubled and the fifth of the chord is omitted.

Because doubling is not a major factor, the issue of whether to use open, close, or neutral structure does not exist when part-writing seventh chords. It is really only possible to discuss the relative proximity of the voices to one another and liken that proximity to close or open structure. Figure 20.15 demonstrates two possible ways to voice a seventh chord built on G. The first chord is similar to a close-structure triad, since the upper three voices are within the span of an octave. The second chord is more like open structure, with the upper three voices considerably more spread out. If the prevailing structure of a part-writing exercise is close structure, then the first example is most appropriate. If the prevailing structure is open, then the second example would be the better choice.

Figure 20.15.   *Possible choices for structure in seventh chords*

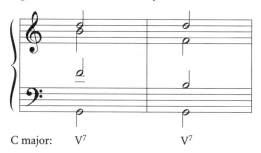

C major: V⁷   V⁷

When part-writing seventh chords, it is again necessary to spell the chords above the staff and underline the names of notes that are already present in the soprano and bass. This will help you keep track of the chord tones so that you will not omit or unintentionally double one.

The most important aspect of part writing that involves seventh chords is the voice-leading movement of the chordal seventh.

The chordal seventh must move stepwise downward.

This chord tone is typically treated as if it were a type of non-harmonic tone that must resolve downward. For now, notice the stepwise motion of the chordal sevenths in the exercises below; more emphasis will be placed on this voice-leading convention in the next chapter.

Practice Box 20.8

Spell each chord above the staff. Determine an appropriate structure based on the soprano line and add inner voices for all the triads. Then determine the placement of alto and tenor notes for the seventh chords. Your goal should be smooth voice leading with as few leaps as possible. Also add a Roman numeral analysis.

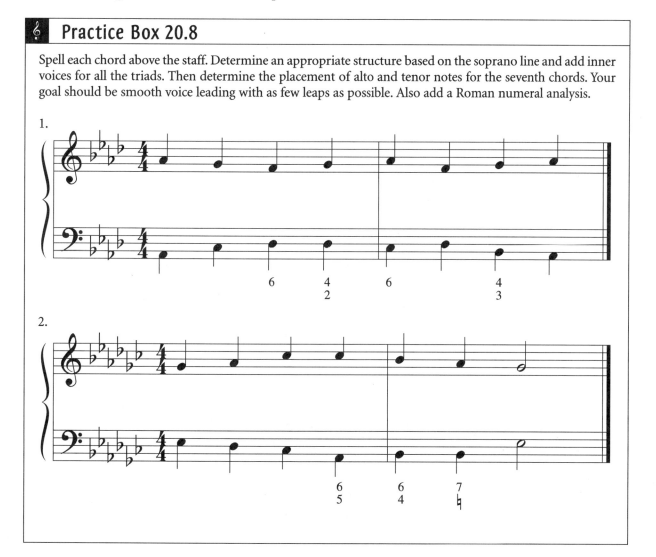

Music for Analysis

Name the qualities of the triads and seventh chords used in the compositions below. Spell the chords above the staff and write the qualities underneath the chords.

Example 20.1.   Dave Brubeck, "Going to Sleep," mm. 1–4

Track 20, 0:00

In this example, the chords in the right hand are accompanied by a boogie-woogie style rhythm in the bass. Analyze the chords found in the treble staff. Not all of them will be seventh chords. Circle the ones that are not.

Example 20.2.   Brubeck, "Pick Up Sticks," mm. 30–35

Track 20, 0:23

AURAL SKILLS

Melody

Sing the following melodies using solfege or numbers. These melodies contain outlines of seventh chords.

Harmony

Sing the following exercises in four-part harmony. All of them contain seventh chords.

Rhythm

Practice these rhythms in simple meters. All contain borrowed divisions of the beat. Notice that in meters where the half note gets the beat, the triplet figure is not beamed, because the notes that make up the figure are quarter notes.

Dictation

Identify the quality of each of the seventh chords that you hear.

1. major-major	major-minor		1. major-major	minor-minor
2. major-major	major-minor		2. major-major	minor-minor
3. major-major	major-minor		3. major-major	minor-minor
4. major-major	major-minor		4. major-major	minor-minor
5. major-major	major-minor		5. major-major	minor-minor

1. major-minor	fully diminished		1. fully diminished	half-diminished
2. major-minor	fully diminished		2. fully diminished	half-diminished
3. major-minor	fully diminished		3. fully diminished	half-diminished
4. major-minor	fully diminished		4. fully diminished	half-diminished
5. major-minor	fully diminished		5. fully diminished	half-diminished

1. major-minor	fully diminished	half-diminished
2. major-minor	fully diminished	half-diminished
3. major-minor	fully diminished	half-diminished
4. major-minor	fully diminished	half-diminished
5. major-minor	fully diminished	half-diminished
6. major-minor	fully diminished	half-diminished
7. major-minor	fully diminished	half-diminished
8. major-minor	fully diminished	half-diminished
9. major-minor	fully diminished	half-diminished
10. major-minor	fully diminished	half-diminished

The following rhythms represent exactly harmonized melodies that you will hear. There will be seventh chords in the progressions. Every time you hear a seventh chord, circle the note where it occurs in the measure.

1.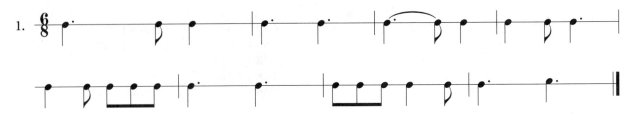

2.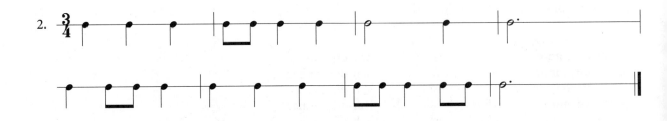

3.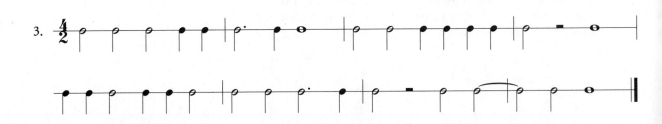

4.

KEYBOARD APPLICATIONS

Play the following chord exercises with both hands.

1.

Continue transposing this exercise up through all twelve possible starting notes.

2.

Continue transposing this exercise up through all twelve possible starting notes.

chapter **21** Dominant and Leading-Tone Seventh Chords

The Dominant Seventh Chord

The dominant seventh (V^7) chord appears more often than any other type of seventh chord. It can be used in all of its inversions in both major and minor keys. In any chord progression, it will be used in the same place as a dominant triad. At cadence points, if it is in root position it can be part of a perfect authentic cadence, provided that the tonic chord is also in root position and that *do* is in the soprano. If the dominant seventh chord is in an inversion, or any chord tone other than *do* appears in the soprano of the tonic chord, then the cadence is imperfect authentic. Figure 21.1 demonstrates both perfect and imperfect authentic cadences with dominant seventh chords.

Figure 21.1. *Authentic cadences using 7th chords*

C major: V^7 I V^7 I
         Perfect authentic   Imperfect authentic
         do in soprano   *mi* in soprano

Here are some examples of dominant seventh chords in actual compositions. Example 21.1 contains the dominant seventh chord in root position and second inversion. Find and label the seventh chords in Examples 21.2 and 21.3.

Example 21.1. Tchaikovsky, Album for the Young, *"Neapolitan Dance-Tune," op. 39, no. 18, mm. 1–11*

Track 21, 0:00

sempre staccato

330

Example 21.2.   Haydn, Piano Sonata no. 38, Hob. XVI/23, 2nd movement, mm. 1–3

Track 21, 0:25

Example 21.3.   Beethoven, Sonatina in E♭, WoO 47/1, 2nd movement, mm. 1–4

Track 21, 0:42

In addition to being used as a harmonic sonority, the V⁷ chord is often outlined melodically. Example 21.4 is a very famous demonstration of that technique from a symphony by Haydn.

Example 21.4.   Haydn, Symphony no. 94 in G Major, "Surprise," 2nd movement, mm. 1–16

Track 21, 0:57

Part-Writing Considerations

As mentioned in the previous chapter, there is one crucial rule that must be observed when part writing any type of seventh chord.

The chordal seventh must resolve stepwise downward.

This means that you must always be aware of the name of the pitch that forms the seventh of any four-note chord. Spelling the chords above the staff is a great help in this process. You might want to develop a practice of putting a small star or asterisk above the chordal seventh when you spell the chord (when spelling the chords in root position above the staff, this will always be the last note that you write).

Locate the chordal seventh in each of the chords in Figure 21.2 and then notice the direction it moves when it resolves to the next chord. In each case, the movement is downward. This downward resolution also dictates the inversion of tonic chord that can follow the third-inversion dominant seventh chord. Since the chordal seventh, which is the fourth scale degree, appears in the bass in this chord, it must move downward to the third scale degree, which means that the tonic chord must appear in first inversion.

Figure 21.2.   *Downward resolution of the chordal 7th*

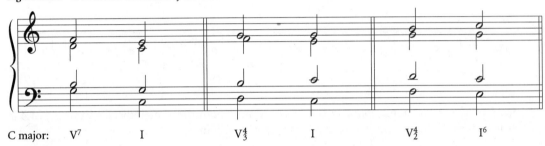

C major: V^7 I V^4_3 I V^4_2 I^6

The resolution of the chordal seventh can be delayed by the insertion of a tonic six-four chord into the progression. This usually happens with a supertonic seventh chord that precedes a cadential six-four chord. Another method of delaying the resolution of a chordal seventh is through the use of a suspension. Despite any type of delay of the resolution, the chordal seventh still must resolve stepwise downward.

Doubling is generally not an issue in seventh chords, since there are four notes in the chord and four voices in the texture in which to place them. However, *it is possible to double the root of a seventh chord and omit the chordal fifth.* This is most often done when the chord is in root position.

One other special circumstance can apply to the voice leading between the dominant seventh and tonic chords. In some cases following a dominant seventh chord, it is necessary to create a tonic chord that has a tripled root. Remember that in this case, the fifth of the tonic triad is omitted. In the example below, this is done to avoid an unusually large leap in one of the inner voices. This scenario will usually be necessary only at authentic cadences.

Figure 21.3.   *Omission of chordal 5th in tonic triad following V^7 chord*

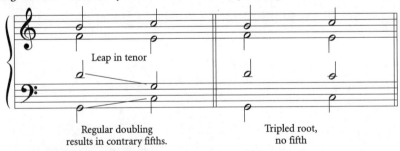

In the first example above, the chordal seventh must resolve downward to an E, which is the third of the tonic triad. Under the normal rules of doubling, the only chord tone remaining, which is G, must go into the tenor voice. This creates a rather large leap in the tenor, accompanied by contrary fifths, which are marked with diagonal lines in the example. In the second version, this leap is avoided by taking advantage of the option that allows us to triple the root of the chord and omit the fifth. This option is usually needed only when the tonic triad is preceded by a dominant seventh chord. It is used to avoid poor voice leading, leaps larger than a fourth in a single voice, and incorrect parallelism.

An alternative to omitting the fifth in the tonic triad is to use an incomplete dominant seventh chord. Just as when a chord tone is omitted in the tonic triad, it is always the chordal fifth, the same holds true for the dominant seventh chord. In the next example, the dominant seventh chord, spelled G–B–D–F, is written with a doubled root and the fifth (D) omitted. Two possible voicings, both of which omit the chordal fifth, are presented in Figure 21.4. This makes it possible to use a complete tonic triad on the final chord. Either of these solutions, omitting the fifth in the tonic triad or in the seventh chord, is an acceptable alternative.

Figure 21.4. *Omission of chordal 5th in V⁷ chord*

Notice the voice-leading characteristics of all four parts. As already discussed, the chordal seventh resolves downward. But the dominant seventh chord also contains the leading tone, and the voice containing that note should resolve upward. In the first measure of Example 21.4, these two notes form a diminished fifth (seen in this example between the soprano and alto). The diminished fifth resolves in contrary motion to a third. In the second measure, the two pitches in question are rewritten to form an augmented fourth, also found in the soprano and alto voices. In this case, the augmented fourth resolves outward to a sixth. These are standard and desirable voice-leading movements for specific components of the dominant seventh chord. Remember that if the leading tone scale degree appears in the soprano, it must resolve stepwise upward. If it appears in the alto or tenor voice, it may resolve to other scale degrees, but resolution to the tonic is always preferable.

It is especially important to spell the seventh chords above the staff. Underline the names of the chord tones that are given to you in the soprano and bass. As you add each note of the chord to your part-writing examples, underline them too. This will help ensure that you do not omit any chord tones.

Practice Box 21.1

Add inner voices and a Roman numeral analysis.

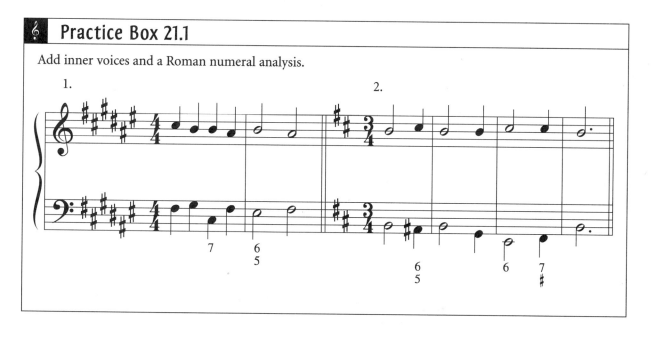

Practice Box 21.1 (continued)

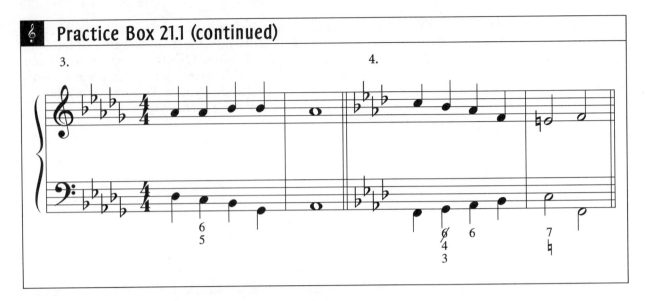

The Leading-Tone Seventh Chord

The leading-tone seventh chord, which is half-diminished in a major key and may be either fully or half-diminished in a minor key, is an acceptable substitute for the dominant triad or dominant seventh chord. The half-diminished seventh is not commonly used in either major or minor keys. Of the two qualities possible for this chord, the fully diminished seventh exerts a far stronger pull toward the tonic than does the half-diminished chord. Since the function of any dominant-type chord is to lead toward the tonic, this pull helps explain the greater frequency with which the fully diminished seventh chord is used.

It should be noted that although the half-diminished chord is diatonic in major keys, it is possible to build a fully diminished leading-tone seventh chord in a major key using an accidental. A lowered sixth scale degree is required to construct this chord. This is called a **borrowed chord,** and the chord is considered to be "borrowed" from the parallel minor scale. A chord spelled B♭–D–F–A♭ is the diatonic vii°7 in C minor. If this same chord is used in C major, it is considered a "borrowed" vii°7 chord. Because the chord contains a note that is not part of the diatonic scale, it is also known as an *altered* chord. Borrowed chords and other kinds of chromatic harmony will be studied in volume 2 of *Theory Essentials*.

Occasionally, as in Example 21.5, the dominant and leading-tone seventh chords are both used in the position of the dominant chord in a chord progression.

Example 21.5.   Mozart, Piano Sonata in C Minor, K. 457, 1st movement, mm. 1–8

Track 21, 1:36

The half-diminished leading-tone seventh chord is much less common than the fully diminished one, but it is seen occasionally. In Example 21.6, the half-diminished leading-tone seventh chord is followed immediately by a fully diminished one in measure 4.

Example 21.6.   *Amy Beach,* The Year's at the Spring, *mm. 1–6*

Track 21, 1:58

Find the leading-tone seventh chord that appears near the end of Example 21.7 and determine its quality.

Example 21.7.   *Schubert, Impromptu, op. 142, no. 1, mm. 1–4*

Track 21, 2:21

F minor: i

The fully diminished seventh chord is one of the most compelling diatonic chords for indicating the name of a key. The only Roman numeral that can ever be assigned to a diatonic fully diminished seventh chord is vii°[7]. Considering that this particular chord quality is only identified with this particular Roman numeral, its resolution will always be to a tonic chord. In other words, the fully diminished chord will always resolve to a chord whose root is up a half step from the root of the seventh chord. Study the chords in Figure 21.5. Notice how the root of each resolves up a minor second to the tonic scale degree.

Figure 21.5.   *Resolving leading-tone 7th chords in minor keys*

D minor: vii°⁷°   i   E minor: vii°⁷°

In each of the measures above, the key is very clearly indicated by the presence of the vii°⁷ chord. Notice how the root of the fully diminished chord resolves up a half step to the tonic scale degree. Both of these examples are in minor, since that is where the fully diminished seventh chord occurs diatonically. Remember that an accidental is necessary to create the leading tone in any minor key.

If we allow the use of an altered tone in a major key to create the fully diminished chord, then it is possible for the vii°⁷ chord to resolve to a tonic in either a major or a minor key. (In a major key, the vii°⁷ chord is *not* diatonic. It can be labeled with a letter "B" under the Roman numeral to indicate that it is "borrowed" from the parallel minor key.) Figure 21.6 demonstrates fully diminished (borrowed) leading-tone seventh chords in major keys.

Figure 21.6.   *Resolving leading-tone 7th chords in major keys*

F major: vii°⁷°   I   G major: vii°⁷°   I
            B   B

Although the key signatures are the same in Figures 21.5 and 21.6, different keys are indicated in each of these figures through the use of fully diminished seventh chords. Also notice that each chord contains an accidental. In minor keys, that accidental is the leading tone. In major keys, the accidental is the lowered sixth scale degree necessary to create the borrowed leading-tone seventh chord.

🎼 Practice Box 21.2

Even without a key signature, it is possible to determine the key for each of these leading-tone seventh chords. Assume that each chord is the fully diminished seventh chord of a minor key. Name the key for each chord.

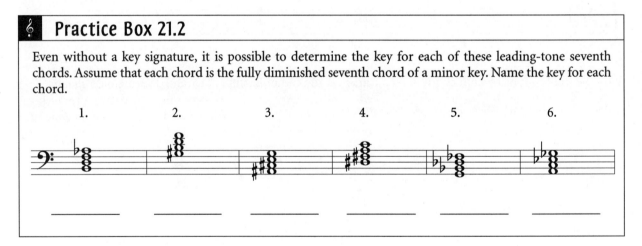

1.   2.   3.   4.   5.   6.

_____   _____   _____   _____   _____   _____

Even when the fully diminished seventh chord appears in inversion, you can still determine the name of the chord of resolution by identifying the root of the vii°⁷ chord and naming the note that is a minor second up (the distance from the leading tone to the tonic). To determine the key for each of the vii°⁷ chords in Figure 21.7, first name the root of each inverted chord. Then think of that note as the leading tone of a key and name the key (the key signature will help). Remember that the easiest way to determine the root of an inverted seventh chord is to look for the second that is formed and name the higher of the two notes.

Figure 21.7.   *Resolving leading-tone 7th chords in inversions*

Root = A♯
Key = B minor

Root = D
Key = E♭ major

Practice Box 21.3

Name the key indicated by each of these leading-tone seventh chords. Spell the chords above the staff in root position.

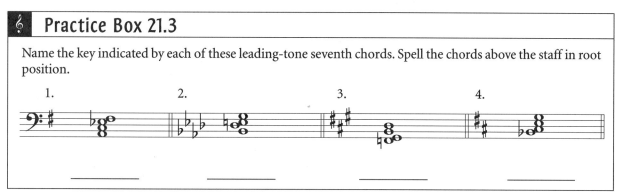

1.   2.   3.   4.

_____   _____   _____   _____

The fully diminished seventh chord is built entirely of minor thirds. These minor thirds create a symmetrical chord, one in which all notes are equidistant. In addition to understanding this principle of chord construction, you should also notice that the chord consists of two interlocking tritones. You should remember that this term can be used to refer to either an augmented fourth or a diminished fifth. The intervals that make up a fully diminished seventh chord are shown in Figure 21.8.

Figure 21.8.   *Intervallic construction of fully diminished 7th chords*

minor 3   minor 3   minor 3

Notice that the distance between the root and the chordal seventh in this chord is a diminished seventh. When inverted, the diminished seventh becomes an augmented second, which is enharmonically equivalent to a minor third. This means that even when inverted, the leading-tone seventh chord retains its symmetrical properties. In fact, because all of the notes are equidistant, even when inverted, the chord can be described from an aural perspective as having no root. This means that you cannot determine the root of the chord just by hearing it. The symmetrical properties of fully diminished seventh chords will be explored in greater depth in volume 2 of *Theory Essentials.*

There are no perfect fifths in a fully diminished seventh chord. Because of that, it is impossible to create parallel fifths (or octaves) in either the approach or the resolution of the chord. However, the half-diminished seventh chord does contain a perfect fifth between the chordal third and the chordal seventh. Therefore, parallelism is a consideration when using a half-diminished leading-tone seventh chord. Consider your voice leading carefully when using a half-diminished chord.

The same part-writing rules that applied to dominant seventh chords also apply to fully and half-diminished seventh chords. The chordal seventh must resolve downward. In fact, it is typical for all voices of a leading-tone seventh chord to resolve with stepwise motion (either up or down). See Figure 21.9.

Figure 21.9.   *Stepwise resolution of all chord tones in leading-tone 7th chords*

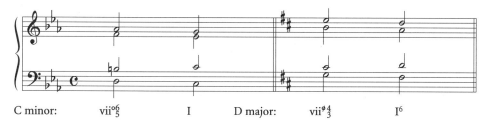

C minor: vii°⁶₅   I   D major: vii°⁴₃   I⁶

Practice Box 21.4

Add inner voices and a Roman numeral analysis. In these exercises, all leading-tone sevenths are in root position.

These examples use leading-tone seventh chords in inversion. You may also find a fully diminished seventh chord used in a major key.

Music for Analysis

Find the dominant and leading-tone seventh chords in these examples.

Example 21.8.   R. Schumann, Papillons, *op. 2, no. 6, mm. 1–4*

Example 21.9.   Mozart, Piano Concerto in C Major, K. 467, 1st movement, mm. 1–8

There are non-chord tones in the melody of Example 21.10. Base your Roman numeral analysis on the left-hand part.

Example 21.10.   R. Schumann, Carnaval, "Chiarina," mm. 1–4

AURAL SKILLS

Alto Clef

Sing these longer melodies, which are written in alto clef.

Chords

Sing the following broken chord progressions in a variety of keys. These progressions include outlines of seventh chords.

1.

D major: I V^7 I

2.

B minor: i V^6_5 i

3.

E♭ major: I   vii°⁷   I

4.

D minor: i   vii°⁷   i

5.

A minor: i   iv V^4_3 i

6.

E minor: i   VI   ii° V^7 i

Rhythm

These exercises combine triplet figures with subdivisions in simple meters. It will be necessary to alternate counting in this manner: "one-la-li, two-e-and-a"; or "one-e-and-a, two-la-li." It may be helpful to practice these exercises with a metronome.

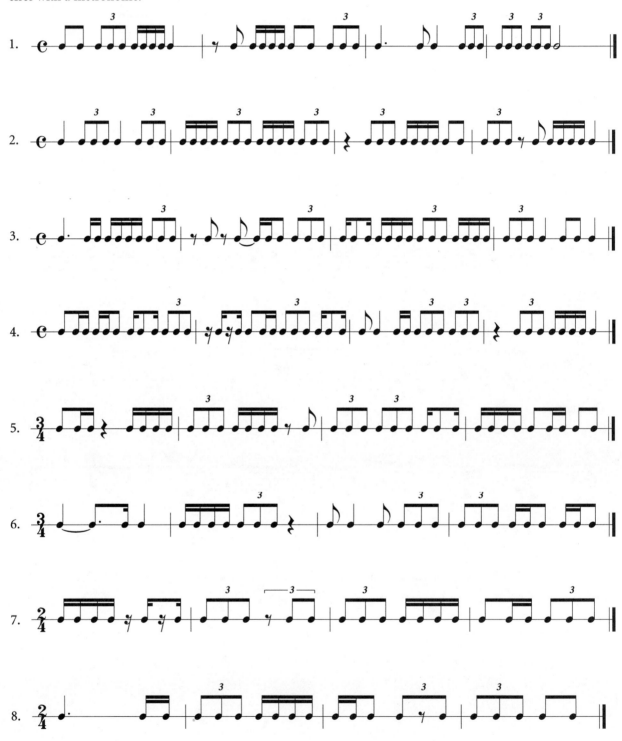

Dual Rhythm

These rhythms should be tapped with both hands. They use simple meters and subdivisions of the beat.

Dictation

Identify the quality of each of these seventh chords.

1. major-major	major-minor	1. major-major	minor-minor
2. major-major	major-minor	2. major-major	minor-minor
3. major-major	major-minor	3. major-major	minor-minor
4. major-major	major-minor	4. major-major	minor-minor
5. major-major	major-minor	5. major-major	minor-minor

1. major-minor	fully diminished	1. fully diminished	half-diminished
2. major-minor	fully diminished	2. fully diminished	half-diminished
3. major-minor	fully diminished	3. fully diminished	half-diminished
4. major-minor	fully diminished	4. fully diminished	half-diminished
5. major-minor	fully diminished	5. fully diminished	half-diminished

1. major-minor	fully diminished	half-diminished
2. major-minor	fully diminished	half-diminished
3. major-minor	fully diminished	half-diminished
4. major-minor	fully diminished	half-diminished
5. major-minor	fully diminished	half-diminished
6. major-minor	fully diminished	half-diminished
7. major-minor	fully diminished	half-diminished
8. major-minor	fully diminished	half-diminished
9. major-minor	fully diminished	half-diminished
10. major-minor	fully diminished	half-diminished

Notate the following melodies in alto clef. Only beat notes and regular divisions of the beat will be used.

1.

2.
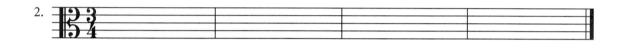

3.

4.

5.

6.

KEYBOARD APPLICATIONS

Play the following chord progressions. Remember to resolve all chordal sevenths downward.

1.   A♭ major
     B♭ major
     E major

sol	*sol*	*la*	*ti*	*do*
I	V$^6_5$	vi	V^7	I

2.   A minor
     G♯ minor
     B♭ minor

do	*do*	*ti*	*do*
i	iv	V$^4_2$	i^6

Notice the quality of the leading-tone seventh chord in the following exercise. It is a borrowed chord.

3.   E♭ major
     F major
     A major

do	*ti*	*do*	*ti*	*do*
I	V$^4_3$	I^6	vii°$^4_3$	I^6

Looking Ahead

You have now learned all the possible qualities of chords that can function as dominants. There are five of them:

1. major triad (V)
2. major-minor seventh (V^7)
3. diminished triad (vii°)
4. diminished minor or half-diminished seventh (vii^{ø7})
5. diminished-diminished or fully diminished seventh (vii°^{7})

Each of these can be considered a **dominant-type** chord. When one of these chords functions as a dominant of the prevailing key, its function can be said to be "primary." Based on its quality and Roman numeral, each has a specific type of resolution to its own tonic chord. For example, the root of a dominant or dominant seventh chord resolves down a perfect fifth to the root of the tonic triad. The root of a diminished triad or diminished seventh chord resolves up a minor second to the root of its tonic.

It is also possible to use a dominant-type chord in a secondary role within a key. Any dominant-type chord has a predictable manner of resolution. If a chord such as G–B–D–F is used in the context of the key of F major, it is not a diatonic chord (the B♮ is not in the key signature). Nevertheless, the chord will continue to function as a dominant-type chord and should resolve to a tonic triad built on C. (See Figure 21.10.) This chord is called a "secondary dominant" because it behaves as if it were the dominant chord of a key other than the primary key of F major.

Figure 21.10.   Secondary dominant in F major

Because it contains an altered tone, this dominant-type triad is not analyzed as if it were part of the key of F major. Its analysis reflects its relationship to the chord that follows it—in other words, the C major triad, which is the dominant of F major. A fraction symbol is used to represent this relationship. Any of the five dominant-type chords listed above can behave in this manner. They can resolve to the following scale degrees: dominant, supertonic, subdominant, submediant, and less commonly, mediant.

Secondary dominant chords will be studied in greater depth in volume 2 of *Theory Essentials*.

chapter 22 Additional Seventh Chords

THEORETICAL SKILLS

The Supertonic Seventh Chord

The supertonic seventh chord is frequently found in both major and minor keys. In a major key, it exists as a minor-minor quality chord. In a minor key, it is most commonly found with a half-diminished quality. The chord is most often used in an inversion. Certainly in minor keys, it is infrequently used in root position because of the diminished triad that forms part of the chord. Examples 22.1 and 22.2 both show the opening measures of compositions that begin with the supertonic seventh chord.

Example 22.1. R. Schumann, Intermezzo, op. 4, no. 4, m. 1

Track 22, 0:00

The example above used the minor ii⁷ chord as the opening sonority of a composition. In the next example, Beethoven used the same chord to open one of his piano sonatas. Determine the inversions that are used for the supertonic seventh chord in both of these examples.

Example 22.2. Beethoven, Piano Sonata, op. 31, no. 3, 3rd movement, mm. 1–8

Track 22, 0:17

There is a secondary dominant chord in the preceding example. Can you find it? To which chord does it resolve?

The chordal seventh of a supertonic seventh chord will resolve downward, just as it did in the dominant seventh chords studied in the previous chapter. Find the chordal seventh in all of the seventh chords above and notice the nature of its resolution. Although the resolution may be delayed for several measures through the use of a cadential six-four chord or non-harmonic tones, you will find that the downward resolution always occurs.

When part writing a supertonic seventh chord in a major key, it is possible to double the third of the chord and omit the fifth. This can happen only in root-position chords.

348

Practice Box 22.1

Add inner voices and a Roman numeral analysis.

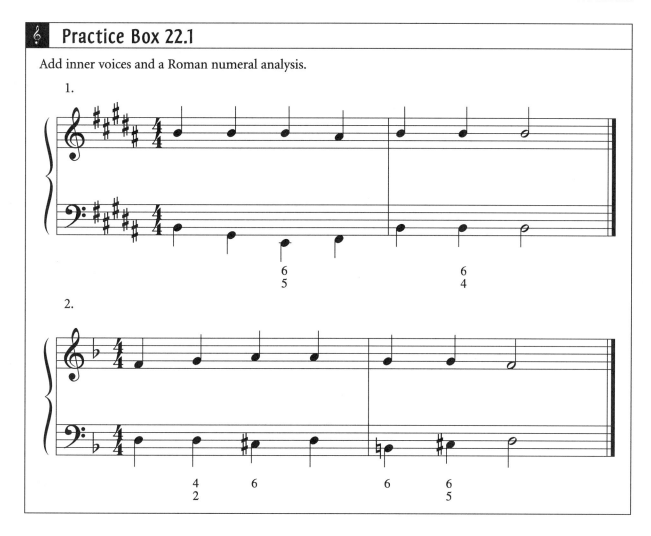

The Subdominant Seventh Chord

The seventh chord built on the fourth scale degree in a major key is the only common diatonic use of a major-major seventh chord quality. The major seventh that forms the outer interval of this chord is highly dissonant and creates a strong pull to the dominant chord. The IV^7 is usually followed by a dominant triad in root position or a cadential six-four chord, creating stepwise movement in the bass voice. It can also be followed by a dominant seventh chord in third inversion, which creates a common tone in the bass voice between the two chords.

The subdominant seventh chord, like all other seventh chords, is also occasionally created through voice-leading movement in one voice, as seen in Example 22.3 from the music of J. S. Bach.

Example 22.3.   J. S. Bach, Chorale, O Ewigkeit, du Donnerwort, *mm. 1–2*

Track 22, 0:38

The subdominant seventh chord is uncommon in minor keys. There are two possible chord qualities in minor, iv^7 and IV^7. When the chord contains the raised sixth scale degree (IV^7) the quality is major-minor. In this case, the chord will have the sound of a dominant seventh chord, but will not behave as if it were a dominant-type chord. For this reason, the IV^7 is seldom found in minor keys.

Practice Box 22.2

Add inner voices and a Roman numeral analysis.

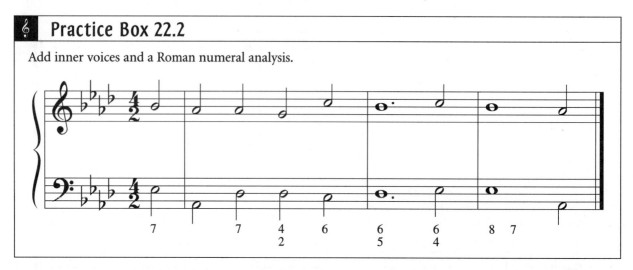

The Mediant and Submediant Seventh Chords

Although these are the least common of the diatonic seventh chords, the mediant and submediant seventh chords are occasionally seen. Both chords are minor-minor in major keys. These chords are virtually nonexistent in minor keys. If they are used in minor keys, both chords are major-major in quality. The half-diminished submediant seventh chord, using the raised sixth scale degree, is extremely rare.

Analyze Example 22.4 to find the seventh chords. There are a variety of seventh chords used, including one submediant seventh. Be careful to distinguish the non-harmonic tones from the chord tones.

Example 22.4.   *Mendelssohn*, Kinderstück, *op. 72, no. 1, mm. 1–8*

Track 22, 0:51

The previous excerpt contains a submediant seventh chord. In Example 22.5 from the Bach chorales, both a mediant and a submediant seventh chord are present. One of the seventh chords is incomplete and is created through the use of a half note. The X on the staff should help you find it. What is doubled in the incomplete seventh chord?

Example 22.5.   J. S. Bach, Chorale, O Ewigkeit, du Donnerwort, *mm. 3–4*

Track 22, 1:13

♪ Practice Box 22.3

Add inner voices and a Roman numeral analysis. The chord with $\frac{8}{6}{3}$ in the figured bass is a first-inversion chord. The 8 is there to indicate that the bass should be doubled, creating irregular doubling in this first-inversion chord. In the following chord, the dashes tell you not to move those pitches created in the preceding chord. (Those notes will remain as quarter notes.) In the third chord of the first measure, there will be only one other moving note besides the bass. After creating the notes indicated by the figures, spell the resulting chord in root position and analyze it.

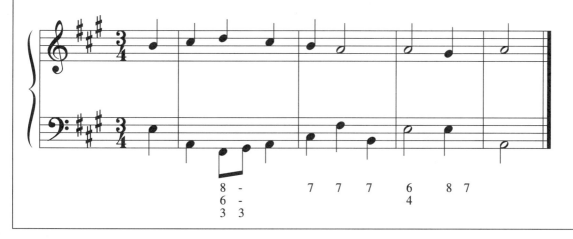

Ninth and Thirteenth Chords

Ninth and thirteenth chords add additional intervals above a chord root. A complete **ninth chord,** with all chord tones present, will contain five notes. A complete **thirteenth chord** will contain seven notes, or all the notes of the diatonic major scale.

Figure 22.1.   All chord tones for 9th and 13th chords

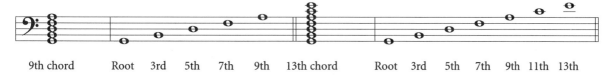

9th chord   Root   3rd   5th   7th   9th   13th chord   Root   3rd   5th   7th   9th   11th   13th

In four-part harmony it is not possible to include all voices of these chords, so it is important to know which chord tones should be omitted. Table 24 shows which voices should be included and which should be omitted.

Table 24.   *Omitted chord tones for four-part harmony using 9th and 13th chords*

	Chord tones included	**Chord tones omitted**
9th chords	Root, 3rd, 5th, 7th	5th
13th chords	Root, 3rd, 7th, 13th	5th, 9th, 11th

Both ninth and thirteenth chords most commonly occur in diatonic harmony on the dominant scale degree. Common Roman numerals for these chords are V^9 and V^{13}. These chords seldom appear in anything other than root position.

In major keys, the dominant ninth chord contains a major ninth above the root of the chord. It is also possible to displace the chordal ninth an octave higher, but never an octave lower, because that would form an interval of a second with the root of the chord. Notice in Figure 22.2 that both the chordal seventh and the chordal ninth resolve downward.

Figure 22.2. V^9 *in a major-key chord progression*

C major: I   ii⁶ V^9 I

In a minor key, the chordal ninth of a dominant ninth chord will create the interval of a minor ninth with the root of the chord. You will notice that the Roman numeral remains the same for either a major or a minor dominant ninth chord, because the foundation triad is major in both chords. Figure 22.3 shows a dominant ninth chord in a minor key progression. Again, the chordal seventh and chordal ninth resolve downward.

Figure 22.3. V^9 *in a minor-key chord progression*

C minor: i   ii°⁶₅ V^9 i

The dominant thirteenth chord is more commonly found in major keys than in minor. In major keys, the chordal thirteenth creates a very distinctive consonant interval with the root of the chord. It may be helpful to think of this interval as a major sixth above the bass (instead of a thirteenth, which is actually a compound interval equivalent to a sixth). The chordal thirteenth often is found in a prominent upper voice (usually the soprano) and often resolves downward by a leap of a third. This is demonstrated in four-voice harmony in Figure 22.4. The chord tones that are present include the root, third, seventh, and thirteenth. Describe the manner of resolution of the chordal thirteenth.

Figure 22.4.   V^{13} in a chord progression

C major: I   V^{13}   I

Here are two examples of ninth and thirteenth chords from actual compositions. Identify the chord tones that are present in the ninth chord in Example 22.6.

Example 22.6.   R. Schumann, Papillons, *op. 2, no. 6, mm. 18–24.*

Track 22, 1:27

There are a number of dominant thirteenth chords in Example 22.7. How does the chordal thirteenth resolve each time?

Example 22.7.   Chopin, Ballade in F Major, op. 38, mm. 41–46

Track 22, 1:43

Practice Box 22.4

Add inner voices and a Roman numeral analysis.

Music for Analysis

The following excerpts contain examples of seventh, ninth, and thirteenth chords. Provide a Roman numeral analysis.

Example 22.8. R. Schumann, Kinderszenen, *"Träumerei,"* op. 15, no. 7, mm. 1–4

Track 22, 2:07

Example 22.9. Mendelssohn, Confidence, op. 19, no. 4, op. 15, no. 7, mm. 5–9

Track 22, 2:34

Example 22.10. Beach, Ariette, mm. 1–16

Track 22, 2:53

AURAL SKILLS

Tenor Clef

Another C clef that is occasionally seen is the tenor clef. It looks just like the alto clef, but places middle C higher on the staff. It is used primarily in music written for the cello and the tenor trombone. Practice these melodies, which use the tenor clef.

Harmony

Sing the following exercises in four-part harmony. They contain a variety of seventh chords.

Rhythm

In a compound meter, the beat is normally divided into three equal parts. Just as in simple meters, it is also possible to have borrowed divisions of the beat in compound meters. The borrowed division would divide the beat into two equal parts instead. This rhythmic figure is called a **duplet**.

The notation of borrowed divisions in compound meters follows exactly the same pattern as in simple meters, using a number placed on the stem side of the note. If the notes are not beamed together, then a bracket is used as well. The notation of this rhythm is shown in Figure 22.5.

Figure 22.5.   Duplets in compound meters

The duplet figure is counted "and one-and-two-and," just as if it were a normal division of the beat in a simple meter.

Practice Box 22.5

Clap and count these rhythms, which contain duplets.

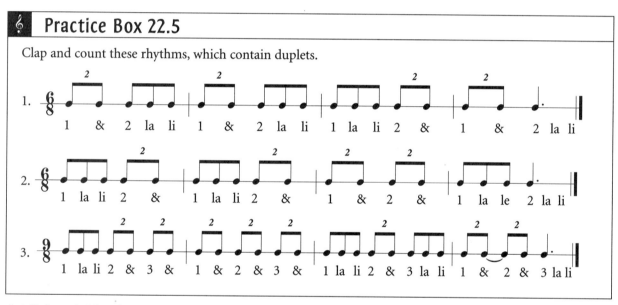

Additional Rhythms

For extra practice, clap and count these exercises.

Dual Rhythm

These rhythms should be tapped with both hands. They use compound meters and subdivisions of the beat.

Dictation

Circle the quality of the seventh chords that you hear.

1. major-major   major-minor   minor-minor   fully diminished   half-diminished
2. major-major   major-minor   minor-minor   fully diminished   half-diminished
3. major-major   major-minor   minor-minor   fully diminished   half-diminished
4. major-major   major-minor   minor-minor   fully diminished   half-diminished
5. major-major   major-minor   minor-minor   fully diminished   half-diminished
6. major-major   major-minor   minor-minor   fully diminished   half-diminished
7. major-major   major-minor   minor-minor   fully diminished   half-diminished
8. major-major   major-minor   minor-minor   fully diminished   half-diminished
9. major-major   major-minor   minor-minor   fully diminished   half-diminished
10. major-major   major-minor   minor-minor   fully diminished   half-diminished
11. major-major   major-minor   minor-minor   fully diminished   half-diminished
12. major-major   major-minor   minor-minor   fully diminished   half-diminished
13. major-major   major-minor   minor-minor   fully diminished   half-diminished
14. major-major   major-minor   minor-minor   fully diminished   half-diminished
15. major-major   major-minor   minor-minor   fully diminished   half-diminished
16. major-major   major-minor   minor-minor   fully diminished   half-diminished
17. major-major   major-minor   minor-minor   fully diminished   half-diminished
18. major-major   major-minor   minor-minor   fully diminished   half-diminished
19. major-major   major-minor   minor-minor   fully diminished   half-diminished
20. major-major   major-minor   minor-minor   fully diminished   half-diminished
21. major-major   major-minor   minor-minor   fully diminished   half-diminished
22. major-major   major-minor   minor-minor   fully diminished   half-diminished
23. major-major   major-minor   minor-minor   fully diminished   half-diminished
24. major-major   major-minor   minor-minor   fully diminished   half-diminished
25. major-major   major-minor   minor-minor   fully diminished   half-diminished

Notate the following melodies in alto clef.

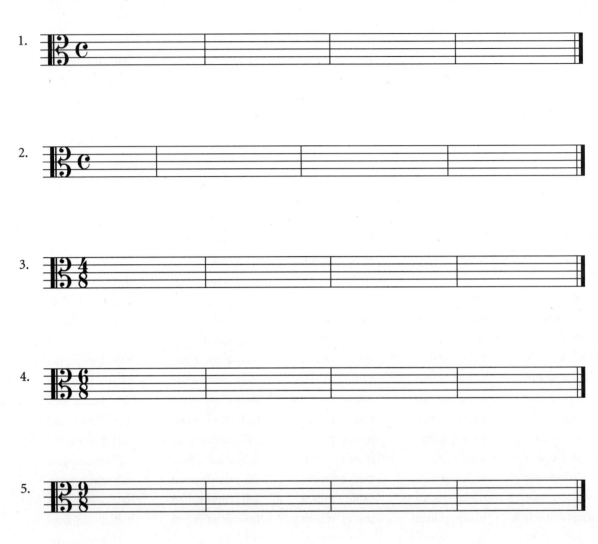

KEYBOARD APPLICATIONS

Play the following chord progressions. You may need to use irregular doubling in order to resolve one of the chordal sevenths properly.

1. B minor
    C# minor
    G minor

me	fa	fa	me
i	ii$^{\phi 4}_{\ \ 2}$	vii^{o7}	i

2. B major
    C♭ major
    D major

sol	sol	fa	fa	mi
I	vi^7	ii^7	V^7	I

chapter **23** Diatonic Modulation

THEORETICAL SKILLS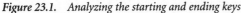

Introduction to Modulation

When we talk about **modulation** in music, we are usually referring to the process of changing keys somewhere within a composition. This means that the tonal center of the piece has shifted from one key, major or minor, to another key, major or minor. This change can be permanent (although that is unusual in music of the Common Practice Period or temporary, and the key signature is not necessarily changed to reflect the new key. If the process is temporary, the change to the new key center can be brief or lengthy.

Modulation can be accomplished through many methods. In this chapter we will be dealing with a process called **diatonic modulation.** This refers to the fact that all chords, including the point of modulation, are diatonic in their respective keys. In volume 2, we will study other methods of modulation. Various methods are utilized to create modulations between keys with certain relationships, such as relative keys or parallel keys.

In Figure 23.1, look at the beginning and the end of the excerpt. Try to determine the starting key and the ending key. Put Roman numerals under the first three chords and the last three chords. For now, don't worry about how the modulation was accomplished or how to demonstrate it in your analysis.

Figure 23.1. Analyzing the starting and ending keys

Key: ___ ___ ___   Key: ___ ___ ___

The starting key and the ending key are not the same, and yet the key signature did not change. The note that signals that the modulation has taken place is the B♭ in measure 3. Since the starting key is C major, which has no sharps or flats in the key signature, the ending of this piece obviously does not take place in that key because B♭ does not exist in C major. That means the modulation took place somewhere before the chord that contains the B♭.

Also, notice the relationship between the two keys. The starting key is C major; the ending key is F major. The key signatures for these two keys, while not identical, are very similar. There is a difference of only one accidental between the two key signatures. This is important because these two scales, C major and F major, contain many scale notes, and therefore several diatonic chords, in common.

Closely Related Keys

Within the topic of diatonic modulation, it is important to understand the concept of **closely related keys,** because it is this principle that governs the keys to which any starting key can modulate. This idea deals with the relationships of key signatures and their degrees of similarity. Keys that have similar key signatures have notes and chords in common, and it is this feature that allows diatonic modulation to take place.

To understand key relationships, first let us look at a pair of key signatures that are not similar. C major has no sharps or flats in its key signature, and B major has five sharps in its key signature. These two key signatures are drastically different. Consider the notes of the two scales. Do they have any notes in common? Only two notes are the same in both scales. Because of this, it is impossible to build a triad that is diatonic in both keys.

Scales as dissimilar as these are said to be **foreign** or **distantly related**. These keys have few or no chords in common. Using the process of diatonic modulation, it would be impossible to modulate from C major to B major or vice versa, because they have no chords in common.

Now we will find some closely related keys for C major. We already know that all keys have a relative key that shares the same key signature. For C major, this key is A minor. These two keys are as closely related as possible. We can demonstrate this relationship in a chart, as seen in Figure 23.2.

Figure 23.2.   Relative keys

However, there are other keys with similar key signatures to those in the figure above. If we add one sharp to the key signature of C major, we get G major. If we add one flat to C major, we get F major. All of these key signatures differ by only one sharp or flat. Figure 23.3 adds these keys to our chart. They are closely related keys.

Figure 23.3.   Relative keys and closely related keys

F major and G major also have relative minor keys that share their key signatures and would also be closely related to C major. Those keys are D minor and E minor. Our finished chart of closely related keys is shown in Figure 23.4.

Figure 23.4.   Complete set of closely related keys for C major

Using another key as an example, the closely related keys for B♭ major would be its relative minor, plus the keys that contain one flat more and one flat less in the key signature.

Figure 23.5.   Complete set of closely related keys for B♭ major

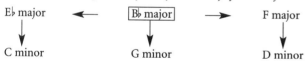

You may notice that each of the major keys listed in the chart above is a fifth away from the starting key of B♭. The same relationship exists between the minor keys listed above. When you add or subtract an accidental from a key signature, you are moving around the circle of fifths. Closely related keys are always next to each other on the circle of fifths.

Almost all keys have five closely related keys. The only exceptions are those keys that have seven sharps or flats in the key signature. C♯ major, A♯ minor, C♭ major, and A♭ minor will only have three closely related keys because it is not possible to add another sharp or flat to these key signatures.

Using the process of diatonic modulation, it is possible to modulate from any key in the chart to any other key in the same chart.

Practice Box 23.1

Name the closely related keys for the following keys. Fill in the blanks on the chart in any order that makes sense to you.

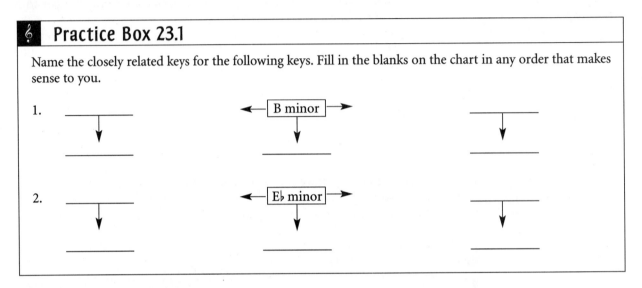

Finding Common Chords

The next process is to identify chords that are the same in the closely related keys. Between any two closely related keys, there will be several chords that are identical—in other words, that the two keys share. We will start with C major and its relative minor. Then we will explore some of the other closely related keys that were identified on the previous page. To begin, choose one of the two keys and list all of the diatonic chord spellings for that key. The spellings for C major are listed in the center column of Table 25. The leftmost column has the Roman numerals for the key of C major. The right column identifies the Roman numerals of those chords that also exist in the key of A minor.

Table 25.   *Common chords between C major and A minor*

C major		A minor
I	C E G	III
ii	D F A	iv
iii	E G B	
IV	F A C	VI
V	G B D	VII
vi	A C E	i
vii°	B D F	ii°

The outer two columns identify the **common chords,** or those chords that exist in both of the closely related keys. You should notice that there are six chords in common between the two keys. Because these two keys are actually relatives, they will have the most chords in common. Now we will compare C major to a key that is not its relative minor but is closely related: D minor. Fill in the Roman numerals for the common chords from D minor in Table 26.

Table 26. *Common chords between C major and D minor*

C major		D minor
I	C E G	
ii	D F A	
iii	E G B	
IV	F A C	
V	G B D	
vi	A C E	
vii°	B D F	

There will be four to six common chords between any pair of closely related keys. When determining common chords, it is necessary only to spell the chords from one of the pair of keys. If you are using one major and one minor key, it is probably easiest to spell the chords from the major key, since there are fewer possibilities.

Practice Box 23.2

Determine the common chords between the following keys.

D major		B minor

F minor		A♭ major

Diatonic Modulation

When a piece of music modulates using diatonic modulation, there is always a point at which the two keys intersect. This chord is the actual point of modulation. It must be possible to analyze this chord diatonically in both keys. This chord is called the "common chord" between the two keys. The common chord must be a diatonic chord in both keys; hence, the modulatory process is called "diatonic modulation." It is also called "common-chord" modulation, or "pivot chord" modulation but those terms can be deceiving, because other styles of modulation also use a chord that is common to both keys (the pivot point), although it may not be a chord that is diatonic in both keys.

Figure 23.6 is the same progression that was presented at the beginning of the chapter. In the Roman numeral analysis of our original progression, we have gone as far as we can go using the key of C major. The G minor chord cannot be analyzed in the key of C major. When we reach this chord, we know that the modulation has already taken place and we are in F major. The asterisk marks the spot where the modulation must take place.

Figure 23.6.   Modulating progression starting in C major

If we look at the chord with the asterisk, D–F–A, we realize that it is a diatonic chord in both keys. This chord has a diatonic Roman numeral that can be assigned to it in either C major or F major. In C major, it is a ii chord; in F major, it is a vi chord. This chord is the point of modulation.

To demonstrate this in our analysis, we use a modulation bracket, which is drawn like this:

This stair-step symbol allows the representation of a single chord in two keys. The analysis for the starting key is written on top of the bracket; the analysis for the ending key is written below it. Using the common-chord modulation bracket, the complete analysis of this chord progression is presented in Figure 23.7.

Figure 23.7.   Analysis of diatonic modulation using the common chord bracket

The modulation from C major to F major is completely described by this Roman numeral analysis. The bracket shows the point of modulation and the dual interpretation of the common chord. Once you determine the Roman numeral for the new key, then the progression must move correctly after that chord all the way to some kind of cadence.

Remember that the chord itself does not change during the process of modulation. Only our interpretation of it changes.

All of the chords used in this progression are diatonic. That is true despite the presence of an accidental on the third chord from the end. It is important to realize that by the time you reach the chord with the accidental, *the modulation has already taken place.* In this case, appearances are deceiving. The B♭ is a diatonic pitch in the key of F major, not an altered tone in C major.

Let's try an example in a harder key. We'll start with a progression in G♭ major, shown in Figure 23.8. Above the Roman numerals, spell each chord. Using the chords of this progression, let's try to modulate to the key of D♭ major. Consider the last chord in the progression below. It can also be analyzed as a diatonic chord in D♭ major. What is its Roman numeral analysis in the new key? Finish the progression to its logical conclusion according to the circle of fifths progression.

Figure 23.8.   Modulating progression starting in G♭ major

Once you have determined that the vi chord in the starting key is also the ii chord in the new key, you should write it in the bracket above.

Now let us consider what happens once we are in the new key. Try to decide how many chords are necessary in order to finish the progression. The first chord analyzed in D♭ major must behave in a specific manner, according to the rules of progression by fifth. Some kind of dominant chord, either a V or vii°, must follow a ii chord. (The dominant chord may be preceded by a cadential six-four chord.) Then the dominant chord must be followed by a chord that forms a cadence, usually a I chord. In the progression above, write in the chords necessary to finish the progression with a cadence in D♭ major. Then spell the remaining chords above the Roman numerals.

The process of modulating to a new key does not alter any of the rules of chord progressions that you have learned. The chord progressions in each key should still conform to the standard circle of fifths progression you learned in previous chapters.

Establishing a Key

When you are constructing a modulation, remember that both keys need to be firmly established with a cadence, usually involving a dominant-to-tonic progression. A modulation that occurs too soon, before the starting key has been completely defined, is generally not effective. The quickest way to establish the starting key is with a I–V–I progression, although it is possible to use a deceptive cadence or to make the process considerably longer or more complex. After the modulation, it is necessary to create a cadence in the new key.

Since the tonic and dominant chords are such strong indicators of a key, they can be problematic when used as chords of modulation. The point of modulation is to move away from one key into another; using a V chord in the bracket can make the modulation sound awkward or unconvincing. The dominant triad is virtually never used as a pivot chord. The I chord is occasionally used as a pivot (becoming the IV) when modulating to the dominant key. However, the most effective modulations are accomplished with pairs that do not include tonic or dominant chords, including the leading-tone triad. Some examples of these effective modulations are shown in Figure 23.9. Notice that they are grouped in pairs, since each chord of the pair can occur in either the starting or the ending key.

Figure 23.9.   Frequently used pairs of common chords

ii |	iv |		IV|	VI|		iii |	vi |
| iv	| ii		|VI	|IV		| vi	| iii

vi |	ii |		vi |	iv |		vi |	ii |
| ii	| vi		| iv	| vi		| ii	| vi

I |	IV|		i |	iv |
|IV	| I		| iv	| i

♭ Practice Box 23.3

Using Roman numerals and a common chord modulation bracket, write a progression that modulates from the key of E major to G♯ minor. Make sure that there is a dominant-to-tonic progression in each key. Spell each chord above your Roman numerals.

E major: I

Sometimes you will find a modulation that appears to involve multiple common chords. Look at the following example.

Figure 23.10.   Multiple common chords between keys

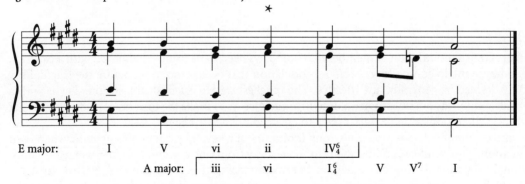

E major: I   V   vi   ii   IV$^6_4$
A major: iii   vi   I$^6_4$ V   V^7 I

The modulation moves from E major to A major. The first chord where you find an accidental indicating that you are in a new key is the next to last chord, with the D♮. This note creates a V^7, which, along with the cadential six-four chord that precedes it, clearly indicates that the piece has moved into A major. Each of the three previous chords in the example can be analyzed in both keys. While it is certainly possible to leave the analysis as shown, several factors should influence the decision.

1. The six-four chord at the beginning of the second measure is clearly a cadential six-four chord in the new key. It does not have a similar function in the starting key; in fact, it does not function as any of the known types of six-four chords—cadential, passing, pedal, or arpeggiated—in the key of E major. Therefore, it is inappropriate to analyze it in both keys.

2. The third chord of the progression can be analyzed as both a vi chord in E major and a iii chord in A major. However, at this point the listener would have no reason to suspect that a modulation is coming and would still aurally comprehend the chord only in E major. This chord probably should be analyzed only in the starting key.

3. By process of elimination, we have arrived at a single common chord, occurring on the fourth beat of the first measure. In almost all diatonic modulations that contain multiple common chords, there will be a logical choice for a single chord on which to modulate. Arriving at the best choice may involve a type of musical detective work, using all that you have learned about progressions and the functions of various types of chords.

Part Writing Diatonic Modulations

Part-writing considerations for diatonic modulations differ in two important ways from the work we have done up till now. The first is that you must determine the point of modulation—in other words, the common chord—unless it is given to you in the exercise. The second is that you will have to determine the starting and ending keys, one or more of which may not match the key signature.

Usually the starting key will match the key signature, but not necessarily. The best way to determine the ending key is to spell the final two chords and then determine what kind of cadence is likely based on the relationship between the roots of the chords. If there is a fifth relationship between the roots of the chords, it is probably an authentic cadence, meaning that the final chord is the I (or i) chord. Root movement of a second between the final two chords, on the other hand, may indicate a half or deceptive cadence.

Practice Box 23.4

Add inner voices and a Roman numeral analysis. The asterisk shows the point of modulation.

1.

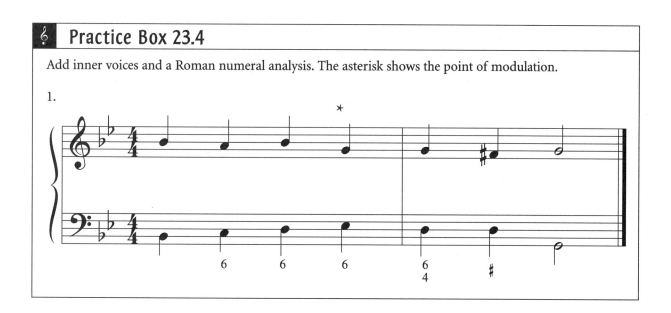

Practice Box 23.4 (continued)

2.
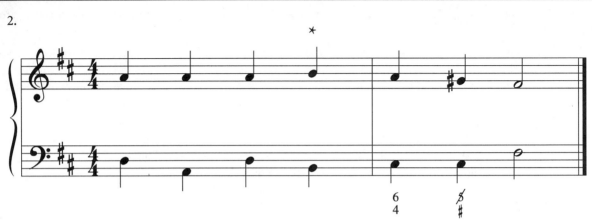

In the next exercises, you will have to determine the point of modulation. It will not be marked with an asterisk.

3.

4.

Practice Box 23.4 (continued)

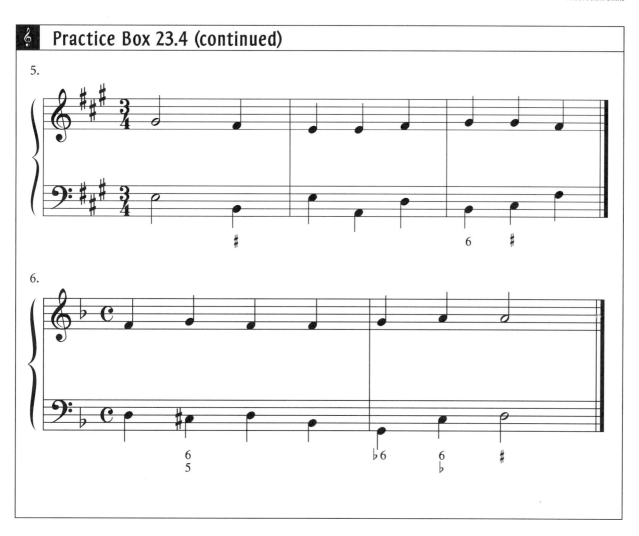

Music for Analysis

Remember that when analyzing diatonic modulations, it is most helpful to find the chord that functions only in the new key (often with an accidental) and look for the modulation prior to that chord.

Example 23.1. Mendelssohn, Songs without Words, *op. 38, no. 2, mm. 1–5*

Track 23, 0:00

Example 23.2. Mozart, Piano Sonata, K. 331, 2nd movement, mm. 49–60

Track 23, 0:22

AURAL SKILLS

Melody

Sing the following melodies with solfege syllables or numbers. All of these melodies contain a modulation. Each exercise has a pair of repeated notes at the point of modulation. (They may be flagged individually to call attention to the point of modulation.) The modulation bracket is used to demonstrate the key. Using solfege or any other sight-singing system, sing the first of this pair of notes in the starting key and the second in the ending key. The first three are done for you. You may need to analyze the other exercises before beginning to sing.

Harmony

Sing the following modulating chord progressions in four-part harmony.

Rhythm

Practice the following rhythms, which contain duplets.

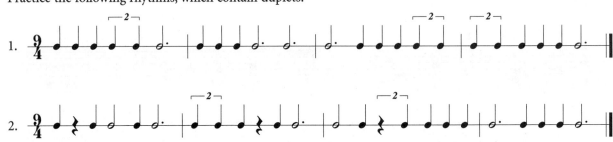

Dual Rhythm

These rhythms should be tapped with both hands. They use compound meters and subdivisions of the beat.

Dictation

The rhythms below represent modulating chord progressions. All are in four-part harmony. Circle the chord where you hear the modulation taking place. The key signatures represent the starting keys for each example. Try to add a Roman numeral analysis and identify the key to which each example modulates.

1.

2.

3.

4.

5.

6.

Notate the rhythms that you hear. They will contain borrowed divisions of the beat in compound meters.

1.

2.

3.

4.

5.

6.

KEYBOARD APPLICATIONS

Practice these exercises using the starting keys that are indicated. Double the bass in the chord of modulation to avoid a leap of an augmented second in the tenor voice.

1.   Starting key:
      D major
      B♭ major
      A major

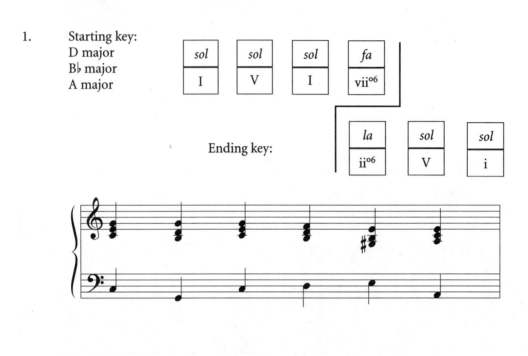

2.   Starting key:
      F major
      A♭ major
      B major

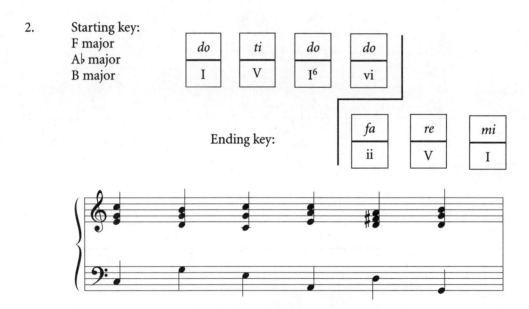

chapter 24 Review of Seventh Chords,
Non-Harmonic Tones, and Modulation

REVIEW CHAPTER

Four-Part Harmony Review

Here is a summary of the rules of part writing that were studied in chapters 13–23.

1. The bass should be doubled in all second-inversion chords. Use open or close structure depending upon the prevailing structure at the point of the six-four chord.

2. The soprano should be doubled in all first-inversion chords, unless the soprano is the leading tone or the voice leading is substantially improved through doubling the bass.

   a. If the soprano and bass notes are the same pitch class, use open or close structure, depending upon the prevailing structure at the point of the first-inversion chord.

   b. If the soprano and bass notes are different pitch classes, choose one of the following structures:

      (1) Neutral structure, in which the soprano is doubled in the tenor voice (generally used with mid-range soprano notes)

      (2) Octave structure, in which the soprano is doubled in the alto voice at the distance of an octave (generally used for relatively high soprano notes in a prevailingly open structure)

      (3) Unison structure, in which the soprano note is doubled in the alto voice on exactly the same pitch (generally used for relatively low soprano notes in a prevailingly close structure)

3. Use irregular doubling in first-inversion chords when the leading tone is in the soprano. Irregular doubling requires the doubling of the bass voice in a first-inversion chord.

4. When consecutive first-inversion triads are indicated, do not use the same structure on both chords.

   a. Check the pair of chords for obvious choices for structure:

      (1) If one of the chords already has the soprano doubled in the bass, use open or close structure on that chord and choose neutral (or octave or unison) structure for the other chord.

      (2) If one of the chords contains a leading tone, do the part writing for that chord first, being careful not to double the leading tone. Choose a different structure for the other chord.

      (3) If there are no obvious choices for either chord, experiment to find a combination that does not cause parallelism. Irregular doubling may be a choice for one of the chords.

5. Doubling is generally not a consideration for seventh chords. Place one note of the chord in each of four voices, based on the best voice leading from the surrounding chords.

6. The chordal seventh must resolve stepwise downward. This downward resolution may be delayed by a cadential six-four chord or a suspension.

7. It is occasionally possible to omit a chord tone in a seventh chord under the following circumstances:

   a. Double the bass and omit the chordal fifth in a root-position seventh chord

   b. Double the chordal third and omit the chordal fifth in a root-position seventh chord (generally used only with the supertonic seventh chord in a major key)

8. Circle and label all non-harmonic tones that are indicated by the figured-bass symbols. It may be necessary to notate the voices before you can identify the type of non-harmonic tone.

9. The 8-7 combination in figured-bass symbols will create a chordal seventh. This chord tone must be handled as described on page 379 (6.) and resolve stepwise downward.

10. Suspension figures (including the figured-bass symbols 9-8, 2-1, 4-3, 7-6, and 2-3) must be prepared and resolved correctly. The suspended note (the first number of the pair) must be preceded by exactly the same pitch in the same voice. It is always necessary to add the voices to the chord preceding the suspension before attempting to write the suspension, in order to determine the proper voice in which the suspension should appear.

Terminology Review

All of the terms below were covered in chapters 13–23. You should study them to make sure they are part of your musical vocabulary.

altered tone	distantly related keys	ninth chord
anticipation	dominant seventh chord	non-harmonic tones
appoggiatura	dominant type chord	passing six-four chord
arpeggiated six-four chord	duplet	passing tone
borrowed chord	escape tone	pedal six-four chord
borrowed division	foreign keys	pedal tone
cadential six-four chord	fully diminished seventh	retardation
cadenza	half-diminished seventh	seventh chord
changing tone	leading-tone seventh chord	subdivision
closely related keys	major-major seventh	suspension
common chord	major-minor seventh	tertian
diatonic modulation	minor-minor seventh	thirteenth chord
diminished-diminished seventh	modulation	triplet
diminished-minor seventh	neighbor tone	
	neutral structure	

🎼 Practice Box 24.1

Identify the errors in the part-writing examples below. The errors will include things such as parallelism, incorrect doubling, incomplete chords, incorrect interpretation of figured-bass symbols, and improper resolution of chord tones and non-harmonic tones. When you find an error, mark it with a circle or parallel lines and try to identify the reason the error occurred. These reasons may include incorrect changes of structure, omission of chord tones, improper voice leading, and incorrect chord progressions, among others. A Roman numeral analysis is not provided, but doing one may help you discover the errors.

1.

🎼 **Practice Box 24.1 (continued)**

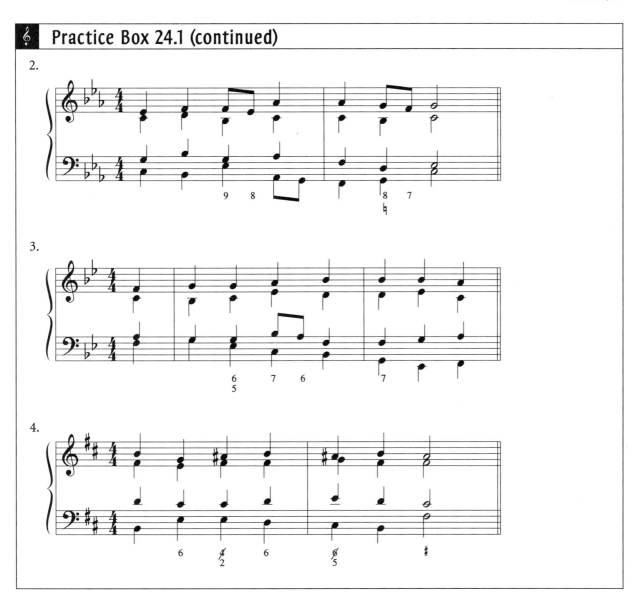

Analysis Review

Here are some complete pieces for analysis. There are common-chord modulations, plus a variety of other diatonic harmonies that you have studied in chapters 13–23. The first two examples, by Robert Schumann, are from the same collection of children's pieces.

Example 24.1.   *R. Schumann,* Album for the Young, *"Wild Rider," op. 68, no. 8*

Track 24, 0:00

Example 24.2. R. Schumann, Album for the Young, *"The Happy Farmer,"* op. 68, no. 10

Track 24, 0:47

Although Example 24.3 is primarily in two-voice counterpoint, it is possible to discern harmonic progressions based on chord outlines. This example modulates several times. Circle and label all non-harmonic tones.

Example 24.3.   *J. S. Bach,* Notebook for Anna Magdalena Bach, *Minuet in D Minor*

Track 24, 1:41

AURAL SKILLS

Melody

Sing the following melodies with solfege syllables or numbers. All of these melodies contain a modulation. It may be helpful to use the techniques shown in chapter 23 to identify the point of modulation with a modulation bracket.

Rhythm

Practice the following rhythms. They consist of a combination of subdivisions and borrowed divisions in compound meters. It may be helpful to practice these exercises with a metronome.

Dictation

Circle the quality of the seventh chords that you hear.

1. major-major   major-minor   minor-minor   fully diminished   half-diminished
2. major-major   major-minor   minor-minor   fully diminished   half-diminished
3. major-major   major-minor   minor-minor   fully diminished   half-diminished
4. major-major   major-minor   minor-minor   fully diminished   half-diminished
5. major-major   major-minor   minor-minor   fully diminished   half-diminished
6. major-major   major-minor   minor-minor   fully diminished   half-diminished
7. major-major   major-minor   minor-minor   fully diminished   half-diminished
8. major-major   major-minor   minor-minor   fully diminished   half-diminished
9. major-major   major-minor   minor-minor   fully diminished   half-diminished
10. major-major   major-minor   minor-minor   fully diminished   half-diminished
11. major-major   major-minor   minor-minor   fully diminished   half-diminished
12. major-major   major-minor   minor-minor   fully diminished   half-diminished
13. major-major   major-minor   minor-minor   fully diminished   half-diminished
14. major-major   major-minor   minor-minor   fully diminished   half-diminished
15. major-major   major-minor   minor-minor   fully diminished   half-diminished
16. major-major   major-minor   minor-minor   fully diminished   half-diminished
17. major-major   major-minor   minor-minor   fully diminished   half-diminished
18. major-major   major-minor   minor-minor   fully diminished   half-diminished
19. major-major   major-minor   minor-minor   fully diminished   half-diminished
20. major-major   major-minor   minor-minor   fully diminished   half-diminished
21. major-major   major-minor   minor-minor   fully diminished   half-diminished
22. major-major   major-minor   minor-minor   fully diminished   half-diminished
23. major-major   major-minor   minor-minor   fully diminished   half-diminished
24. major-major   major-minor   minor-minor   fully diminished   half-diminished
25. major-major   major-minor   minor-minor   fully diminished   half-diminished

Harmonic Dictation

One line of the texture is provided for you. Add the bass or soprano, inner voices, and a Roman numeral analysis. All of these exercises modulate.

1.

2.

3.

4.

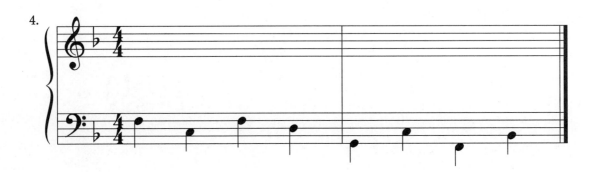

Add soprano and bass lines, inner voices, and Roman numeral analysis. Only the starting notes are given to you. All of these exercises modulate.

5.
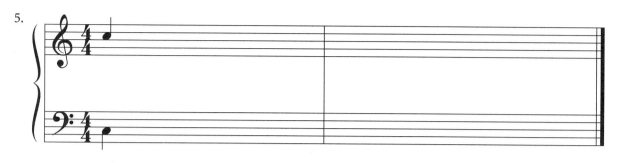

6.

7.

8.
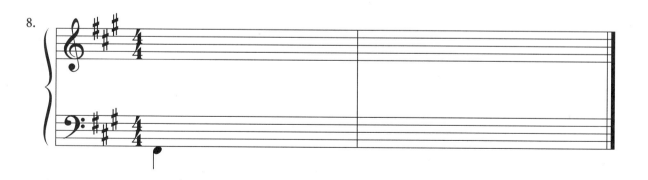

KEYBOARD APPLICATIONS

Practice these exercises using the starting keys indicated.

1.   Starting key:
      B minor
      F♯ minor
      D minor

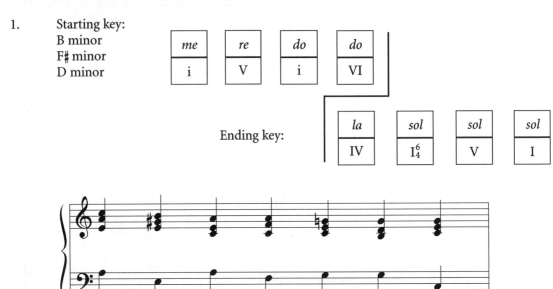

2.   Starting key:
      C minor
      C♯ minor
      F minor

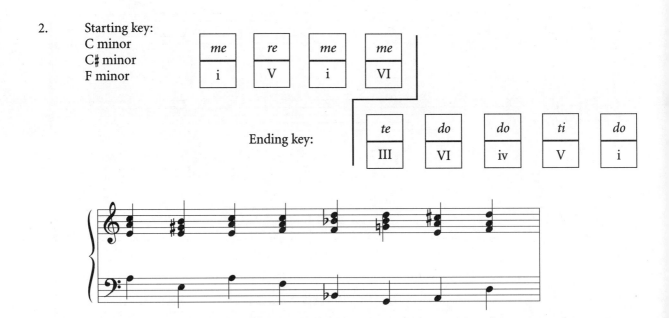

PRACTICE BOX ANSWERS

Practice Box 1.1
G, A, F, B, D, G, E, C, F, E, B, F   F, E, G, C, A, A, B, G, E, F, D, G

Practice Box 1.2
C, A, F, B, G, A, C, D, B, E   D, A, E, C, B, G, D, C, F, E

Practice Box 1.3

Practice Box 1.4
1. F♯   2. A♭   3. C♯   4. G♭   5. A♯   6. B♭

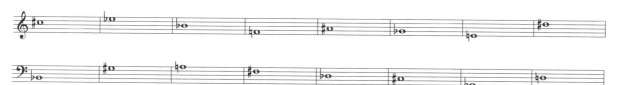

Practice Box 1.5
1. A♯ and B♭   3. C♯ and D♭   5. C and B♯

2. D♯ and E♭   4. G♯ and A♭   6. F♯ and G♭

F, C, B, E

Practice Box 1.7
1. 𝅝   4. ♪ + ♪ + ♪ + ♪

2. 𝅝   5. ♪ + ♪

3. 𝅗𝅥   6. ♩ + ♩ + ♩ + ♩

Practice Box 1.8
3 ♪   2 ♩

Practice Box 2.1

Practice Box 2.4

A major, A♭ major, G♭ major, B major, D major, F major, E♭ major, G major, F♯ major, C♭ major, B♭ major, D♭ major

Practice Box 2.5

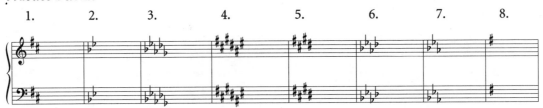

Practice Box 2.9

1. 6   2. 3   3. 3   4. 3

The number of counts is always a multiple of 3.

5. 𝅗𝅥.   6. ♩ + ♩ + ♩   7. 𝅝.   8. 𝅗𝅥 + 𝅗𝅥 + 𝅗𝅥

Practice Box 3.1

4th, 6th, 3rd, 2nd, 8ve, 7th   5th, 6th, 8ve, 4th, 7th, 3rd

Practice Box 3.2

Practice Box 3.3

Practice Box 3.4

1. major 2nd   2. minor 3rd   3. major 6th   4. minor 7th   5. major 2nd   6. major 6th
7. minor 2nd   8. major 6th   9. minor 2nd   10. major 6th   11. minor 6th   12. major 7th

Practice Box 3.5

1. aug 4th	2. perf 4th	3. dim 5th	4. dim 5th	5. perf 4th	6. perf 5th
7. aug 5th	8. perf 5th	9. dim 5th	10. perf 4th	11. dim 4th	12. perf 4th

Practice Box 3.6

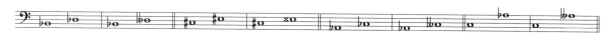

Practice Box 3.7

minor 3rd   major 3rd   minor 6th   minor 7th

Practice Box 3.8

1. major 2nd	2. minor 7th	3. major 3rd	4. minor 6th
5. aug 4th	6. dim 5th	7. minor 3rd	8. major 6th

Practice Box 3.9

Practice Box 3.10

1. major 10th   2. perfect 11th   3. perfect 12th   4. minor 10th

Practice Box 4.1

1. D, D minor   2. F♯, F♯ minor   3. C, C minor

Practice Box 4.2

1. E minor   2. G♯ minor   3. G minor   4. A♯ minor

Practice Box 4.3

1. B♭ major   2. A♭ major   3. C♭ major   4. B major

Practice Box 4.4

G major, E minor

It would take four people to sing this example. The stems are seemingly turned in the wrong direction to indicate the separate voices on the staff.

Practice Box 4.5

Practice Box 4.6

Practice Box 4.7

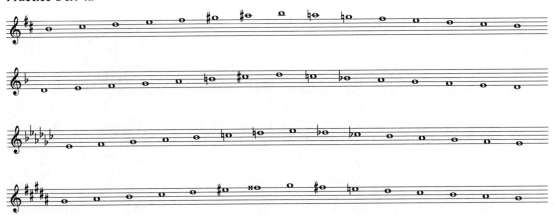

Practice Box 4.8

1. F# minor   2. A minor   3. C# minor   4. E minor
5. D# minor   6. F# minor   7. B♭ major   8. G major
9. D♭ major   10. B♭ major

Practice Box 5.1

1. G   2. D   3. C   4. B♭   5. F#   6. G♭

Practice Box 5.2

Practice Box 5.3

Practice Box 5.4

Practice Box 5.5

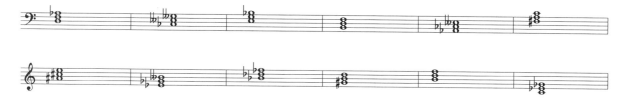

Practice Box 5.6

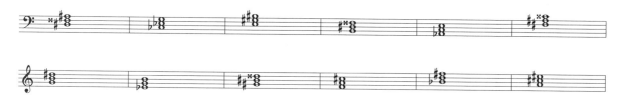

Practice Box 5.7

Practice Box 5.8

1. D aug	2. A♭ major	3. C dim	4. B aug	5. F minor	6. D♯ dim
7. E major	8. F♭ major	9. D♭ major	10. C♯ major	11. E♭ aug	12. G♯ dim

Practice Box 5.9

1. F A C♯, augmented   2. A♯ C♯ E, diminished   3. D F♯ A, major
4. G♭ B♭ D♭, major   5. E♭ G B, augmented   6. C♯ E G♯, minor

Practice Box 5.10

D minor	C minor	G diminished	B♭ major	B minor	A♭ major
2nd inv.	1st inv.	2nd inv.	root position	1st inv.	2nd inv.

Practice Box 5.11

1. A C E   2. A C E   3. B D F   4. D F A   5. F A C   6. G B♭ D

Practice Box 5.12

1. G♯ B D   2. A♭ C E♭   3. B D F♯   4. C E♭ G   5. F♯ A C   6. E♭ G♭ B♭
   1st inv.   2nd inv.   1st inv.   root position   1st inv.   2nd inv.

Practice Box 6.4

1. 2   2. 3   3. 3   4. 2   5. 4   6. 4

Practice Box 7.1

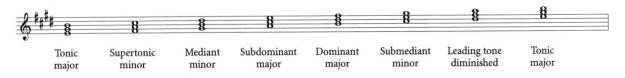

Tonic   Supertonic   Mediant   Subdominant   Dominant   Submediant   Leading tone   Tonic
major   minor   minor   major   major   minor   diminished   major

Practice Box 7.2

G major: I   I   vi   V⁶   I   IV   V   IV   I⁶   IV   V₄⁶   I   I

$\text{G major:} \quad I \quad I \quad vi \quad V^6 \quad I \quad IV \quad V \quad IV \quad I^6 \quad IV \quad V^6_4 \quad I \quad I$

Practice Box 7.3

Tonic   Supertonic   Mediant   Subdominant   Dominant   Submediant   Subtonic   Leading tone   Tonic
minor   diminished   major   minor   major   major   major   diminished   minor

Practice Box 7.4

C E♭ G   B♭ D F   E♭ G B♭   A♭ C E♭   D F A♭   C E♭ G   G B♮ D   C E♭ G
   i   VII   III   VI   ii°6 i^6_4 V   i

Practice Box 7.5

1. imperfect authentic   2. perfect authentic   3. perfect authentic

Practice Box. 7.6

B major: I   iii   vi   ii   V   I   G minor: i   VI   iv   V   i
   i   VII   III   VI   ii°   V   i

Practice Box 8.1

Practice Box 8.2

Practice Box 8.3

These are some of the possible solutions for exercises 9–14.

Practice Box. 8.4

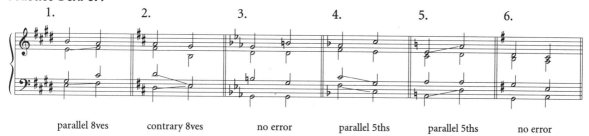

Practice Box 8.5

1. contrary   2. similar   3. parallel   4. parallel   5. contrary   6. parallel

Number 4 should not be used in four-voice harmony

perfect authentic
cadence

Practice Box 9.1

Practice Box 9.2

A♭ M: I   V   I   G M: I   V   I

Practice Box 9.3

G M: V   I   A♭ M: V   I   B M: V   I   D mi: V   i   F♯ mi: V   i

Each soprano line is *re-do*.

Practice Box 9.4

D M: I   V   I   B♭ M: I   V   I   A M: I   V   I

Practice Box 9.5

G mi: i   V   i   E mi: i   V   i   F mi: i   V   I

Practice Box 9.6

C mi: i   V   F M: I   V   E M: I   V

Practice Box 9.7

C mi: i   V   i   iv   I

Practice Box 9.8

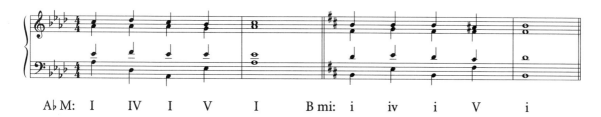

A♭ M: I   IV   I   V   I   B mi: i   iv   i   V   i

Practice Box 10.1

D M: I   ii   V   I   E♭ M: I   ii   V   I

The soprano line must be moved down from the tonic to the supertonic chord to create contrary motion with the bass voice.

Practice Box 10.2

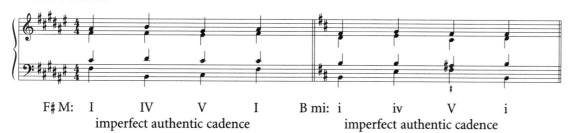

F♯ M: I   IV   V   I   B mi: i   iv   V   i
        imperfect authentic cadence   imperfect authentic cadence

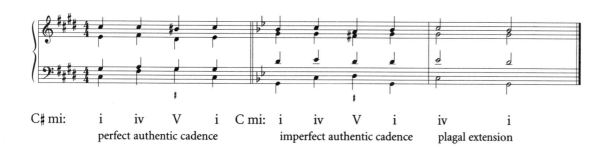

C♯ mi: i   iv   V   i   C mi: i   iv   V   i   iv   i
      perfect authentic cadence   imperfect authentic cadence   plagal extension

Practice Box 10.3

Possible soprano lines are demonstrated. There are other solutions.

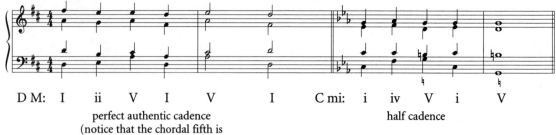

D M: I   ii   V   I   V   I   C mi: i   iv   V   i   V

perfect authentic cadence   half cadence
(notice that the chordal fifth is
omitted in the final tonic triad)

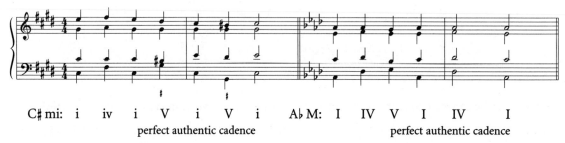

C♯ mi: i   iv   i   V   i   V   i   A♭ M: I   IV   V   I   IV   I

perfect authentic cadence   perfect authentic cadence

Practice Box 10.4

D♭ M: I   IV   V   vi   A M: I   IV   V   vi

Practice Box 10.5

E mi: i   iv   V   VI   A mi: i   iv   V   VI

Notice that the soprano is doubled in the alto voice in the first example and in the tenor voice in the second example.

Practice Box 10.6

A♭ M: I   ii   V   I   D M: I   IV   V   I

Notice the parallel motion between the soprano and bass at the point of root movement by second. This creates the need for irregular doubling on the second chord of each of these pairs.

Practice Box 11.1

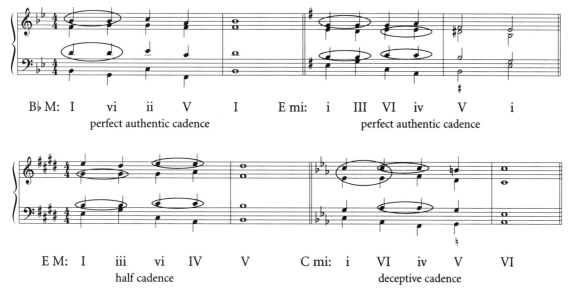

In the soprano line for 4, you must keep the common tone where the bass line moves by the interval of a third. Use parallel motion at the deceptive cadence, with irregular doubling on the final chord.

Practice Box 11.2

Practice Box 11.3

Practice Box 12.1

1. 2nd chord, incorrect doubling (soprano is doubled), incorrect Roman numeral (iii)
   parallel 5ths between second and third chords
   parallel 5ths between 4th and 5th chords (change of structure)

2. 2nd chord, incorrect Roman numeral (VII)
   incorrect Roman numerals on last three chords (iv, V, I)
   parallel 5th and 8ves between 1st and 2nd chords (soprano moves parallel to bass)
   4th chord incomplete (no A)
   parallel 5ths between 4th and 5th chords
   6th chord, incorrect doubling, sharp has been omitted

3. 3rd chord, incorrect Roman numeral (VI), incomplete chord (no D)
   chord progression does not follow the circle of fifths (i, VI, i and III, V)
   4th chord, soprano is out of range, incomplete chord (no F)
   5th chord, incorrect structure (upper 3 voices are not evenly spaced)
   final chord, incorrect doubling (bass is not doubled)

4. 3rd chord, incomplete (no F♯)
   4th chord, incorrect Roman numeral (vi), crossed voices (alto and tenor)
   5th chord, crossed voices (alto and tenor)
   6th chord, incorrect doubling

Practice Box 13.1

Practice Box 13.2
These represent possible soprano lines that can be added to the given bass lines. There are also other solutions.

Practice Box 13.3
These represent possible bass lines that can be added to the given soprano lines. There are also other solutions.

Practice Box 14.1

| 1. F♯ | 2. A | 3. E♮ | 4. D♯ | 5. C | 6. E♯ | This note is always the leading tone. |
| 7. A | 8. E | 9. F | 10. A♭ | 11. D♭ | 12. F♯ | This note is always the fourth scale degree. |

Practice Box 14.2

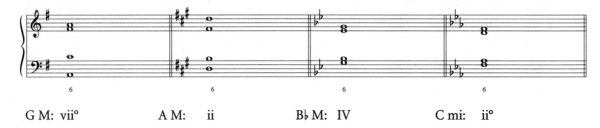

G M: vii°   A M: ii   B♭ M: IV   C mi: ii°

Practice Box 14.3

F M: I   ii   V   I   B M: I   IV   V   I

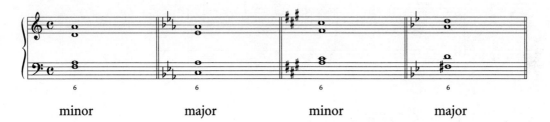

A M: I   vi   ii   V   I   B mi: i   ii°   V   i

Practice Box 14.4

minor   major   minor   major

Practice Box 14.5

G M: vii°   E mi: ii°   D M: IV   B mi: VI   B♭ M: V   G mi: VII   B M: vii°   G♯ mi: ii°

E♭ M: vii°   C mi: ii°   A♭ M: I   F mi: III   B M: vi   G♯ mi: i   F mi: V

Practice Box 14.6

A mi: i   ii°   V   i   i   iv   i   D♭ M: I   V   vi   ii   I   V   I

E M: I   V   vi   ii   I   V   I   F M: I   IV   V   I   IV   V

Practice Box 14.7

E♭ M: I   I   IV   V   I   F♯ mi: i   ii°   V   i   iv   i

E mi: i   III⁺   VI   ii°   V   i   F♯ M: I   vi   V   I   ii   V   I

D mi: i   V   i   VI   iv   ii°   V   A M: V   I   IV   I   V   vi

Practice Box 15.1

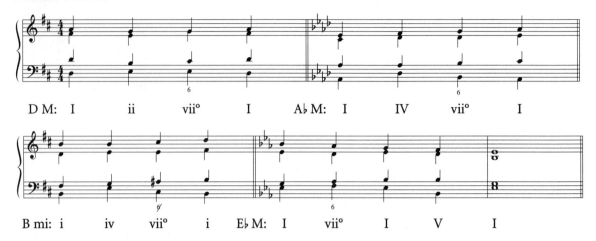

Practice Box 15.2
1. PAC, plagal extension   2. IAC   3. deceptive   4. half   5. IAC   6. deceptive

Practice Box 15.3

Practice Box 16.1

Bb M: I   V   I   V   I   IV vii° I   E mi: i   VI   iv   i   IV   V   i

Practice Box 16.2

C# M: I   V   I   IV   I vii° I   F mi: i vii° i   iv   V   i   iv   i

Practice Box 16.3

Eb M: I   vi   vi   vi   ii   I   V   I   G# mi: i   i   i   iv   i   V   i

Practice Box 16.4

B M: I IV I IV I V I   F mi: i VII III iv iv V i   iv   i

D M: V   I   I   I   vi   IV   V   V   I

C mi: V   i vii° i   ii° i   V   i

Practice Box 17.1

Practice Box 17.2

In the example above, the 5 6 pattern cannot be a non-harmonic tone, because the vii° chord is necessary to form a cadence.

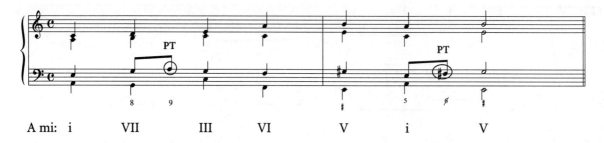

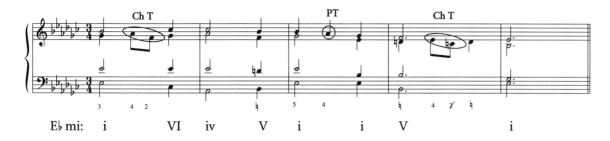

E♭ mi: i   VI iv   V   i   i   V   i

Practice Box 18.1

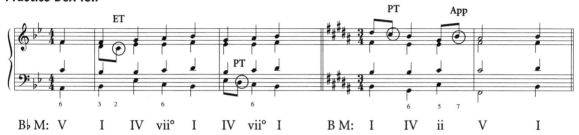

B♭ M: V   I   IV vii° I   IV vii° I   B M: I   IV   ii   V   I

Practice Box 18.2

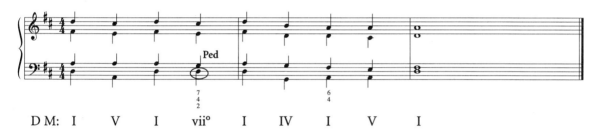

D M: I   V   I   vii°   I   IV   I   V   I

Practice Box 19.1

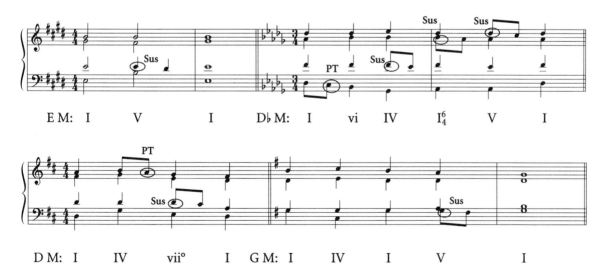

E M: I   V   I   D♭ M: I   vi   IV   I$^6_4$ V   I

D M: I   IV   vii°   I   G M: I   IV   I   V   I

Practice Box 19.2

Practice Box 19.3

B♭ M: I   vi   ii   V   I   V   I   G M: I   vii°   I   IV   V   I

B M: V   I   iii   vi   ii   V   I

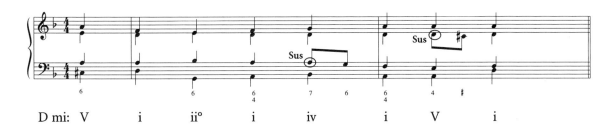

D mi: V   i   ii°   i   iv   i   V   i

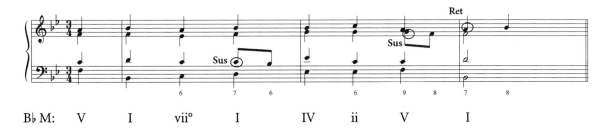

B♭ M: V   I   vii°   I   IV   ii   V   I

Practice Box 20.1

Practice Box 20.2

1. major-minor   2. diminished-minor   3. diminished-diminished   4. major-major   5. minor-minor

Practice Box 20.3

1. D F A C, minor-minor, 2nd inversion
2. A C E G, minor-minor, 3rd inversion
3. D F A♭ C♭, diminished-diminished, 1st inversion
4. G B♭ D F, minor-minor, root position
5. G B D F♯, major-major, 3rd inversion
6. F A C E, major-major, 2nd inversion

Practice Box 20.4
1. A C# E G   2. G B D F   3. B D F A   4. A C E♭ G   5. C E G B   6. B D F A

Practice Box 20.5
1. B D# F# A#   2. C E♭ G B♭   3. B D# F# A   4. A♭ C E♭ G♭

Practice Box 20.6

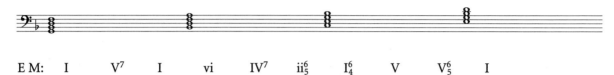

E M: I   V⁷   I   vi   IV⁷   ii⁶₅   I⁶₄   V   V⁶₅   I

Practice Box 20.7

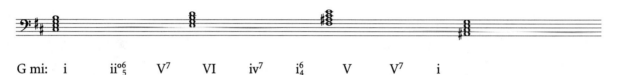

G mi: i   ii°⁶₅   V⁷   VI   iv⁷   i⁶₄   V   V⁷   i

Practice Box 20.8

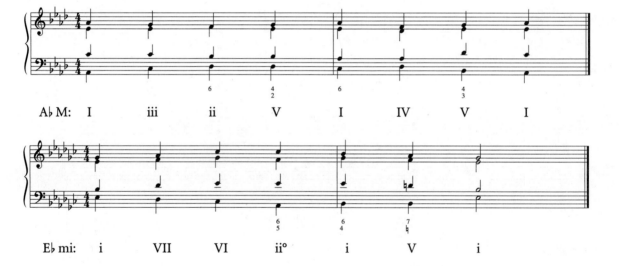

A♭ M: I   iii   ii   V   I   IV   V   I

E♭ mi: i   VII   VI   ii°   i   V   i

Practice Box 21.1

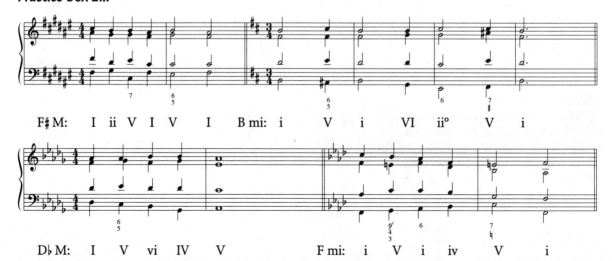

F# M: I   ii   V   I   V   I   B mi: i   V   i   VI   ii°   V   i

D♭ M: I   V   vi   IV   V   F mi: i   V   i   iv   V   i

Practice Box 21.2
1. C minor   2. A minor   3. B minor   4. E minor   5. A♭ minor   6. B♭ minor

Practice Box 21.3
1. G major   2. F minor   3. A major   4. D major

Practice Box 21.4

Practice Box 22.1

B M: I   vi   ii   V   I   IV   I

D mi: i   ii⌀   V   i   IV   V   i

Practice Box 22.2

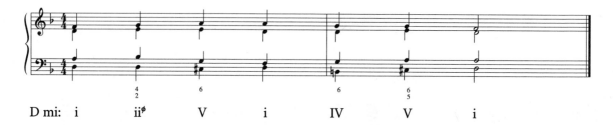

A♭ M: V   I   IV   V   I   ii   I   V   V   I

Practice Box 22.3

A M: V   I   IV vii° I   iii   vi   ii   I   V   V   I

Practice Box 22.4

D mi: i   VI   iv   ii°   V   i   G M: I   vii⌀   I   IV   ii   V   I

Practice Box 23.1

1. B minor, D major, G major, E minor, A major, F♯ minor
2. E♭ minor, G♭ major, D♭ major, B♭ minor, C♭ major, A♭ minor

Practice Box 23.2

D major		B minor
I	D F♯ A	III
ii	E G B	iv
iii	F♯ A C♯	
IV	G B D	VI
V	A C♯ E	VII
vi	B D F♯	i
vii°	C♯ E G	ii°

F minor		A♭ major
III	A♭ C E♭	I
iv	B♭ D♭ F	ii
	C E♭ G	iii
VI	D♭ F A♭	IV
VII	E♭ G B♭	V
i	F A♭ C	vi
ii°	G B♭ D♭	vii°

Practice Box 23.3

E major:	I	V	I	iii	vi		
G♯ mi:					iv	V	i

Practice Box 23.4

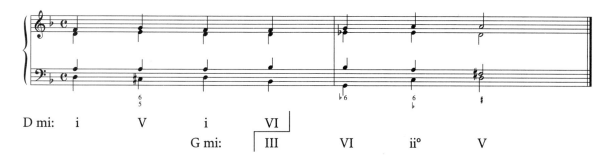

D mi: i   V   i   VI⌐
              G mi: └III   VI   ii°   V

Practice Box 24.1

1. chord 2, chordal 7th does not resolve downward
    chord 4, incorrect doubling (bass should be doubled)
    chord 5, incorrect doubling (bass should be doubled)

2. chord 4, incomplete (no chordal 5th)
    chords 4–5, parallel octaves (passing tone does not prevent parallelism)
    chord 6, chordal 7th does not resolve downward

3. chords 1–2, parallel octaves (soprano and bass)
    chord 3, incomplete chord (no chordal 7th)
    chord 4, suspension is not prepared
    chord 6, chordal 7th does not resolve downward
    last chord, incorrect doubling

4. chord 2, preferable to double the soprano (unison doubling)

COMPOSER INDEX

INDEX